# Computer Programming

PN 9090279 3

# Computer Programming
## Fourth edition

J. Rothwell, J. Edgar, M. Spink and D. Duret

NCC BLACKWELL

Copyright © J. Rothwell, J. Edgar, M. Spink and D. Duret, 1996

First published in 1981 as *Programming Techniques and Practice* by Alan Chantler, reprinted 1987. A fully revised and updated edition published in 1992 and this edition published by:

NCC Blackwell Ltd
108 Cowley Road
Oxford OX4 1JF
UK

Blackwell Publishers Inc.
238 Main Street
Cambridge, Massachusetts 02142, USA



*Library of Congress Cataloging-in-Publication Data*
Computer programming/J. Rothwell . . . [et al.]. – 4th ed.
   p.  cm.
   Rev. ed. of: Computer programming/P. Blacklock. 3rd ed. 1992.
   Includes bibliographic references and index
   ISBN 1-85554-655-8 (alk. paper)
   1. Electronic digital computers – Programming.   I. Rothwell, J. (Janet)
   II. Blacklock, P. (Phil). Computer programming.
QA76.6.C6348   1995
005.1 – dc20                          95-39330
                                     CIP

ISBN 1-85554-655-8

*British Library Cataloguing in Publication Data*
A CIP catalogue record for this book is available from the British Library

Typeset in 10 on 12pt Palatino and Helvetica
Printed in Singapore

# Contents

# Preface

This book has been written primarily for students who are following the National Computing Centre's International Diploma in Computer Studies (IDCS). However, it is suitable for all students who are studying an introductory course in computer programming.

Programming is essentially a practical activity and while we have used pseudo-code throughout this book, you will learn more – and get a lot more enjoyment and satisfaction – if you code up the examples and exercises into a language such as C or Pascal and test them on your computer.

In addition, there are plenty of exercises for you to try, some of them taken from past examination papers, and specimen answers are provided. Do try them and discuss them with your tutors if you find that your answers are different to ours. You may not necessarily be wrong! There are often a number of ways of programming any particular problem.

We hope that you find this book meets your needs. We have researched the syllabus and are confident that if you understand everything and can put it into practice, you will have no problems in passing your course. Good luck!

# 1

# An introduction to programming

## Objectives

At the end of this chapter you should

❏ understand the three control constructs of structured programming
❏ be able to apply these three constructs to simple problems in your chosen computer language
❏ understand what a variable is and how different simple data types require differing amounts of memory
❏ understand the purpose and use of pseudo-code.

## 1.1 Introduction

This chapter is concerned with the three basic elements of programming: accepting data, processing it and outputting the results. Whatever programming language you use these elements form the basis of all useful programs. For major data processing the data to be accessed may be of a massive quantity, the processing relatively trivial and the output of information repetitive. On other occasions the data input may need complicated and subtle processing to ensure accurate and meaningful output. The different languages available have, by tradition as well as design, become associated with different sorts of applications. COBOL is associated with commercial data processing, FORTRAN with science and engineering, Pascal with teaching, BASIC with interactive personal computing and so on. In the end, however, all programming problems depend upon the accurate and careful use of the basic elements forming the computer language.

It is possible to plan and, hence, produce designs for programs without needing to become directly concerned with the finer details of any one particular computing language – in fact it is very useful to be able to do this since the peculiar grammar of individual languages can interfere with the planning and design phases of program production.

Most of the programming chapters in this book are concerned with the basic techniques of structured programming. Explanation of techniques and algorithms have to be applicable to all readers and again we do not want the syntax of a particular computer language to interfere with our explanation of the basic requirements which are universal. For this reason all our algorithms are illustrated with pseudo-code. This code will suffice for all questions in the examinations for the IDCS. There are summary examination questions for each chapter which will help you to be successful in this examination and also in many other computer programming examinations as well.

Pseudo-code is one of the tools that can be used to write a preliminary plan that can be developed into a computer program; it is **not** a standard language, although programmers usually use terms within it that closely resemble the actual language to be used. Its purpose is to describe the algorithm (the method of solving the problem) in a form that can be easily understood and translated into the actual programming code required. The syntax of the language to be used and fine detail of the program are ignored until writing the source code, i.e. the program to be compiled. Usually the variables to be used are described in the pseudo-code using meaningful names from which the reader can deduce the purpose.

We do recommend that you learn to translate pseudo-code into your own computer language. Programming is a practical subject and the enjoyment of applying your skills is gained by producing reliable and successful computer programs. When you can translate the principles described in this book into one practical computer language you can, with relative ease, repeat the process with any other.

The syntax and power of computer languages is variable; good programming practice is common to them all.

The following sections deal, in turn, with the control construct sequence, selection and iteration.


## 1.2 Sequence

At the end of this section you should be able to:

- ❏ understand what we mean by a programming sequence and have been introduced to the pseudo-code for input assignment and output
- ❏ understand the difference between simple data types and why these data types are required.

A sequence of actions always takes place in a computer program. The normal sequence is

$$\text{input} \rightarrow \text{process} \rightarrow \text{output}.$$

Data are accepted, a process is performed on the data and the results are returned to the user or retained for use again at a later stage.

The following example illustrates this sequence.

## Example 1.1

This is the pseudo-code code required to input three numbers from the keyboard of a personal computer and output the result.

```
use variables : number1, number2, number3 of type integer
accept number1, number2, number3
sum = number1 + number2 + number3
print sum
end program
```

The program starts with a declaration of variables followed by an instruction *accept* which tells the computer to take the numbers from the keyboard and store them as the variables *number1*, *number2* and *number3*.

The next line instructs the computer to add together the contents of the stores identified by number1, number2 and number3 and place the answer in a store identified by the name sum. Lastly the instruction *print sum* outputs the answer on the printer.

We will now consider these concepts in more detail.

## Variables and variable names

A variable is a data item whose value can change during the processing of the program. The computer program needs a name to use so that it can access and manipulate the data when commanded to do so. This name is the *identifier* for that variable. The name chosen must conform to certain rules so that the computer programs you are using to build your program do not get ambiguous instructions. This means that you cannot use names that the computer uses to make up the programming language. These words are called reserved words and you should have access to a list of these whenever you are writing a program. Punctuation marks and spaces may also have a special meaning within the grammar or syntax of the computer language you are learning. These also cannot be used as part of a variable name.

You should make sure that you know how to use valid variable names.

## Good practice

A very useful guide to choosing a variable name is to **use a name that is meaningful in the context of your program.** For example, in the above program *sum_* is used for the variable which is used to **hold the sum of the three numbers.** Using this rule will help to make your programs easier to understand.

## Variable types

The compiler also needs to know what **type** of data is being used because it will have a different way of dealing with whole numbers, fractional numbers and characters. As you will see later, the type of data being used has a great influence on program design.

Whole numbers are usually called integers; fractional numbers are usually called reals or floats; letters are usually called characters and names are usually called strings.

The program example used above uses whole number variables, i.e. of type integer.

## Constants

Data items are sometimes required to keep their values throughout the program hence the term **constant.** The computer still needs to know a name for the constant and its data type so that it can be manipulated as required during the program.

Constants and variables obey the same rules and can be compared or used together in arithmetic expressions as long as they are of the same data type.

The following exercise will reinforce the concepts of simple data types.

## Exercise 1.1

Choose an appropriate data type for variables to be used in each of the following situations:

- ❏ a variable used for a metric measurement
- ❏ a variable used to count a number of people
- ❏ a variable used to calculate a total sum of money
- ❏ a variable used for a choice between five letters.

## Assignment and calculations

In the pseudo-code statement

$$sum: = number1 + number2 + number3$$

a calculation is performed and the result assigned or copied into the location identified by the variable name sum. Computer languages provide all the usual operators for arithmetic. The signs used in our pseudo-code are

| | |
|---|---|
| + | meaning add |
| − | meaning subtract |
| * | meaning multiply |
| / | meaning divide |

For the moment this is all we will use in our examples.

It is important to understand that the code just written first performed the calculation and then assigned the value to the identifier (the name used for a particular variable) sum. An assignment is **not** the same as the logical operator equals '=' which we use so often in mathematics. To help you remember this difference our pseudo-code uses the sign ':='.

An assignment such as *sum:= sum + number* means that the calculation sum + number is to be performed and then the result assigned to the identifier sum.

## *Example 1.2*

The following pseudo-code describes an algorithm (a logical method or plan) which will accept two numbers from the keyboard and calculate the sum and product displaying the answer on the monitor screen.

A new pseudo-code command is introduced – *display* which indicates output to the screen.

```
use variables: sum, product, number1, number2 of type real.
display "input two numbers"
accept number1, number2
sum: = number1 + number2
print "The sum is", sum
product: = number1 * number2
print "The product is", product
end program
```

## *More complex calculations – the order of precedence*

The order in which a calculation is evaluated is very important since the end result can differ according to which operation is given precedence, i.e. performed before the other. The following simple example illustrates the problem. The expression $a:= 2 * 3 + 4$ could be calculated in two different orders. Perform the addition first: $3 + 4 = 7$. Then the multiplication: $2 * 7 = 14$.

The value assigned to a would be 14. Alternatively the multiplication could be performed first: $2 * 3 = 6$ and then the addition $6 + 4 = 10$. The value assigned to a would be 10.

Having rules for the order of precedence of the arithmetic operations avoids this ambiguity – you should have encountered them during your early mathematics lessons. The way expressions are worked out by a computer are very similar to the rules you should have learnt at that stage in mathematics and are

(1)  do operations in brackets first
(2)  evaluate any exponentiation (e.g. finding the cube of a number)
(3)  then any multiplication or division operations
(4)  and lastly addition and subtraction.

## Example 1.3

In the assignment statement $a = b + c * (d + e)$ what is the value assigned to $a$ when $b = 2, c = 3, d = 4$ and $e = 5$?

Evaluate the bracketed component first: $(d + e)$ is $(4 + 5)$, i.e. 9. Next do the multiplication: $c * 9, 3 * 9$, i.e. 27. Lastly the addition: $b + 27... 3 + 27$, i.e. 30.

## Exercise 1.2

Evaluate the following expressions to find the value assigned to *a*

(a)   $a = 5 * 3 + 2 * (4 + 5)$
(b)   $a = 5 + 3 * 2(3 - 1)$.

In these expressions $b = 2, c = 3, d = 6$

(c)   $a = b * b - 4 * d * c$
(d)   $a = b + d + (c - d/c)$
(e)   $a: = b * b - d * d + c$.

## Summary exercise 1A

(1) Write a program which will calculate the area of a circle using the formula area = pi * radius * radius.
(2) Write a program which will calculate to the nearest square metre the amount of carpet needed to cover the floor of a room on input of the length and width of the room.
(3) Write a program which will output the square and the cube of any number input.
(4) Explain the meaning of the term 'a reserved word'.

## 1.3 Selection

This section describes how to:

❑ choose alternative actions as a result of testing a logical condition
❑ produce code to test a sequence of logical tests.

### *Making choices*

There are many occasions where a program is required to take alternative actions. For example, there are occasions where we need to take action according to the user choice as in a menu of options where the user is required to input alternative choices and in consequence the program must act on that choice. All computer languages therefore provide a means of selection. Usually it is in the form of an if statement and our pseudo-code is no exception to this.

We shall use the if statement together with logical operators to test for true or false as shown below.

$$\text{if } a = b \text{ print "}a = b\text{"}$$

The action is **only** taken if the test result is true.

The logical operators used in our pseudo-code are:

$=$    is equal to
$>=$   is greater than or equal to
$<=$   is less than or equal to
$<>$   is not equal to

Hence if $a <= b$ translates to 'if $a$ is greater than or equal to $b$'.

### *Exercise 1.3*

**(a)** If $a = 1$, $b = 2$, $c = 2$ write down true or false to describe the results of these tests:
$a > b$ is?
$b = c$ is?
$2 * a = b$ is?
$c > a$ is?

**(b)** Given $x = 5$, $y = 6$ what is the result of the following code: if $x > y$ display '*abcde*'; if $x < y$ display '*xyz*'.

### *An example program*

The following example shows how the selection control structure is used in a program. The problem is to offer to the user a menu of choices which will enable the input of two numbers and the calculation of the sum, difference or product of the numbers. Here is the pseudo-code.

*use variables: choice, of type character*
  *ans, number1, number2, of type integer*
*display "choose one of the following"*
*display "m for multiply"*
*display "a for add"*
*display "s for subtract"*
*accept choice*
*display "input the numbers you want to use"*
*accept number1, number2*
*if choice = m then ans = number1 * number2*
*if choice = a then ans = number1 + number2*
*if choice = s then ans = number1 − number2*
*display ans*

## Logical links

There are many occasions when we need to extend the conditions that are to be tested. Often there are conditions to be linked.

In everyday language we say things like 'If I had the time and the money I would go on holiday'. The 'and' means that **both** conditions must be true before we take an action. We might also say: 'I am happy to go to the theatre or the cinema'. The logical link this time is 'or'. Conditions in if statements are linked in the same way. Conditions linked with an 'and' only result in an action when all conditions are true. For example: if $a > b$ and $a > c$ then display '$a$ is the largest'. Conditions linked with an 'or' lead to an action when **either** or both conditions are true.

## Exercise 1.4

Using the given following conditional statements write down either action or no action for the cases described.

**(a)** if $a >= b$ OR $a = c$
  when $a = 3$, $b = 3$, $c = 3$ the result is?
  when $a = 2$, $b = 3$, $c = 3$ the result is?
  when $a = 2$, $b = 3$, $c = 2$ the result is?
  when $a = 5$, $b = 3$, $c = 3$ the result is?
**(b)** if $a = b$ AND $b >= c$
  when $a = 3$, $b = 3$, $c = 2$ the result is?
  when $a = 3$, $b = 3$, $c = 5$ the result is?
  when $a = 3$, $b = 2$, $c = 1$ the result is?
  when $a = 3$, $b = 3$, $c = 3$ the result is?

## An example program

The problem is to input an examination mark and test it for the award of a grade. The mark is a whole number between 1 and 100. Grades are awarded according to the following criteria:

>=   80 distinction
>=   60 merit
>=   40 pass
<     40 fail

The pseudo-code is

*use variables: mark of type integer*
   *accept mark*
   *if mark >= 80 display "distinction"*
   *if mark >= 60 AND mark<80 display "merit"*
   *if mark >= 40 AND mark <60 display "pass"*
   *if mark < 40 display "fail"*

An **if** statement on its own is often not the neatest way of solving a problem. A more elegant set of conditions can be created by adding an **else** statement to the if statement. The **else** statement is used to deal with situations such as in the following examples. A person is paid at top value for category 1 work otherwise pay is at normal rates. This leads to logical statements such as:

*If the work is category 1 pay-rate is top else pay-rate is normal.*

The else statement provides a neat way of dealing with the alternative condition.
   In pseudo-code we write

*If work = cat1 then p-rate: = top else p-rate: = normal.*

## Exercise 1.5

Using the following conditional statements write down the actions that will result for the values given.

**(a)** if $a = b$ print 'yes' else print 'no'
   $a = 2, b = 2$
   $a = 3, b = 4$
**(b)** if $a > b$ AND $a > c$ print '$a$' else print '$b,c$'
   $a = 3, b = 4, c = 3$
   $a = 5, b = 4, c = 2$
   $a = 5, b = 2, c = 6.$

## Exercise 1.6

Write the pseudo-code to describe an algorithm for the following program. The program is to calculate the wages of a sales executive according to the following rules. If the sales executive has been with the company more than three years he or she has a loyalty bonus of 10%. The wage is calculated at rate of 15% on sales.

## The case statement

Repeating the if then/else statements a number of times can be somewhat confusing. An alternative method provided in a number of languages is to use a selector determined by the alternative conditions that are needed. In our pseudo-code this will be called a case statement.

The case statement is frequently used for choosing between options such as those found in screen menus.

The code located by the case selector is a simple text output as shown in the example below. However, the size of the code required is as large as is needed to solve the problem. This construct will be encountered again in Chapter 4.

## Example 1.4

The following program segment outputs a message to the monitor screen describing the insurance available according to a category input by the user.

```
use variables: category of type char
accept category
IF category = U THEN DISPLAY "insurance is not available"
ELSE if category = A then DISPLAY "insurance is double"
ELSE if category = B then DISPLAY "insurance is normal"
ELSE if category = M then DISPLAY "insurance is medically dependent"
ELSE DISPLAY "entry is invalid"
```

This is expressed in a case statement as

```
ACCEPT category
DO case of category
CASE category = U
    display "insurance not available"
CASE category = A
    display "insurance is double"
CASE category = B
    DISPLAY "insurance is normal"
```

*CASE category = M*
    *DISPLAY "insurance is medically dependent"*
*OTHERWISE DISPLAY "entry is invalid"*
*ENDCASE.*

## Exercise 1.7

Write the pseudo-code to describe an algorithm for the following description. An index is set to the numbers 1, 2, 3 or 4 according to a given job code. Index 1 is a four-person job and is expected to last three days. Index 2 is a two-person job and is expected to last four days. Index 3 is a one-person job and will last five days. Index 4 is a two-person job and will last seven days. Each person is paid at $100 per day. Using a case statement write the pseudo-code that will process these conditions and calculate the expenditure for each.

## Summary exercise 1B

Write a pseudo-code for each of the following program descriptions.

**(a)** Write an algorithm which will ask a user to input a number between 1 and 100 and will output an error message if the number is not in range.
**(b)** Given the three lengths *a*, *b* and *c* write an algorithm to determine, on input of values for *a*, *b* and *c*, if a triangle can be drawn. (No side can be greater than the sum of the other two.)
**(c)** Write the pseudo-code to present on the monitor screen a menu of choices which allows the user to choose between three houses available for rent. On entering the choice details of the house concerned are output to the printer. House 1 costs $200 per month and is a one-bedroom flat with a car-parking area. House 2 costs $400 per month and is a two-bedroom terrace with a garage. House 3 costs $800 per month and is a three-bedroom detached house with air-conditioning and a double garage.

## 1.4 Iteration

At the end of this section you should understand how to control iterations which:

❏ test at the start of a block of code: a **while do** iteration
❏ test at the conclusion of a block of code: a **repeat until** iteration
❏ are controlled by a count given from known conditions: a **for do** iteration.

The power of a computer lies in its ability to do things time and time again without becoming tired, bored or inaccurate. Repeating the same action or set of actions is called iteration. The commands used to create iterations are all based on logical tests. There are three constructs for iterations in our pseudo-code.

The first iteration we shall describe always completes at least once, since the logic test used to terminate the loop is at the end of the code which constitutes the loop.

Repeat an action or block of actions **until** (a true condition) this type of loop is often used for validating numbers since the test must always be performed.

## *The repeat until loop*

The syntax is

```
REPEAT
a statement or block of statements
UNTIL a true condition
```

## *Example 1.5*

A program segment which repeatedly asks for entry of a number in the range 1 and 100 until a valid number is entered.

```
REPEAT
DISPLAY "Enter a number between 1 and 100"
ACCEPT number
UNTIL number >0 AND number <= 100
```

Another common use is to allow repetition of a menu of options as in this example.

## *Example 1.6*

A survey has been carried out to discover the most popular sport. The results will be typed into the computer for analysis. Write a program to accomplish this. Here is the pseudo-code

```
REPEAT
    DISPLAY "Type in the letter chosen or Q to Finish"
DISPLAY        "A: Athletics"
DISPLAY        "B: Swimming"
DISPLAY        "C: Football"
DISPLAY        "D: Badminton"
DISPLAY        "Q: end data:"
```

```
ACCEPT letter
   IF letter = 'A' then athletics = athletics + 1
   IF letter = 'S' then swimming = swimming + 1
   IF letter = 'F' then football = football + 1
   IF letter = 'B' then badminton = badminton + 1
UNTIL letter = Q
DISPLAY "Athletics scored" athletics "votes"
DISPLAY "Swimming scored" swimming "votes"
DISPLAY "Football scored" football "votes"
DISPLAY "Badminton scored" badminton "votes"
```

## Exercise 1.8

(**a**) Write the pseudo-code for an iteration which outputs the square of the number input until the number entered is 999.

(**b**) Write the pseudo-code segment that will ask for a name to be input until 20 names have been typed or the user types stop.

## The while loop

The second type of iteration we will look at is the **while** iteration. This type of conditional loop tests for the terminating condition at the beginning of the code block; thus no action is performed at all if the first test causes the terminating condition to evaluate as false.

The syntax is

```
WHILE (a true condition).
   a statement or block of statements
ENDWHILE
```

## Example 1.7

A program segment to print out each character typed at a keyboard until the character 'q' is entered.

```
WHILE letter <> 'q'
   DISPLAY "The character you typed is", letter"
   ACCEPT letter
ENDWHILE
```

Since a while loop will only take action after it has tested the variable some form of initialization is often necessary. In the following example this is achieved by accepting the first input before and outside the while loop.

## Example 1.8

Write a program that will output the square of any number input until the number input is zero.

> *Use variable: number of type real.*
> *DISPLAY "Type in a number or zero to stop"*
> *ACCEPT number*
> *WHILE number <> 0*
> *square:= number * number*
> *DISPLAY "The square of the number you input is" square*
> *DISPLAY "Type in a number or zero to stop"*
> *ACCEPT number*
> *ENDWHILE*

## Exercise 1.9

(a) A sentence is complete when the last character entered is a full stop. Write a section of pseudo-code that will continue to accept characters counting them on input and will output the number of characters in the sentence when the full stop is entered.

(b) Write a program segment that will test a number on input to ensure it is in the range 0 to 10 and will output an error message if the number is out of range.

## The for do iteration

The third type of iteration, which we shall use when the number of iterations is known in advance, is a **for do** loop. This, in its simplest form, uses an initialization of a variable as a starting point, a stop condition again depending on the value of the variable. The variable is incremented on each iteration until it reaches the required value.

Our pseudo-code syntax will be:

> *FOR (starting state, stopping condition, increment)*
> *Statements*
> *ENDFOR*

## Example 1.9

```
FOR (n = 1, n <= 4, n + 1)
DISPLAY "loop" n
ENDFOR
```

This fragment of code will produce the output

```
loop 1
loop 2
loop 3
```

Note how the variable used as the loop counter is also used to output the loop number.

It is very important to be aware of any use of the counting variable. If the value within the loop is changed, the count will change. Do **not** do this without a very clear reason for changing the behaviour of the loop.

## Example 1.10

A program to calculate the sum and average of a series of numbers. The pseudo-code solution is

```
use variables: n, count of type integer
    sum, number,average of type real
DISPLAY "how many numbers do you want to input?"
ACCEPT count
FOR (n = 1, n <= count, count + 1)
    ACCEPT number
    SUM:= sum + number
ENDFOR
average:= sum/count
DISPLAY "The sum of the numbers was", sum
    DISPLAY "The average of the numbers was" average
```

## Summary exercise

(1) (a) What is a reserved word.
   (b) Explain the difference between a variable and a constant.
   (c) Explain the essential difference between a **repeat until** iteration and a **while do** iteration.
(2) Consider the following pseudo-code statements:

```
overdrawn:= balance < 0;
If overdrawn then...
```

What data type is overdrawn?'

**(3)** Write pseudo-code for a program to output the sum of two numbers until the user chooses to stop.

**(4)** Write a program that will accept the input of 20 results which are entered as *a*, *b* or *c*. Add the result appropriately to the variables *scoreA*, *scoreB* and *scoreC* as the results are entered and in conclusion output the total of each of these variables.

**(5)** Write a program that will offer the user the choice of three calculations: to calculate the area of a circle using the formula area = 3.142 $* r * r$, calculate the circumference of a circle $C = 2 * 3.142 * r$ or calculate the volume of a sphere $V = 4/3 * 3.142 * r * r * r$. The program should offer the user the opportunity to continue to input data and choose the calculation or to stop the program.

# 2
# Analysis of data and problems

## Objectives

At the end of this chapter you will be able to:

❑ describe the system development process
❑ understand the function of the program stage
❑ analyse problems using top-down design
❑ draw data structure diagrams
❑ understand and draw file structures.

In Chapter 1 we considered the basic elements of structured programming. Before we consider more complex programming structures it will be useful to see where the programming component fits into the design and installation of a computer system.

It will become clear that methods of planning the programming process will help in program construction and we will introduce some of the basic concepts and tools that are helpful to this process.

Systems analysis and design is a challenging and complex subject. There are well-documented formal methods which are widely applied to this subject which are beyond the scope of this book. Here, we shall only consider the outline of the systems development life cycle and where the programmers become involved in the process.

## 2.1 The traditional system development life cycle

This can be described in different ways but it is characterized basically by the following seven sequential phases:

**(1)**  initial study
**(2)**  requirements analysis
**(3)**  systems analysis
**(4)**  design
**(5)**  coding
**(6)**  testing
**(7)**  implementation and production.

The model shown in Figure 2.1, sometimes called the waterfall model, is an effective way to develop and control the diverse activities of a development system process.

At the end of each phase, there is a control of the work and the achievement of the goals of the phase can be evaluated. From then, there are three possibilities for the development of the project.

❑ The results of the evaluation are satisfactory (e.g. the goals of the specific phase have been reached) and the development can go onto the next phase.

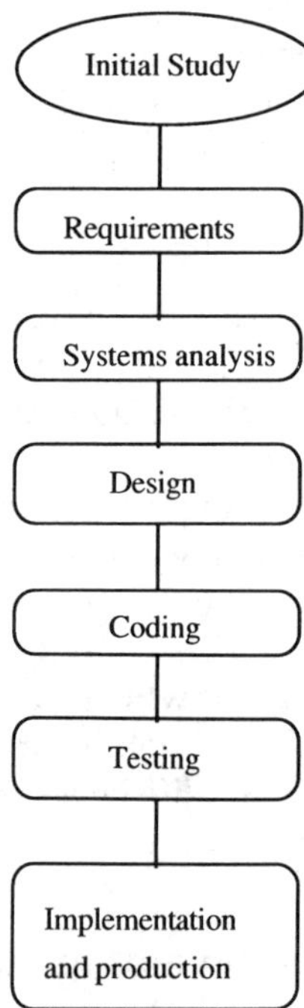


**Figure 2.1**

❑ The results of the evaluation are not completely satisfactory (e.g. some parts of the program need to be clarified, or improved). Therefore more work needs to be done on this phase before going onto the next one.
❑ The results are very poor and the entire project might be discontinued, or restarted.

Once a phase is completed it is better not to return to a previous phase, however, this may be necessary in some specific cases.

### 2.1.1 The initial study

The main purpose of this stage is to assess the feasibility of the project. It is very important to define the problem in user terms as precisely as possible. A solution cannot be developed if the problem is not clearly stated and understood. At the end of this stage, the minimum outputs are:

❑ a brief description of the proposed system which could include the hardware and software specification
❑ an estimation of the project cost
❑ a possible completion date for the work.

### 2.1.2 Requirements analysis

At this stage an accurate and complete set of user requirements is produced to determine the characteristics of an acceptable solution. This information is obtained mainly via direct interviews with current and future users of the system.
  A requirements analysis document contains the following information:

❑ a clear understanding between the user and the developer over the proposed system or solution
❑ a list of the existing and new tools, facilities and people available for developing the solution
❑ a schedule for the next stages of the project with the deliverables for each stage.

### 2.1.3 Systems analysis

The objective of the system analysis stage is to describe in detail a solution that will fully meet the user requirements. That is, the user requirements from the previous stage are translated into data processing terms which can be understood by the system designers, programmers and testers. This includes a description of:

❑ the inputs to the process

❏ the operations the system performs for each input
❏ the output obtained for the corresponding input.

*The input to the process.* The developer begins by defining the type of input that will be processed by the system. Data may be from either external or internal sources, or from a combination of both.

An example of external data input might be information from a manufacturing plant or simply from a motor for monitoring purposes. In such a case it is necessary to use special equipment to convert this information from its analogue form into a digital one that can be processed by the computer. This information can already be digital (keyboard or another digital system) and therefore be imported directly to the system.

If the input is already stored in a file (internal data input) the storage format must be specified so that it can be read.

Numerical input can have maximum and/or minimum values and data which are not within that range could be ignored or consider as errors. However, it is a frequent mistake to set boundaries if the user does not think it is necessary. It might be more convenient for the implementation, but, as a result of this, some data will be ignored.

The input can be a command and there must be a protocol which specifies the number of parameters and their formats. The first parameters of the input command can specify the action to be carried out by the process and the other parameters can be numerical values related to the action. For example START,1,0.1 could be an input command controlling a motor which will start motor number 1 at the speed of 0.1 rad/s.

*The process and the output.* Output can be obtained in various formats depending upon the processing action. At this stage, it should be kept in mind that the system analysis document should not define how the system will work but it must define what the system will do to meet the user requirements. Therefore, for any given input, the process and the associated output should be clearly determined. This includes prompts and terminal messages, error messages and warning reports, graphs, computed results, etc.

## 2.1.4 Design

The design stage describes how the solution will be built to meet the user requirements as specified at the previous stage. The final set of programs is produced directly from that description so it has to be a detailed, technical, logical definition of the final system.

Complex problems cannot be solved in one step so they are divided into a set of subproblems which can be more easily solved. This decomposition process results in a set of programs and modules interacting with each other.

A system test plan needs to be developed for each program or module which will be used in the next stage to ensure that they meet their individual specifications.

All these programs and modules in the system are defined in terms of their inputs, outputs, and required functions and process. The interaction parameters (timing, performance requirements) between each of the system's programs and modules are defined explicitly.

The decomposition process can be described by a system flow chart, which shows the three elements of program, data and their interaction. Although still used by many analysts, it has several disadvantages as an aid to viewing a system and it is becoming more common to use data flow diagrams (DFD), logical data structures (LDS) and the entity life history. The DFD illustrates the data movement in the system by showing the flow of information.

At this stage, the use of formal program design techniques and programming standards are recommended. The designer selects proper data structures and algorithms for the implementation of the input and output data and the system functions. The final details may be left until the coding stage.

As this is the last stage before the coding of the new system, it should also be considered whether the programs are developed internally, externally or both. The system can either be developed from scratch or from parts which will be purchased as complete packages or from an independent programmer who will produce the required code from the program specifications.

## 2.1.5 Coding

The objective of this stage is to produce software programs that make up the system. Ideally, the coding should start when the previous phase (the system design) is completed, and should not return to it. However, some additional design of the program and modules is always necessary even if the system design is good.

These programs and modules need to be tested according to the system test plan developed in the previous phase and they should meet their individual specifications. This task is carried out at the same time the program is being created.

This phase is complete when all code is written and documented, and error-free compiled. The system is then ready to be tested which is the next phase of the life cycle.

## 2.1.6 Testing

In the previous stage, modules were tested in isolation, therefore the next step is to test them as a group to see how they interact with each other. Then the system must be tested in each environment that it is likely to be used. For example, the programs might have been developed on machines using the latest technology, but the user might be working with older machines which were specified in the requirements analysis phase.

Finally, the software is tested by users. First, it will be in a controlled environment to ensure that it meets the user's requirements and then in a live environment by some 'friendly' users to find uncovered problems.

This is not always possible as some applications cannot tolerate errors. A nuclear reactor control, a flight control support in aircraft or patient monitoring in intensive care units in hospitals must be completely error-free before they are tested in a live environment. The only way to test this software is by simulating the live environment. For example, the simulation program of a nuclear reactor will be developed to test the system which will control it.

### 2.1.7  Implementation and production

When all the previous stages have been completed to the satisfaction of everyone involved, the system is then ready for implementation. This phase is very costly but it is also necessary to keep good records with previous and new clients. Basically, after the installation of the system, it must be kept operational and updated according to the need of the users.

## 2.2  The programmers' role

Now that we have had an overview of the system development process it is easier to see where the programmers fit in. It is clear that this occurs in the coding, testing, implementation and production stages.

After the design stage and after detailed program specifications have been drawn up, the systems analyst will call on the programming team to develop the programs which fulfil the functional requirements of the system.

The most important feature of a computer program is that it functions correctly, that is, it does what it is supposed to do! Therefore, it is essential to plan a reliable development life cycle and to follow it as closely as possible.

## 2.3  The software development life cycle

This development of software has stages that are very similar to the systems development stages.

The initial input to the coding process is the functional specification that the program must fulfil. The programming team then commence the design of the program followed by production of the working code which is then tested. The code, if required, is amended until the working program can be integrated into the proposed new or updated system. Feedback from the system testers as a result of their review of the program or requirements to update or alter some program functions then creates a new cycle of software development.

In summary, the software development life cycle consists of the following stages:

❑ specification
❑ design
❑ implementation
❑ testing
❑ review and maintenance.

These stages are considered in more detail later in the book

## 2.4  The design process: structure diagrams

Diagrammatic techniques are widely used in the design process of all branches of engineering – software engineering is no exception to this. Just as architects have their drawings and engineers their blueprints, software engineers have diagrams particularly suitable for their uses. Later in the book a number of these techniques are discussed in detail, however we have chosen to use structure diagrams as our basic diagrammatic tool. This is because such diagrams are easy to construct and can be used to produce illustrations of outline plans and of both data and program structures. The technique is well suited to the structured programming approach upon which we have based our approach throughout this book.

### The basic techniques

At the end of this section you should be able to construct structure diagrams which show the relationship between the components of the structure and how these components occur as a sequence, and where there are iteration and selection components.

A structure diagram is a way of describing the relationship of the component parts of the structure to the whole. As an example consider students in a class: the class is the whole and the students are the components. Using our new terminology we can say that the class is an iteration of students and show this on a diagram in the following way.

A rectangle is drawn to represent the class and beneath this another rectangle is drawn to represent the students. To show that there are a number of students – an iteration – we draw an asterisk (*) in the top right-hand corner of the box. The structure diagram is shown in Figure 2.2 overleaf.

The class may not all do the same course some may, for example, choose different options. Let us suppose that the students may choose to study course A or course B. The diagram now must include a selection component. This is

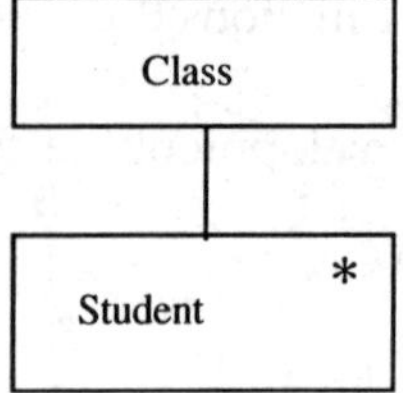

**Figure 2.2**  Iteration.

indicated by rectangles drawn below the selection stage and indicating the selection by placing a small circle in the top right-hand corner of the box. The diagram of the class structure now becomes as shown in Figure 2.3.

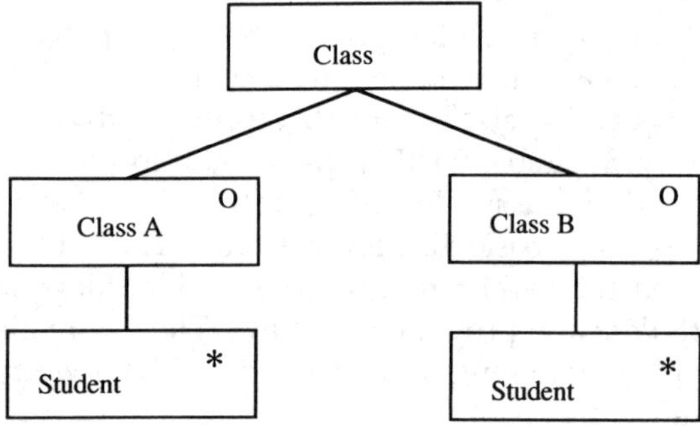

**Figure 2.3**  Selection.

The lowest levels of the components are shown as the hierarchy descends through the diagrams. The sequence of the structure diagram is indicated by the order reading from left to right as illustrated in the following example. An examination paper consisting of four questions which must be answered in the order question A then B, C and D would be shown as a structure as in Figure 2.4.

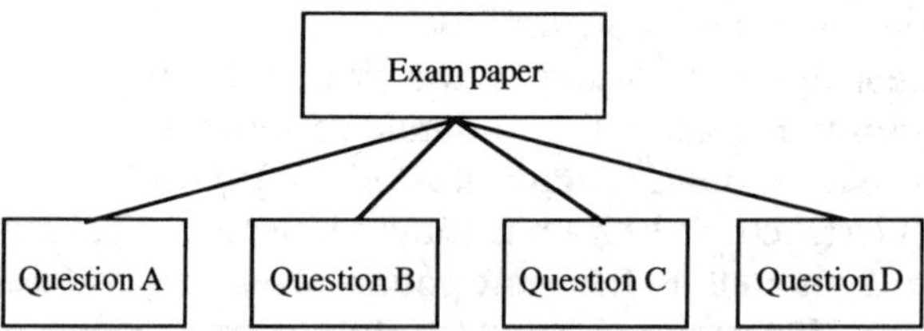

**Figure 2.4**  Sequence.

To summarize:

❏ rectangles are used to indicate components. Components may be further subdivided
❏ sequence is indicated by reading from left to right
❏ a rectangle containing an asterisk placed at the top right-hand side indicates an iteration
❏ a box containing a small **circle placed at the top right-**hand corner indicates one part of a selection.

Figure 2.5 shows a representation of iteration and selection.

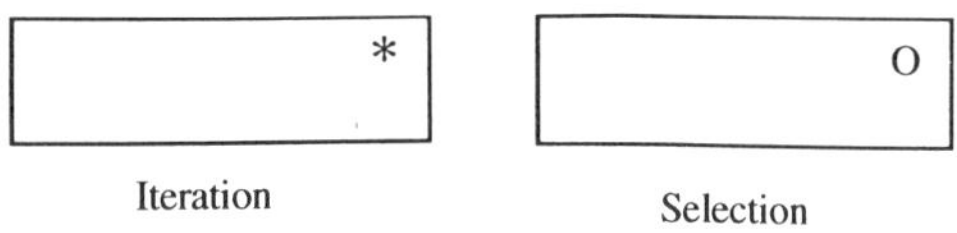

Iteration      Selection

**Figure 2.5**   Representation of iteration and selection.

## *Examples*

(1)  A chess set can be described in a data structure diagram. It is formed of a repetition of pawns, castles, bishops and knights, and the other single pieces as shown in Figure 2.6.

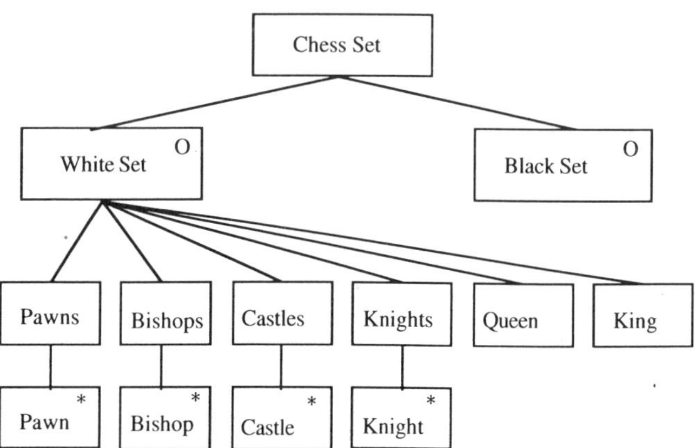

**Figure 2.6**   Structure diagram of a chess set.

(2)  A sports club maintains records of its members showing category of membership and payment details. Life members do not need payment details. The structure diagram of the sports club records is shown in Figure 2.7.

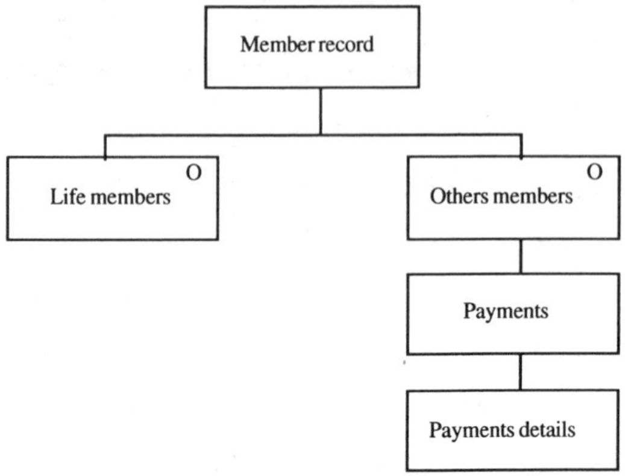


**Figure 2.7**   Data structure diagram of sports club records.

## *Exercise 2.1*

**(a)** Draw a structure diagram to show a pack of cards organized into the four suits (spades, hearts, diamonds and clubs).

**(b)** The students in a school are organized into classes. Draw a structure diagram to show the relationship between the school, the classes and the students.

**(c)** Draw the structure diagram to describe a book which commences with a preface followed by a number of chapters and concluded with an epilogue.

**(d)** Draw a structure diagram to show how library books are organized in alphabetical order (only consider the first letter of the author's surname and do not show any more than authors up to letter E).

**(e)** Draw a diagram to show the structure of a play organized into three acts each with a number of scenes.

## 2.5   Data structure diagrams

In Chapter 1 we stated that there are three control constructs – sequence, selection and iteration – and we have seen that these components can be easily illustrated on a structure diagram. Structure diagrams can therefore be used to describe both data and program structures. In this section we are going to look at the file data structure.

We have chosen to discuss the file data structure at this point for two reasons. Firstly, computer-based files are extremely important structures in data processing applications; secondly, file structures are easily described using data structure diagrams. Therefore the two concepts, files and data structure diagrams, can be described together – each concept assisting in the comprehension of the other.

## *Organizing information: files*

The need for organizing information has always existed and the maintenance of files of related information preceded the invention of computers. Most people will be familiar with the idea of organizing data in this way.

The structure of a file to be used for computer processing is defined using the terms file, record and field.

A file is composed of records. Each record contains data organized in a defined structure. The components of this record are called fields.

In the previous section we used as an example a class of students. If we were to organize information about this class for a computer application we would construct a file, the components of which would be students' records and the record fields would hold the information needed about each student.

As an example let us suppose that the file organization is as follows:

```
File name        Class a1
record name      student
record details   name: John
                 address: flat 1, main street, suburb a, city 12
                 exam code 5
```

Figure 2.8 shows the structure diagram of class file.

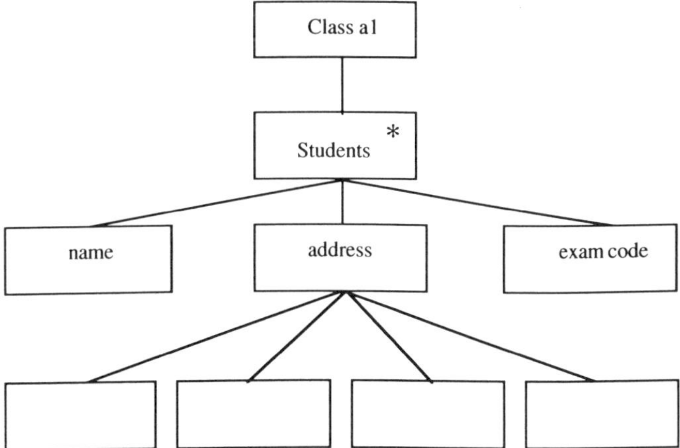


**Figure 2.8**   Structure diagram of class file.

Since a file is a collection of records it is shown as an iteration, the top level box is drawn to represent the file, the next level is the box showing an iteration of records which on the next level is shown as a sequence of fields.

## Designing record structures

The fields in a record must be carefully designed to contain all the data that might need to be referenced for the provision of information from the file. This task would be performed in conjunction with a client and forms a part of the system specification required by a programmer before building a program.

For applications where a database applications package such as Dbase3 Plus or Excel, are to be used, the design of the record structure has to be accomplished before the database files can be created.

Since the file contents are determined during the system design we shall concentrate on emphasizing the importance of choosing the correct data type for the record fields. It is worth emphasizing again that good programming practice recommends the use of meaningful variable names for the fields and the record.

## Example

A stock file is required to contain the following information: the name of a stored item, a product code, the number in stock, the price of the item and the re-order level. A suitable record structure might be:

```
record name    stock-item
field names    data types, and sizes
item-code      String of 8 characters
quantity       Integer
price          Real
re-order       Integer.
```

## Exercise 2.2

(a) Design a file structure that would contain appropriate data for members of a sports and social club. The club has different categories of membership and in consequence different subscription rates. Subscriptions are payable each January.

(b) Design a file structure for the patients at a medical centre. Draw a structure diagram for this file.

(c) A warehouse stores details of stock held on a file whose records hold information on each product in the form:

<pre>
product number    6 digits
product name      18 characters
quantity in store 4-digit number
price per item    a decimal number
supplier name     24 characters
</pre>

Give an appropriate file structure for this. (NCC 2/93.)

**(d)** An employee file contains details of the employee as follows: employee name, monthly salary, tax deducted, employee number. Design an appropriate record structure for this file.

## 2.6 File structure on a computer

The data structure of files maintained on a computer is more complex than we have previously discussed. In order for the operating system to keep track of and maintain files a header record and a trailer record are needed. The header record is used to store details about the file (e.g. the file name, file type, etc.) and this is the first record on the file. Data records follow and the file ends with a trailer record containing the end of file marker and other housekeeping details. See Figures 2.9 and 2.10.

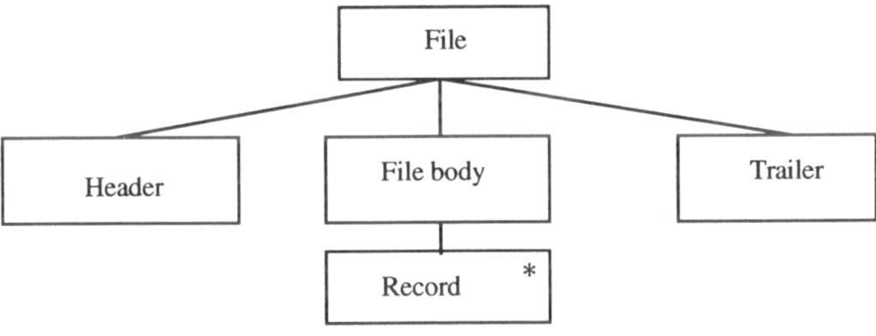


**Figure 2.9**   Structure diagram of a file – 1.

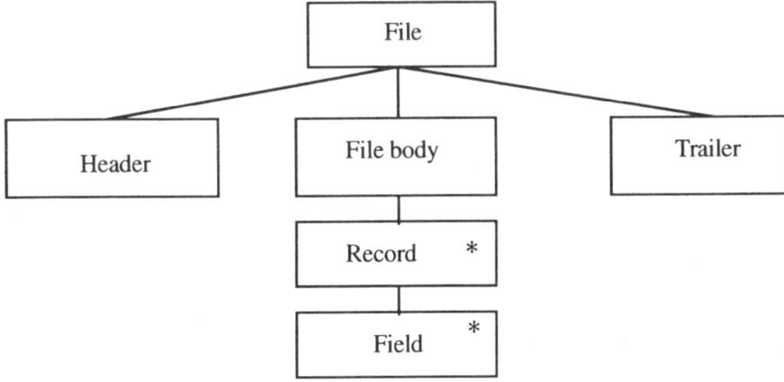


**Figure 2.10**   Structure diagram of a file – 2.

The programmer does not normally need to worry about the header and trailer areas since the operating system will deal automatically with their creation and maintenance.

The data records can also have a more complex organization than that previously discussed.

There may be fields, for example, that are subdivided into more fields giving more detailed information or allowing areas for alternative information.

## Structure diagram of a file

Figure 2.11 shows a structure diagram of file with three layers.

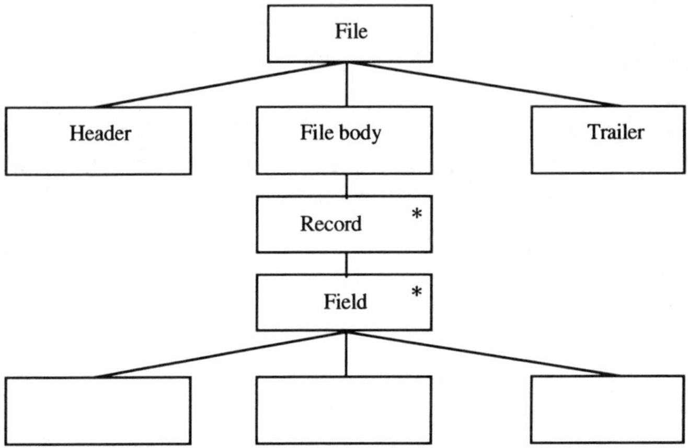


**Figure 2.11**   Structure diagram of a file with three layers.

## Exercise 2.3

Produce the data structure diagram for the following file:

Stock file:
Each main record is followed by as many trailer records as there are outstanding orders for that part.
Main record:
Part No: Description (up to 30 characters)
Quantity in stores
Minimum re-order quantity
Delivery lead time (weeks)
Current price
Flag indicating development part – not used in production

Trailer records:
    Order number
    Order quantity
    Order week number

## Fixed and variable length records

A fixed length record is one in which the number of characters allowed in each record can be predetermined. This occurs when the data can be well defined and will remain in the same format for each record. In addition, each field can be given a sensible maximum size to cope with alterations in field size.

## Example

Part of a staff record might be designed as shown in Figure 2.12. Each of the field sizes can be reasonably determined – a sensible maximum can be decided for the surname and the initials and fixed sizes for the other fields. In records such as this it is easy to determine the position of each record and consequently the algorithms needed to access the record access are relatively straightforward. It is also possible to determine the total data volume and hence ensure appropriate backing storage is available.

| Field name | size in characters |
| --- | --- |
| surname | 20 |
| initials | 15 |
| marital status | 1 |
| sex | 1 |
| category | 4 |

**Figure 2.12**  Part of a staff record.

## Variable length records

There are occasions when the records in a file are required to store variable amounts of data and it is not sensible to allow the field lengths sufficient spare capacity to cope with the variation since the storage space required would be highly inefficient in the use of the backing store.

In the staff file example this could occur if it was required to maintain details of previous work experience when considerable variation will occur between employees. An estimate of maximum storage space for such a record could mean considerable wastage. In such a case the more complex processing requirements needed to deal with variable length records may be justified. It is the responsibility of the design team to ensure that the processing/storage trade-off is chosen sensibly.

## 2.7  Organizing files for processing

### File types

We have seen that files are a collection of records which a program accesses as required by the system needs and that files are kept on backing storage which is either tape or disk.

The files may be organized on the backing storage using a number of methods. The method decided for file access and hence file organization is another system design decision and the method decided demands different programming techniques. We need therefore to understand how these files are organized.

The file types to be described are:

❑ serial file
❑ serial sequential file
❑ indexed sequential file
❑ relative file.

*Serial file.* Each record is written after the last record in the current file. These files are often called sequential files in programming languages because both types of files are handled in the same way by the compiler. Records in a serial file are sequenced in the order in which the data were generated. Examples include memory dumps, archival files and records of events.

*Serial sequential file.* This is a file that has been sorted in the order of one of the record fields. This field is described as the key field because it is used for the identification of the record during processing. Discussions of file handling are dealt with later in the book, but it is important to understand the concept of the key field.

Records can be arranged in sequence of one or more key fields. In this case we talk about the primary key and the secondary key. A physical analogy is a library where books are stored in alphabetical order and then sorted again on the subsequent sequence of letters in the authors name. For example, a book with author Andrews and a book with author Amiss will both be found in the section on authors whose name begins with the letter A which can be considered the primary key, however, the book by Amiss will be found stored before the book by Andrews since the secondary key sort will place the letter m before the letter n.

Another example could be a transaction files arranged in customer account number, then item-number order. Primary key: account-number; secondary key: item-number.

*Indexed sequential file.* Indexed sequential file organization uses two 'files'. As the file is created an index is set up. The index contains the key field from each record stored in sorted sequence, along with the address of the corresponding record. It is then possible to use the index in the additional file to directly access the required record therefore this file is found on direct access media.

Problems may occur as file maintenance continues. The disk portion (the prime area) allocated to the record file may need to be expanded to a secondary or overflow area If the index is not maintained in key sequence access times become inefficient and the file will need to be re-organized. Examples include the key word index at the end of a book.

*Relative or direct access files.* The term 'random access' is also used in this context. These files must be on direct access storage devices – for personal computer users this means your disk drive. Records can be found by direct addressing, i.e. a record key can be used for converting to a unique record location. To use this technique space is allocated to all the expected records to be stored and each record has a unique address. The key chosen in the record structure is directly related to one of these unique addresses, thus providing quick and direct access. The disadvantage of this method is that space must be allocated to all expected records and in actual usage there may be many record slots not used. The key conversion also relies on the record key being numeric and thus direct addressing is not suitable for all applications.

Indirect addressing can allow more efficient use of disk space and also cope with alphanumeric keys. The technique is called 'hashing'. A special mathematical technique when applied to the chosen record key will result in the storage address of the required record. Hashing algorithms must be capable of producing a good uniform distribution of records on the disk file. Since it is possible to generate the same address from different records allowance must be made for such 'collisions' and the algorithm must minimize the generation of identical addresses.

Direct access files are used in on-line applications such as flight reservations systems where speed of access is crucial.

## Programming operations on files

Programmers are concerned with either the creation of an external file or the maintenance of files, i.e. the alteration of the file contents by adding, amending or deleting files.

Each programming language has its own commands for file operations and although there are significant syntactical differences between the various languages there are basic operations that all languages must provide. These are

❑ opening a file; that is making the file available for manipulation
❑ reading records from the file into the immediate access store so that the program can access the fields and operate on the data
❑ writing new or amended records to the file and finally closing the file on conclusion of the operations.

The programming sections in subsequent chapters deal with these problems, and Chapter 3 on formal structured design methods has a more detailed analysis of a number of file-handling procedures.


## 2.8  Analysing the problem: program structure diagrams

The second level of the software life cycle is concerned with the design of the programs. The systems analyst will have provided a detailed program specification and the programming team leader will allocate tasks to the team.

Sometimes, however, a programmer will be faced with the problem of individual commissions. In these situations it is very important to insist on a proper program specification. If you are not clear about what needs to be achieved you can get into a cycle of confusion that can be expensive and frustrating for both the programmer and the client.

Having achieved a satisfactory program specification the next step is to analyse the problem and hence produce a design. The technique to be described in this section is known as top-down stepwise refinement.

The 'top-down' technique is an approach widely used in problem solving of all types. It is a divide-and-conquer method and is very useful in group working. It is extremely simple and yet very powerful.

Essentially the problem is studied and the major components established in outline only. (It is important not to be distracted by detail at this stage.) Having established each of the major components the technique is repeated for each part until the stage is reached at which the actual solution to the components becomes definable in terms of simple actions. This is easily illustrated by means of an outline structure diagram which will show the components of the problem and their sequential relationship (see Figure 2.13).

The process is known as 'stepwise refinement' because the approach takes place in a sequence of clearly defined steps, each one of which provides a more precise analysis of the problem. Each layer of the structure diagram represents the components required to solve the problems considered in the layer above.

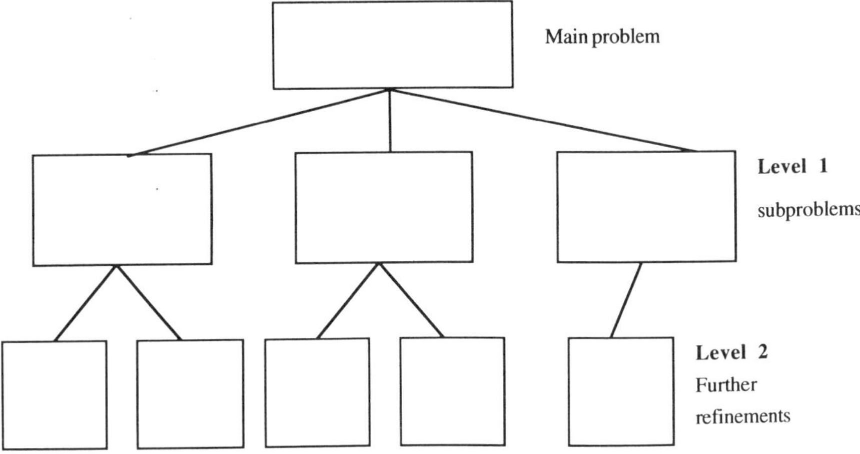

**Figure 2.13**   Hierarchical block diagram.

## Designing a top-down modular program

Structured programming provides an ideal environment for the top-down approach. Every structured program has one module which provides the top-down logic for the whole program. In the C language it is the function called *main* (normally written at the beginning of the program). This contrasts with Pascal, which has its main procedure at the end of the program. In COBOL it is the first paragraph in the procedure division.

This module normally controls the three basic functions of initializing, processing and closing down the program. In each of these stages you can expect to find similar sets of tasks whatever the program being written. Of course this is a great help when you become familiar with these expected routines.

Examples of initialization routines are: requesting library routines, opening files, and defining headings. Examples of processing tasks are: computations, reading and processing records, comparing values, and requesting data from the user. Examples of closing tasks include: closing files, producing concluding hard copy, and final user messages.

We have mentioned before that a structured program should only consist of three constructs: sequence, selection and iteration. It should be no surprise therefore that the techniques used to construct data structure diagrams are directly applicable to program structures. We now add to these structures the conditions that apply to the paths through the program structure.

A repetitive programming task such as reading records until the end of the file is reached is shown as an iteration in Figure 2.14. A task such as choosing

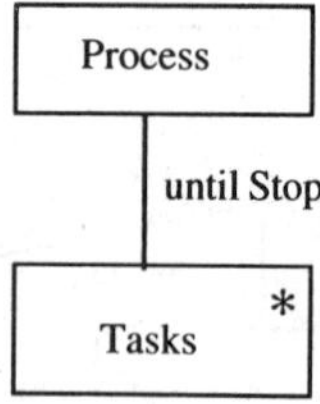


**Figure 2.14**

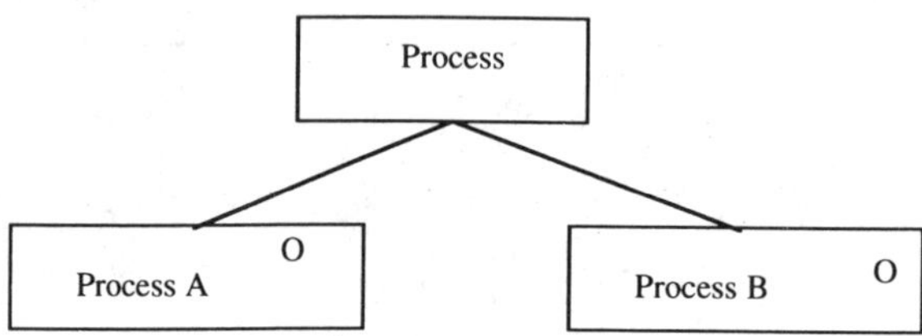


**Figure 2.15**

from a menu of options is shown as a selection in Figure 2.15. Note that the terminating condition for these tasks is written above the rectangle which is in effect the header box for that task.

## Exercise 2.4

Draw a program structure segment to show:
(a) Choosing between procedure A and procedure B.
(b) Repeating an action until the user entry is stop; output message 1 if A > B otherwise output message 2.

## Selection of tasks

On some occasions no action will be taken as one of the results of a logical test in which case the resultant box will be left blank or the line only will be drawn (see Figure 2.16).

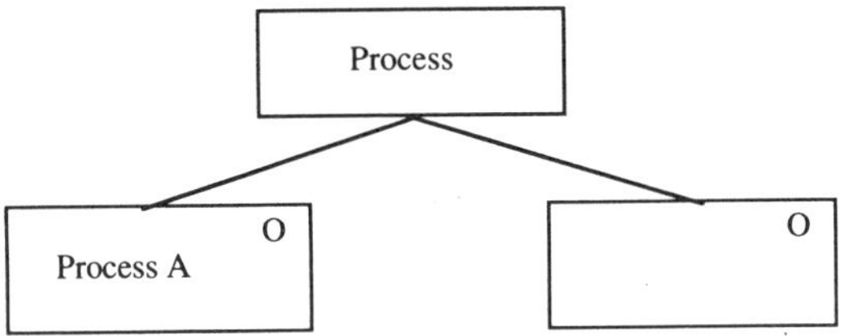


**Figure 2.16**

## *Exercise 2.5*

(a) Draw a section of a structure diagram from an element called 'draw' which allows the user to draw a circle upon inputting a C, a box upon inputting a B or to quit upon inputting a Q.

(b) Draw a section to show a record being read and written to a new file if it contains the field NCC.

## *Jackson structured programming*

The process of using data structure diagrams and program structure diagrams is the basis of a widely known formal method called Jackson structured programming (usually abbreviated to JSP). This technique will be studied later in this book. The use of a top-down method of solution is **not** dependent on using JSP. The technique can be used in the production of pseudo-code or even written as a list of structured tasks.

Programmers should not be restrictive in their choice of planning tools unless of course it is a particular company policy to always use a prescribed approach. The advantage of using a prescribed approach is that the conformity with standards makes it much easier to maintain programs. There is, however, a widely held belief among programmers that too much prescription prevents innovation and creativity.

We will conclude this chapter with an example which will be a useful precursor to Chapter 3.

## *Example of the production of a small structured program*

*Specification.* The program is to read a file of records consisting of a person's name and a set of examination marks, each one a percentage score. The average mark for each student is to be calculated and then assessed for a grade. The grades are pass if >39, merit >59, distinction >79. The results are to be written to a new file.

*Step 1.* The top layer! Considering the problem in outline we can see that we must

    access files
    process each record
    close files.

*Step 2.* Further thought gives us the next level of tasks. Accessing the files will require that we open files for reading/writing. The processing task will be to set up a loop to read in the records.

*Step 3.* The accessing files elements are concluded but the processing tasks require further refinement. These are read record to appropriate variables and use these values to calculate the mean from which we can establish grade and then write the result to the file.

*Step 4.* The above tasks require further action. However, this turns out to be the last layer. Note the end of each component refinement is reached when the actual programming actions can be listed. These are in order to calculate the mean. The actions are: read mark field add to total variable and divide by number of marks assigning result to mean variable. To assess the grade the actions are: compare mean with grade boundaries, write result to grade variable. Lastly to write to file we must write the name variable and the grade variable to record fields in new file.

*Step 5.* You will notice that the terminating sequence has been left appropriately to the last! In fact this is still at step 1 level and the actions required to refine this are to close the files and send an appropriate user message.

Figure 2.17 shows the development of a structured program.

## Summary exercise

A program is to be written to read a number of records consisting of a sales executive's name and the sales made during the week. It is to calculate the commission due to be paid to the sales executive as a percentage of sales and is to include a bonus if sales are greater than $5000. The

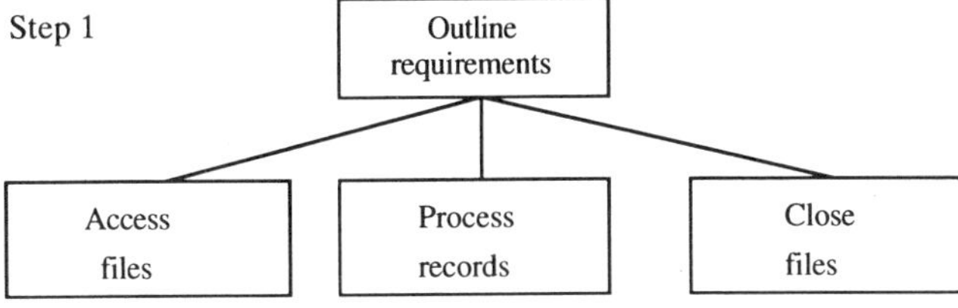


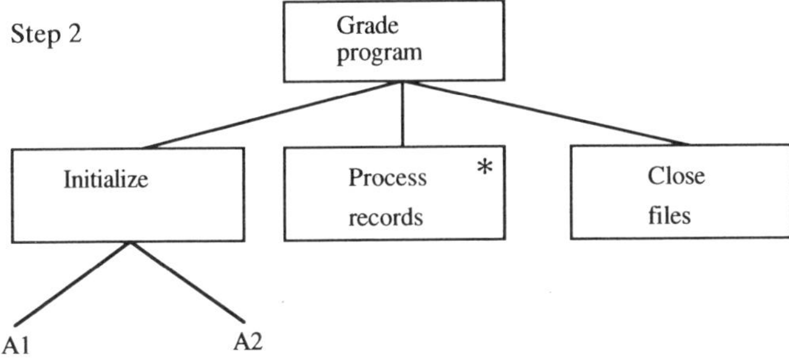


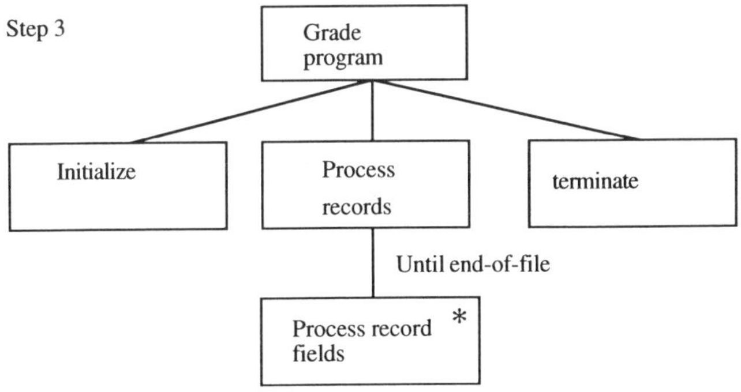


**Figure 2.17**   Development of a structured program (Steps 1–3).

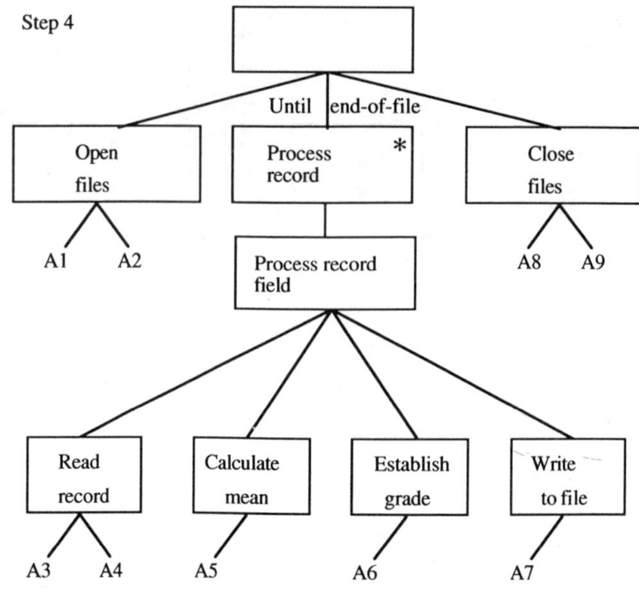



A1   Open input file for reading marks, etc.
A2   Open output file to write results
A3   Read name to output file name record
A4   Read marks and add to total
A5   Divide total by number of marks finding average
A6   Compare average with grade boundaries and determine grade
A7   Write grade to output file grade record
A8   Close files
A9   Output finished message

**Figure 2.17 (continued)**   Development of a structured program (Step 4).

calculations are to be written to a new file, each record containing the executive's name, the commission and the bonus if any. Draw a top-down diagram to illustrate the structure of such a program.

## 2.9 Summary

At this stage we can summarize the basic principles of top-down structured program design:

❏ the problem is analysed using the technique of stepwise refinement

❑ the design includes only three constructs: sequence, selection and iteration. As you have seen from the diagrams just drawn, these program components are self-contained and do not have cross-connections to other components. There is in effect one way in and one way out

❑ programs constructed in this way are easier to maintain and document.

# 3
# A formal structured design method – Jackson structured programming

## Objectives

When you have completed this chapter you will be able to:

❑ understand the application of a formal design method
❑ be able to construct an preliminary program specification by using input/ output data structures
❑ be able to produce the detailed requirements in terms of conditions and actions before coding a program.

## 3.1 Introduction

So far we have considered the three control constructs of sequence, iteration and selection that are required to structure programs. We have also studied data structures and top-down design. It is now time to formalize these methods by the chosen technique of Jackson structured programming (JSP).
  This technique:

❑ uses top-down stepwise refinement
❑ only uses the three control constructs
❑ bases the program design on the structure of the data to be processed.

The steps to be followed in every case are:

(1) Starting with the program specification, produce data structure diagrams of the data to be input for processing, and the data to be output.
(2) Produce a program structure that reflects the requirements of the data structures ensuring correspondence between program and data structures.

(3) Analyse the program structure in a top-down manner to produce an increasingly more specific program structure, by refining each layer of the design until all the necessary actions and conditions have been identified at their appropriate levels.

Our earlier work on data structures showed us how to produce physical data structure diagrams. A programmer is interested in matching the data structures with the program specification. This may well mean that an interpretation of the physical structure is required because all components of the physical DSD may not require processing and a different emphasis may be placed on some components and not others.

## *Example 3.1*

A stock record file is organized into sections by content, in this case children's, men's and women's clothes. The data on children's clothes are to be extracted and updated. The physical DSD is shown in Figure 3.1 and the logical DSD in Figure 3.2. The logical data structure reflects the fact that no processing is required of the records in the sections for both men's and women's clothing.

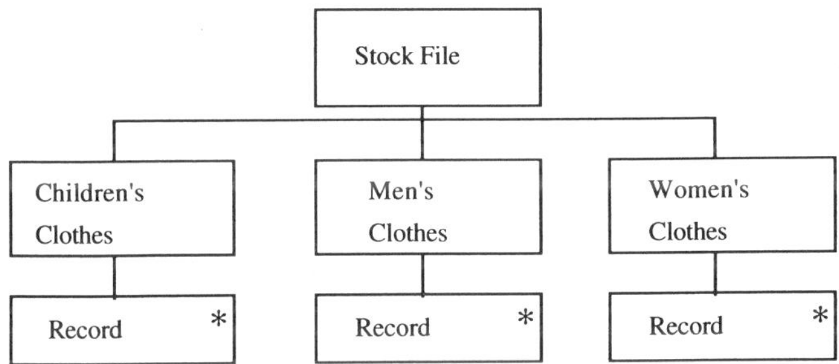

**Figure 3.1**   Physical DSD of stock record file.

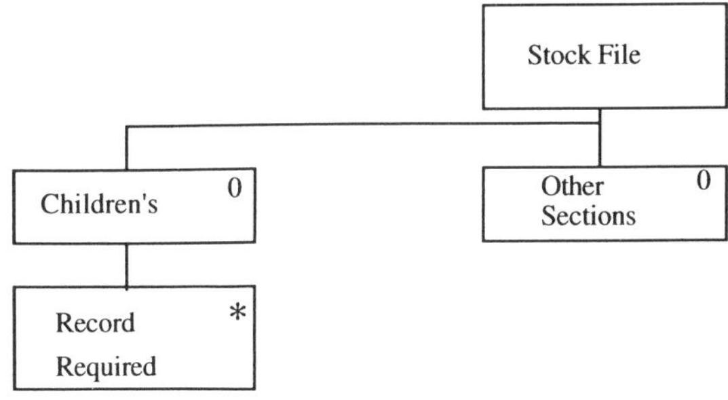

**Figure 3.2**   Logical DSD of stock record file.

## Example 3.2

A transaction file has been created by inputting the information about sales and purchases in batches. Each batch has a header record followed by the records with the details of the sales or purchases. The batches of records are input as they are received and therefore can occur in any order and any number. A report is required totalling the sales and purchases. Figure 3.3 shows the DSD of the transaction file and Figure 3.4 shows the sales component amended to indicate cash or credit sales.

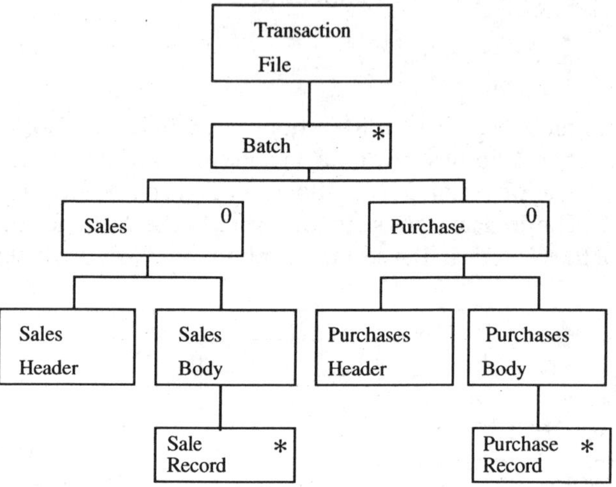

**Figure 3.3**   DSD of transaction file.

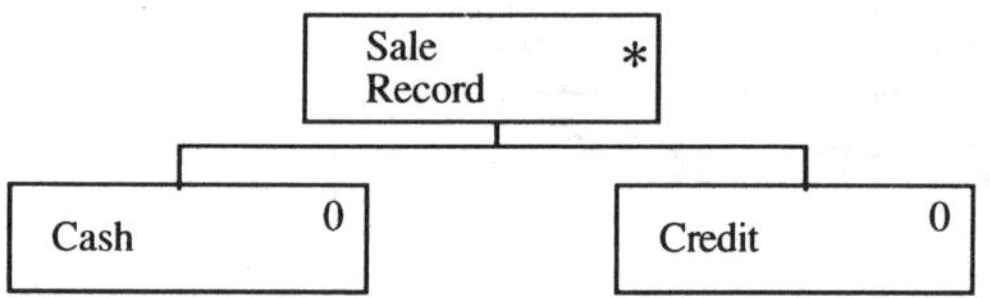

**Figure 3.4**   Amended DSD of transaction file.

## Exercise 3.1

A file contains records of students sorted into undergraduates and post-graduates. Undergraduate students pay fees at rate A and postgraduates at rate B. Students from other countries pay fees at rates E for undergraduates and at rate G for postgraduates.

(a) Draw the logical DSD when it is required to produce a list of all the students who have paid their fees.

**(b)** Draw the logical DSD for a program listing overseas postgraduate students.

**(c)** Draw a DSD for a program listing undergraduates who have not paid their fees.

## 3.2  Establishing the program structure

The program structure is established by determining the input and output data structures and combining them to produce the program structure. As you have already seen, the output requirements are of great value in determining the logical data structure of the input file. The input and output data structures must correspond to each other. That is, each data component of the input structure must have a matching component in the output structure.

To determine the program structure, we first compare the input and output data structures and, starting from the top down, identify the components that correspond to each other. (Corresponding components will be in the same relative place as each other – the input component is processed to produce the output component.) The data structures are then combined to produce a program structure. This process is illustrated in the following two examples which have been chosen to cover two common types of file processing requirements.

*Example 3.3  Using one input file to produce one output file or report*

For this example the input file is organized sequentially. It contains details of spare parts that have been ordered by garages. The garages have been grouped together in areas and the spare parts orders grouped together for each garage.

The requirement is to access this file and produce a total of the value of the orders by garage. Figure 3.5 on the next page shows the physical DSD of the input file.

Since the output requirement does not need to include the area of each garage, the logical DSD does not include this component. Figure 3.6 overleaf shows the logical DSD of input file.

The report structure is to have a heading followed by a one-line summary of each garage's total order value and a footer containing the total of all orders. Figure 3.7 overleaf shows the DSD of the report.

Now that we have produced the input and output DSDs, we now look for correspondences in the structures. A correspondence occurs when the same number of instances occurs between the data components. They can only occur if the input component is to be processed to become the output component. Figure 3.8 on page 47 shows the representation of correspondences.

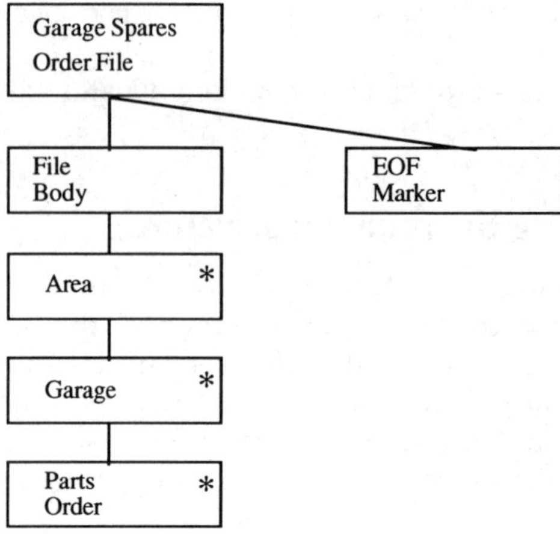


**Figure 3.5** Physical DSD of input file.

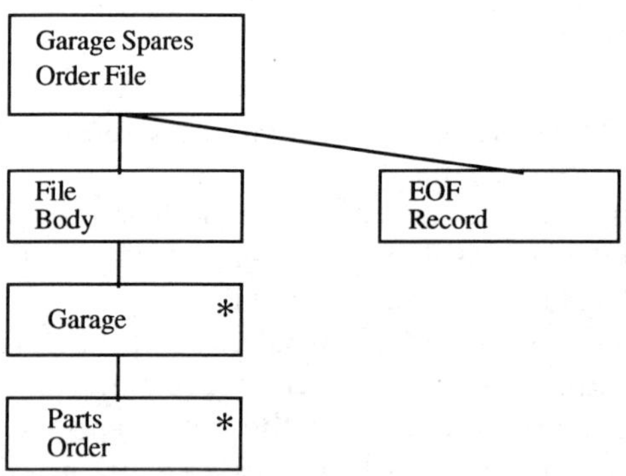


**Figure 3.6** Logical DSD of input file.

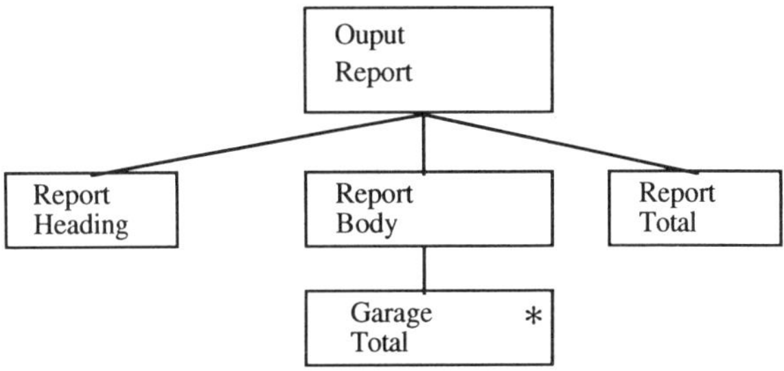

**Figure 3.7**   DSD of report.

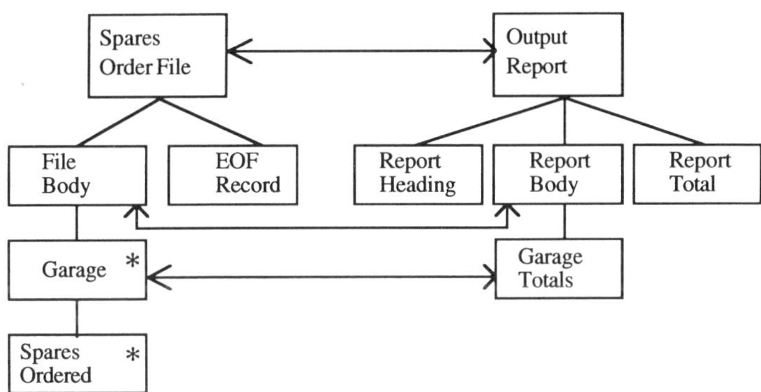

**Figure 3.8**   Representation of correspondences.

Next the two data structures are compared. If necessary, dummy components are added so that the structures are identical. From this we identify the shape of the program structure. Figure 3.9 overleaf shows the input/output data structure comparison for the input and Figure 3.10 shows the input/output data structure comparison for the output.

The resulting program structure is shown in Figure 3.11 on page 49 which you will notice has the following properties:

❏ each data component is related to only one program component
❏ each program component is related to only one input and/or one output component.

The last step is to analyse this preliminary program structure in more detail in order to begin constructing the program.

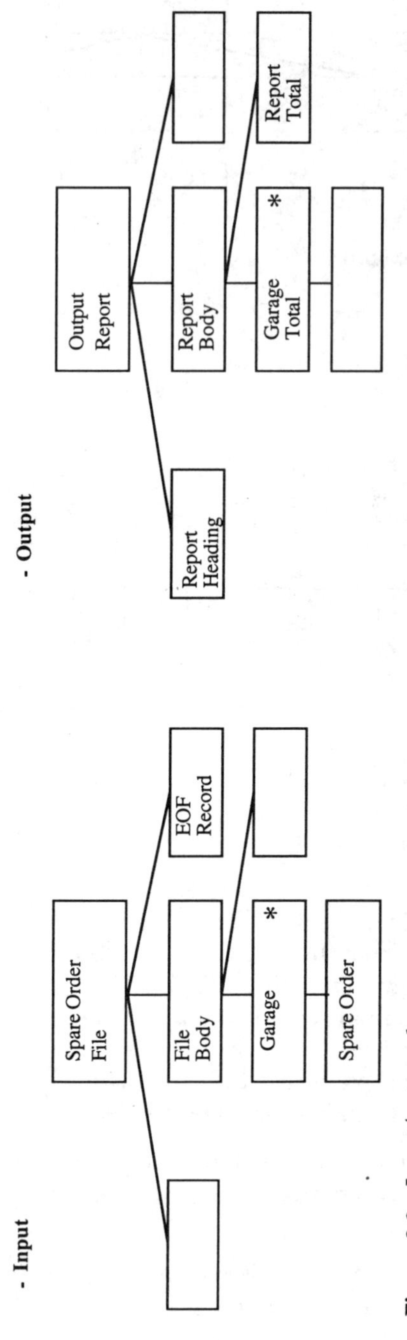


**Figure 3.10**   Input/output data structure comparison – output.



**Figure 3.9**   Input/output data structure comparison – input.

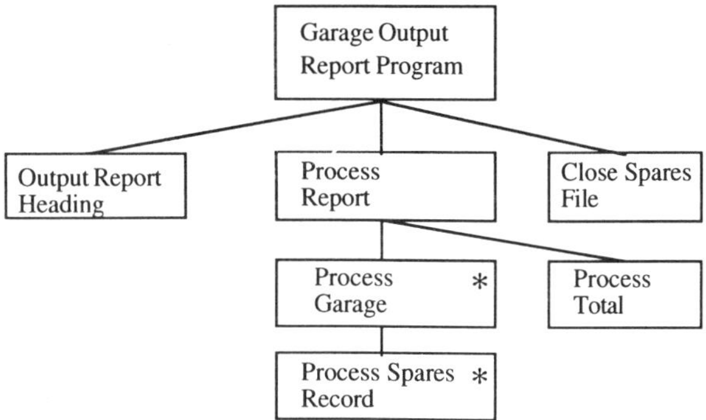

**Figure 3.11**   Program structure.

## Example 3.4  Two input files and one output file

In this more complex example the program specification is as follows. A transaction file is used to update a master file and produce a new master file. The transaction file is sorted in ascending order on the same key as the master file. The update process is to be performed sequentially. The records are matched by comparing the keys of the two files. If the record keys on the master and the transaction file match, then the transaction record is used to update the master record, a new master record is written to the new file and the keys on the next pair of records compared. If the transaction key is greater than the master key, then the master record is written to the new file and the next master record is read in. If, however, the master key is greater than the transaction record, then the transaction record is used to create a new master record and the next transaction record is read in. No deletions will be required.

This process is continued until both files have been completely processed. If the master file ends before the transaction file, new records are created until

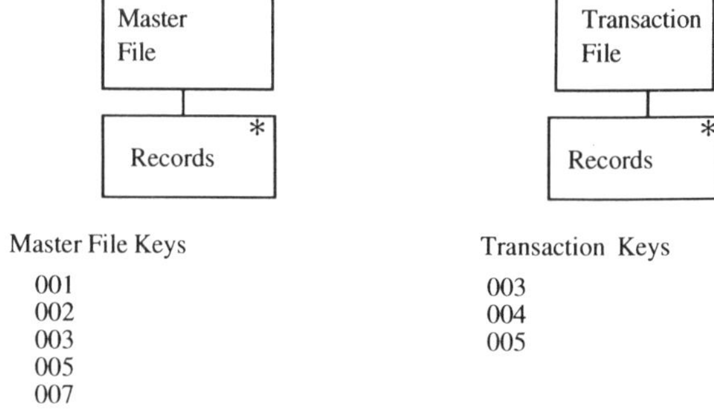

**Figure 3.12**   Physical DSDs of files.

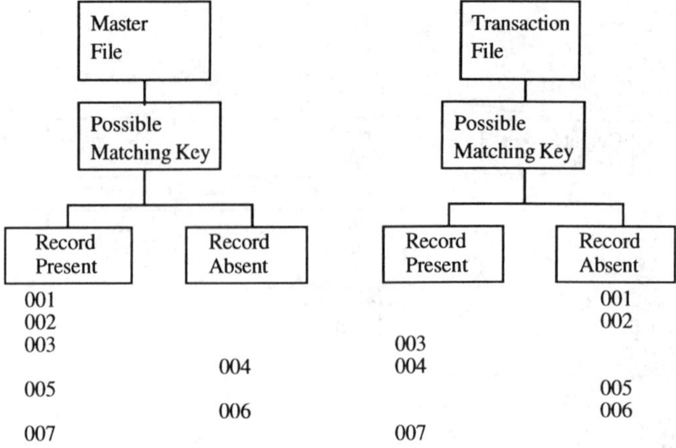

**Figure 3.13**   Logical data structure.

the transaction file ends. If the transaction file ends before the master file, the master file records are copied until the master file ends.

The first step is to consider the physical data structure of the two files. These are shown in Figure 3.12. For this example assume that the record keys are as shown in the diagram. The presence or absence of a key is relevant to the processing requirements and is illustrated in Figure 3.13.

All possible combinations of keys – absent or present – are shown under the logical DSD. For instance:

records present on the master are 001, 002, 003, 005, 007
records present on the transaction are 003, 004, 007
records absent on the master are 004, 006
records absent on the transaction are 001, 002, 005, 006.

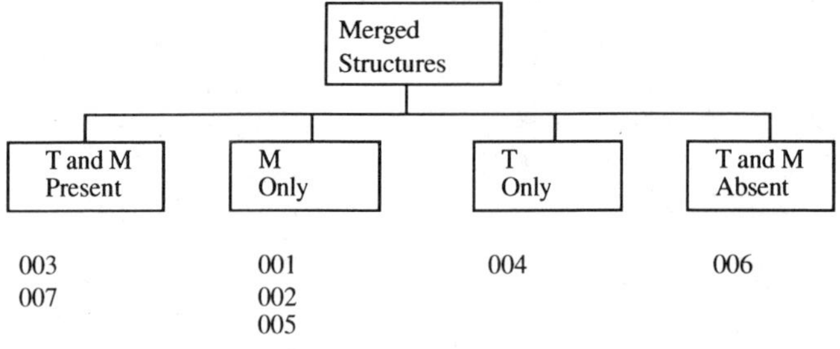

**Figure 3.14**   Revised logical DSD.

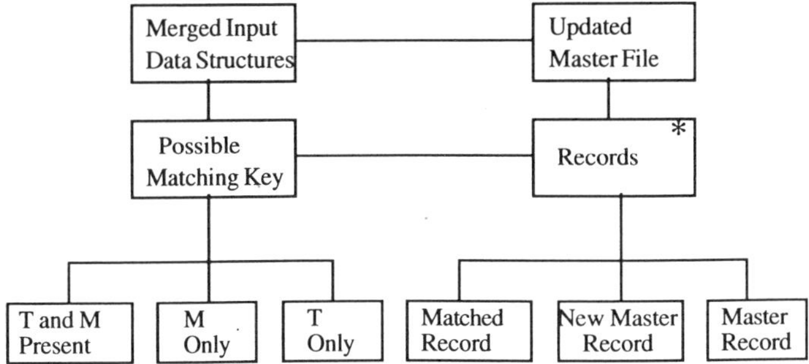

**Figure 3.15**  Matching input and output structure diagrams.

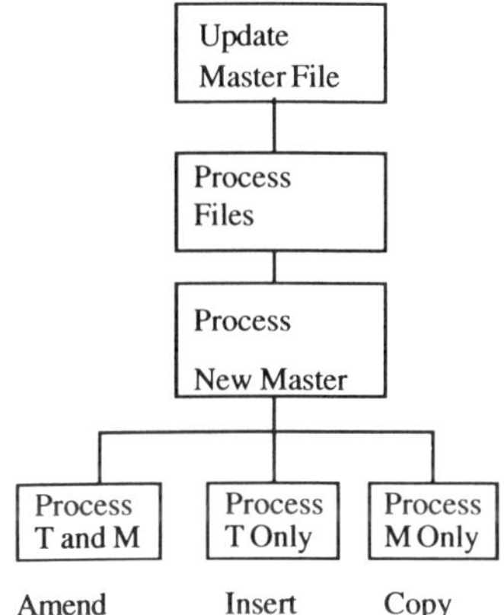

**Figure 3.16**  Preliminary program structure (PSP).

The aim of the computer program is to merge these structures, so a more representative DSD can be produced by combining them into a new logical DSD.

Figure 3.14 shows the revised logical DSD which is much easier to use and covers the required combination of data. In this example the program specification excludes the situation where there are no records to be processed on either the transaction or the master, so the final matching diagrams for input and output data structures are as shown in Figure 3.15.

An initial structure for the program, known as a preliminary program structure (PPS), can now be clearly seen – Figure 3.16. This PPS is be used to determine the processing details that will be required at each level. This is addressed in the next section.

## 3.3 Detailed program design

In the last two examples, we began to develop our programs by drawing data structure diagrams for input and output to produce preliminary program structures. We will now look at how PPSs are used to produce detailed designs for our programs. Once again, this is a systematic procedure; it identifies the elementary program operations (i.e. the conditions or actions that can be converted to one or a few lines of code). This stage can also produce further refinements of the final program structure by reminding programmers of earlier considerations and perhaps drawing their attention to processing difficulties which were not obvious at the earlier stage. We would emphasize that a formal design technique is a tool designed to help us and, although extremely useful, it must not obstruct the design process.

The first consideration in converting the PPS into a detailed design is to consider the conditions that must be applied to the iterations and selections. We need to answer questions such as: 'what determines the conclusion of an iteration?' and 'what conditional tests apply to the selections?'.

We do this in a top-down manner, progressing downward through the levels of the program structure from the top to the bottom.

We illustrate this process applying it to the update program whose program structure was determined in Example 3.4.

When we examine the preliminary program structure diagram the first conditional situation we meet is the need to control the input of the records from the input files. When do we terminate this process? Since all of the old master records are to be amended or copied and any new transactions are to be made into new master records, then the condition is when an end of file record is reached for both files.

In order to be systematic, we number the possible conditions as they arise. In this case we have

C1 = end of file record for the master file
C2 = end of file record for the transaction file.

The next conditions to be determined are the selections which call processing to amend, insert, or copy a record. The records are processed by reading in a transaction record and then a master record and comparing the keys. The possibilities are that the transaction and old master record keys match or the keys do not match. If the keys do not match then the transaction key is greater than the master key or the transaction key is less than the master key.

The conditions are therefore

C3: transaction key = master key
C4: transaction key < master key
C5: transaction key > master key.

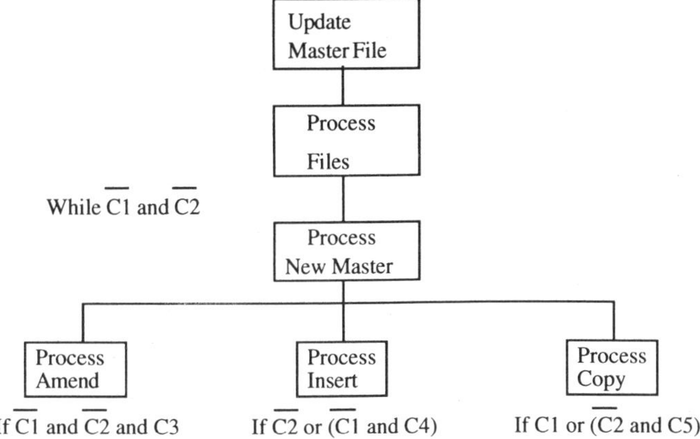



**Figure 3.17**   Program structure conditions added.

The complete list of all possible conditions is (EOF is end-of-file)

C1: EOF (master file)
C2: EOF (transaction file)
C3: transaction key = master key
C4: transaction key < master key
C5: transaction key > master key.

These simple conditions can now be combined to provide the iteration control constructs for the program and are be added to the PPS as shown in Figure 3.17. Note the overbar represents **not**, i.e. $\overline{C1}$ means **not** C1.

The iteration control construct list is

| | |
|---|---|
| WHILE $\overline{C1}$ AND $\overline{C2}$ | until both files reach EOF record |
| IF $\overline{C1}$ AND $\overline{C2}$ AND C3 | if both files not ended and match occurs |
| IF $\overline{C2}$ OR ($\overline{C1}$ AND C4) | if transaction not ended or (transaction key < master key and master not ended) |
| IF C1 OR ($\overline{C2}$ AND C5) | if transaction ended or transaction not ended and transaction key > master key). |

## Actions list

The next step is to consider the actions required for initialization and termination and include them in the actions list. When drawing up the actions list, we examine the lowest level of each elementary component and decide what actions are required to complete the program structure.

For our example the actions list is:

*Initialization*

(1)   The transaction file and the old master file must be opened for reading.

(2)   The new master file must be opened for writing.

*Termination*

(3)   Close transaction file.

(4)   Close master file.

(5)   Close new master file.

(6)   Stop program.

*Input*

(7)   Read master file record.

(8)   Read transaction file record.

*Output*

(9)   Write new master record.

*Processing*

(10)   Update existing master record.

(11)   Create new master from transaction.

(12)   Copy old master record.

The diagram with these actions added is shown in Figure 3.18.


## Reading ahead

If we now examine Figure 3.18, it is clear that the program cannot proceed unless there are records available for comparison at the start of the program. To overcome this problem it is necessary to read the first two records before

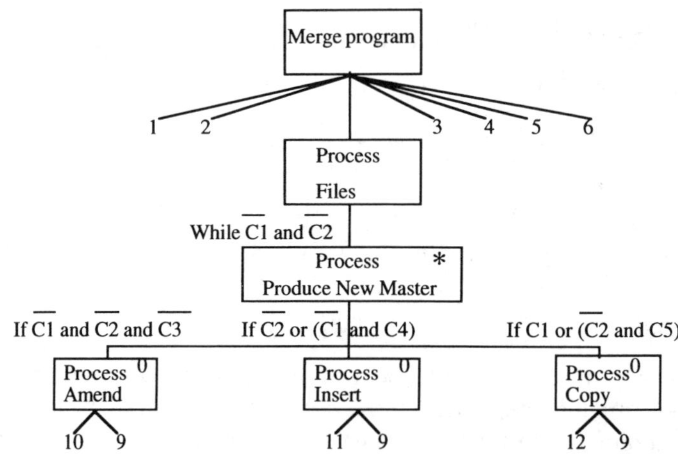


**Figure 3.18**

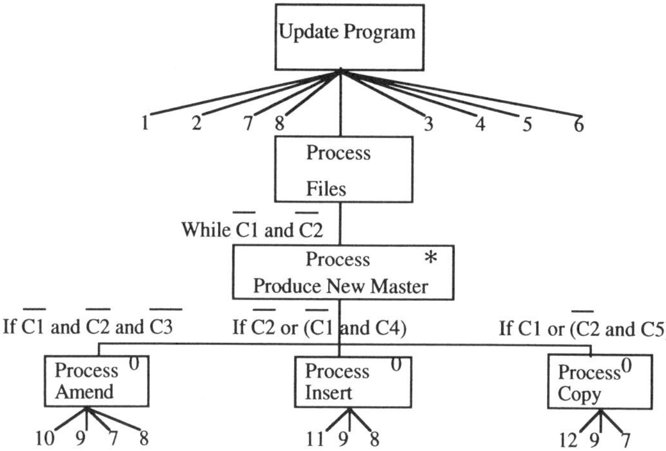

**Figure 3.19**

any processing takes place. This is a recognized technique which is known as 'reading ahead'. It is commonly required when processing sequential files.

Returning to our example, we need to add actions (**7**) and (**8**) at the initialization stages. We must also read into the record area a 'replacement' for any records that have been processed. The diagram now becomes as shown in Figure 3.19. However, this diagram does not conform to the JSP rule that elementary operations must only be allocated to elementary components, so we need to further refine our diagram.

The final solution is shown in Figure 3.20.

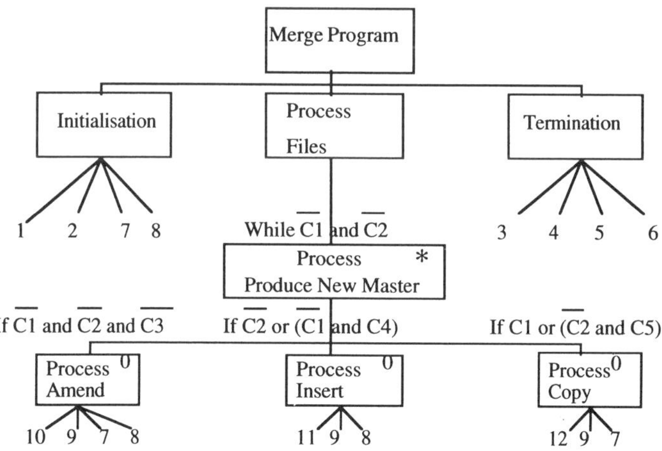

**Figure 3.20**

These examples have been of file processing. The technique is equally applicable to other types of processing problems.

## 3.4  Summary: steps in the application of JSP

(1)  Produce data structure diagrams for the input and output data.
(2)  Use these diagrams to produce a preliminary program structure by looking for correspondences and matching the data structure 'shape' to that of the program structure.
(3)  Examine the program structure and determine the conditions and the actions that complete the final details required to fulfil the program specification.

### Summary exercise

(1)  A college has converted its student application file to a computer system. Each department arranges interviews and records these results in groups as unconditional acceptances, conditional acceptances and reflections. These are maintained on a course file in batches with a course code header at the start of the three groups. The course tutor for each course requires a listing of the student acceptances under the course heading
   (a)  draw the input and output data structures and show correspondences
   (b)  produce a program structure
   (c)  produce condition and action lists and enter them appropriately on the diagram.
(2)  The master stock file contains details of each item in stock including a re-order level. A program is required which will output a report indicating all stock which has reached or fallen below the re-order level. The report is to have a heading and list the item code and the present stock level.
   (a)  Draw the logical data structure of the master file and the report.
   (b)  Draw the program structure diagram in its final form including conditions and actions.

# 4

# Further programming techniques – procedures and functions

## Objectives

At the end of this chapter you will understand:

- ❏ how procedures, functions and subroutines form the building blocks of a structured program
- ❏ what local and global variables are and when they are used
- ❏ what procedure parameters are and how to use them.

## 4.1 Introduction

We have seen how the top-down design process essentially splits a problem into its component parts until a stage is reached where building a solution becomes much easier. Programs written in this way are often called modular programs.

Procedures and functions are the building blocks which are needed to complete this process. Each structured computer language has its own way of providing these components, e.g. the language Pascal, which was designed to teach the concepts we have been using, has both procedures and functions, whereas C has only functions and the original BASIC only provided subroutines.

We have designed our pseudo-code so that we can use both procedures and functions in our example programs. When we want to use a procedure or a function we shall call it simply by using its name.

The difference between a procedure and a function will be that a function will return a value after a call, while a procedure will do a particular task but

**not** return a value. Since the function will return a value, the data type of the function must be declared.

The pseudo-code for a procedure will be

*PROCEDURE name(parameters and their data types)*
*the procedure code*
*ENDPROCEDURE*

The pseudo-code for a function will be

*FUNCTION name(parameters and their data types) data type of the function*
*the function code*
*ENDFUNCTION*

the value returned from the function will be shown using the command *RETURN*.


## 4.2 Local and global variables

Most languages provide a facility where variables may be declared either locally or globally.

A global variable is one that, after declaration, is available to every part of the program. Any procedure or function may use the variable. This means that in order to ensure that one procedure or function does not interfere with another, it is very important to keep track of what the global variables are doing.

A local variable, however, is only declared and used within the procedure or function in which it is declared. The values of local variables are normally lost as soon as the procedure or function call has concluded.

The safest and easiest way to keep track of variables is to confine them (as far as is possible) to local use. That is, only use variables within individual procedures, **not** throughout the whole program.

Another point to remember is that global variables use memory all the time the program is running, and not just when they are needed.

In our pseudo-code, global variables are listed at the start of the code; local variables within the procedure or function where they are needed.

We will now illustrate these concepts with a pseudo-code program.


*Example 4.1*

This is a program to provide a simple quiz on capital cities, basic mathematics or simple chemistry. The structure diagram is shown in Figure 4.1. The procedure names chosen for this example are capital, maths and chem. The procedures are called from the first block of code, which we have called the main procedure. Remember all procedures and functions will start with the name and finish with the statement ENDPROCEDURE.

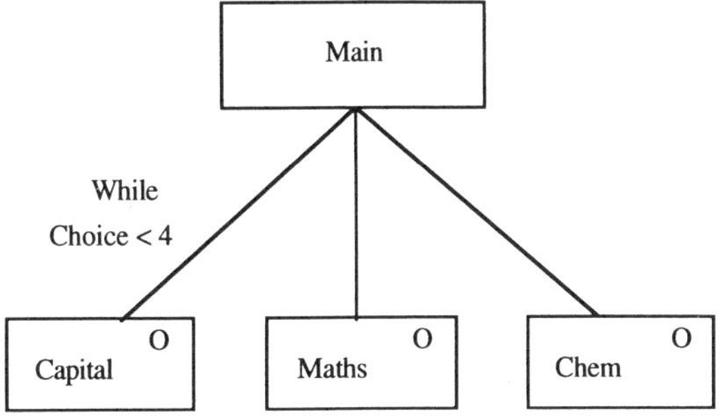


**Figure 4.1**

Here is the pseudo-code. There are no global variables.

*PROCEDURE main (The highest level procedure in the structure)*
*choice is a local variable of type Integer*
*choice: = 0*
*WHILE choice < > 4*
*DO*
  *DISPLAY "Choose which quiz you would like to try"*
  *DISPLAY "Type in the quiz number"*
  *DISPLAY "1. Capital Cities"*
  *DISPLAY "2. Basic Maths"*
  *DISPLAY "3. Chemical symbols"*
  *DISPLAY "4. End the program"*
*REPEAT*
  *ACCEPT choice*
  *IF choice < 1 or choice > 4 DISPLAY "Error: choose again"*
*UNTIL choice > 0 and choice < 5*
*IF choice = 1 then Capital (First procedure call)*
*IF choice = 2 then Maths  (Second procedure call)*
*IF choice = 3 then Chem  (Third procedure call)*
*ENDO*
*ENDPROCEDURE*
*PROCEDURE Capital (start of procedure capital)*
*answer is a local variable of type String*
*score is a local variable of type Integer*
*score: = 0*
*DISPLAY "What is the capital city of England?"*
*ACCEPT answer*
*IF answer = London then score := score + 1*
*DISPLAY "What is the capital city of France?"*
*ACCEPT answer*

*IF answer = Paris then score := score + 1*
*DISPLAY "What is the capital city of Japan?"*
*ACCEPT answer*
*IF answer = Tokyo then score := score + 1*
*DISPLAY "your score is", score*
*ENDPROCEDURE*
*PROCEDURE Maths (start of procedure maths)*
*number is a local variable of type Integer*
*score is a local variable of type Integer*
*score: = 0*
*DISPLAY "What is the square of 16?"*
*ACCEPT number*
*IF number = 256 then score := score + 1*
*DISPLAY "What is the square root of 81?"*
*ACCEPT number*
*IF number = 9 then score := score + 1*
*DISPLAY "What is the denary value of the hexadecimal number 21?"*
*ACCEPT number*
*IF number = 33 then score := score + 1*
*DISPLAY "your score is", score*
*ENDPROCEDURE*
*PROCEDURE Chem (start of procedure Chem)*
*symbol is a local variable of type String*
*score is a local variable of type Integer*
*score: = 0*
*DISPLAY "What is the chemical symbol for sodium?"*
*ACCEPT symbol*
*IF symbol = Na then score = score + 1*
*DISPLAY "What is the chemical symbol for chlorine?"*
*ACCEPT symbol*
*IF symbol = Cl then score = score + 1*
*DISPLAY "What is the chemical symbol for lead?"*
*ACCEPT symbol*
*IF symbol = Pb then score = score + 1*
*DISPLAY "your score is ", score*
*ENDPROCEDURE*

In the simple example above it is clear that main procedure is calling the three
lower level procedures. These do not then call other procedures, although in
more complex problems, there will of course be further calls to other levels.

You may notice that the variable score has been used as a local variable within
the quiz procedures. This declaration does not affect any other procedure since
the value of score is discarded as soon as the procedures conclude. If score had

been declared globally the value from each procedure would continue to accumulate thus giving incorrect answers after the first procedure call.

There is no limit to the number of calls that can be made to a procedure or function and (as you will see later) some languages allow functions or procedures to call themselves! This is clearly a great advantage because it means that we do not have to repeatedly rewrite the code. In fact, once a reliable solution has been found a library of such solutions can be maintained for use whenever they are needed. This technique can be expanded further and reliable routines established which can then be used whenever similar algorithms are required.

Languages such as C, which have a relatively small set of programming commands, are provided with large libraries of prewritten routines which can save a great amount of time and effort!

## Exercise 4.1

Give four advantages of using procedures or functions in a program.

## 4.3  Using parameters and returning values from functions

The term 'parameter' is used to describe variables which are used in a procedure or function and which will accept values passed to the procedure or function when it is invoked. The technical term for the value passed is argument. This complicated definition is best illustrated by some practical examples.

### Example 4.2

To write a procedure called addup which uses two parameters. We remind you that the pseudo-code syntax for using parameters will be to put them in brackets with their data type written next to them.

Note that from now we are going to simplify the declaration of variables in the pseudo-code by omitting the words 'of type' and replacing them with a colon. For example, variable name of type String becomes variable name: String.

```
PROCEDURE addup(a,b: Integer)
variable answer: Integer
answer:= a + b
DISPLAY ("The sum is", answer)
ENDPROCEDURE
```

Whenever it is needed to use this procedure it is called by writing

```
addup(identifier1, identifier2)
```

The identifiers are supplied by an earlier part of the program. The procedure would be used like this:

```
DISPLAY ("enter two numbers")
ACCEPT number1, number2
addup(number1, number2)
```

The complete code is therefore:

```
PROCEDURE main
   DISPLAY ("enter two numbers")
   ACCEPT number1, number2
   addup(number1, number2)
ENDPROCEDURE
PROCEDURE addup (a,b: Integer)
variable answer: Integer
   answer:= a + b
   DISPLAY ("The sum is", answer)
ENDPROCEDURE
```

## Example 4.3

This example describes a procedure that will output to a monitor screen a character chosen by a user. It will repeat this a number of times (also chosen by the user). The program pattern is as follows:

```
PROCEDURE main
variables choice: Character, n: Integer
choice = Y
WHILE choice = Y
   DISPLAY "What character would you like output to screen"
   ACCEPT choice
   DISPLAY "How many times do you wish this to sent"
   ACCEPT n
   design(choice, n)
   DISPLAY "Do you want another design : type Y IF you do"
   ACCEPT choice
ENDWHILE
ENDPROCEDURE
PROCEDURE design (char: Character, number: Integer)
variable times: Integer
FOR (times=1, times<=number, times+1)
   DISPLAY char
ENDFOR
ENDPROCEDURE
```

## 4.4 Functions

A simple example found in most languages are the functions provided to work out the trignometrical values, such as the sine, cosine or tangent of an angle. For example

*ACCEPT x*
*DISPLAY sin(x)*

This short piece of code would display the sine of any value you input. The sine function accepts the argument you input for $x$, works out the value of $sin(x)$ and returns the answer to be output to the monitor screen. Note that functions can be used on the right-hand side of an assignment.

In our pseudo-code we will write the functions using the same construct as that for procedures, but using the term ENDFUNCTION to show the finish of the code and the word RETURN to indicate the identifier sending the value back to the calling place. The call may come from any other procedure or function.

Now that our example programs are becoming more complicated, it is a good time to remind you that pseudo-code is not concerned with program details. It is a planning tool and a useful method of demonstrating program algorithms. These program examples are kept simple to avoid losing the new ideas in the complexity of the code. Nevertheless this program can be used to form the basis of a reasonably challenging piece of coding. Additions you might like to include could be:

❑ validation of the input to the menu
❑ clearing the screen
❑ positioning the screen messages.

Other interesting additions you could look at, if your programming language allows them, are:

❑ the use of colour to make user messages more interesting
❑ screen layout commands to provide attractive presentations.

A most important point is that the test of a good program is 'Does it fulfil the specification reliably?' Remember there is no one correct solution in terms of the coding, only in terms of the program specification. Testing is covered in some detail later on.

We shall now look again at the simple mathematics example program used earlier and use it to illustrate the concept of parameters to functions, and how a value is returned from a function.

You will recall that the program steps required were:

(1) present to the user a menu of choices
(2) accept the choice and do the calculation or end the program.

The structure diagram is shown in Figure 4.2.

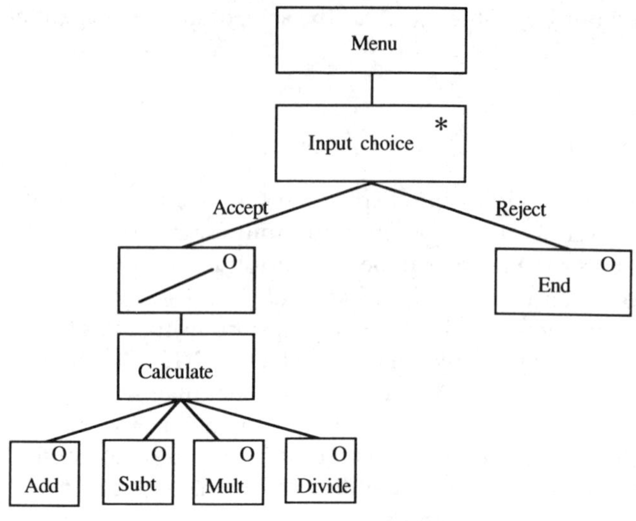


**Figure 4.2**

*main program*
*opening-message*
*screen menu*
*end program*

*PROCEDURE opening_message*
*DISPLAY "this is a simple mathematics program"*
*DISPLAY "it will offer you a choice of calculation to be performed on any two*
*numbers you input"*
*ENDPROCEDURE*
*PROCEDURE menu*
*DISPLAY "Enter your two numbers"*
*ACCEPT number1, number2*
*DISPLAY "Now choose your calculation type"*
*DISPLAY "when you are finished type the number 5"*
*REPEAT*
  *DISPLAY "1: addition"*
  *DISPLAY "2: subtraction"*
  *DISPLAY "3: multiplication"*
  *DISPLAY "4: division"*
  *DISPLAY "5: endprogram"*
  *ACCEPT choice*

```
DO CASE OF choice
   CASE choice = 1
   result: = addup(number1,number2)
   DISPLAY result
CASE choice = 2
   result: = subtract(number1,number2)
   DISPLAY result
CASE choice = 3
   result: = multiply(number1,number2)
   DISPLAY result
CASE choice = 4
   result: = divide(number1,number2)
   IF result < > 0 DISPLAY result
UNTIL choice = 5
ENDPROCEDURE
FUNCTION addup(a,b: Integer): Integer
   answer: Integer
   answer:= a+b
   RETURN answer
ENDFUNCTION
FUNCTION subtract(a,b: Integer): Integer
   answer: Integer
   answer:= a−b
   return answer
ENDFUNCTION
FUNCTION multiply(a,b: Integer): Integer
   answer: integer
   answer:= a*b
   return answer
ENDFUNCTION
FUNCTION divide (a,b Integer): Integer
   answer: Integer
   IF b=0
   DISPLAY"You cannot divide by zero"
   answer = 0
 · ENDIF
   ELSE answer:= a/b
   return answer
ENDFUNCTION
```

## 4.5 Summary

There a number of important reasons for using the procedures and functions:

❏ the code can be built to reflect a structured design with procedures echoing the design at each level of the top-down process
❏ tasks that are needed repeatedly within a program can be coded once and then called when needed
❏ a smaller size of procedure makes them easier to test and debug leading to greater overall reliability
❏ variables can be confined to the procedure in which they are used thus eliminating unexpected side-effects in other parts of the program and also avoiding unnecessary use of memory.

## 4.6 Arrays: sorting and searching

### The array

*One-dimensional arrays.* This type of array is a sequence of simple data types which can be referenced by the position they occupy in the sequence. The normal programming method of referencing an array is to use the array name followed by a subscript containing the element number. The array is stored in the computer in adjacent memory locations and each memory location would have an identifier composed of the array name followed by the appropriate subscript. An array is an iteration of homogeneous data. The data structure diagram is shown in Figure 4.3.

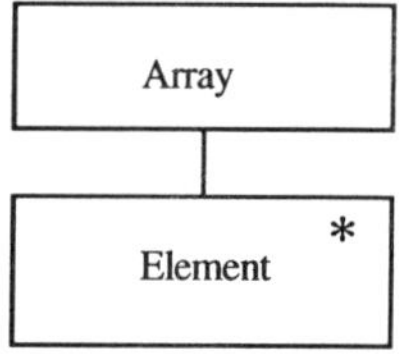


**Figure 4.3**

The array elements can be simple or complex data types, but they must all be the same, i.e. homogeneous.

### Example 4.4

A list of numbers can be defined as an array. An array named 'numbers' contains 23, 34, 45, 56 in that order. Each member can now be identified as: 23 is number[1] , 34 is number[2], 45 is number[3] and 56 is number[4] .

### Example 4.5

'Name' is defined as an array of characters so if the word James is stored in the array called name then J is name[1], a is name[2], m is name[3], e is name[4] and s is name[5].

## Exercise 4.2

A deck of 52 cards (no joker) is sorted into the suit sequence of hearts, clubs, diamonds and spades with each suit in ascending order of value. Defining this structure as the array called cards, answer the following questions.

(**a**)  Name the cards identified by cards[3], cards[51], cards[27].

(**b**)  What are the identifiers for the queen of hearts, the jack of diamonds and the ace of spades?

*Two-dimensional arrays.* The elements of an array can be complex data types. It is clearly necessary to have the ability to have an array of words such as a list of employee names or of book titles. Since a word is an array of characters then an array of names is in fact a two-dimensional array and in some languages has to be declared as such.

The convention in this case is to use two subscripts. We shall show this by a practical example.

## Example 4.6

The array is called name-list and consists of five names of no more than 15 characters.

    james
    janet
    alexander
    lee
    zacharia

The letter m in the name james can be precisely located as name-list[1][3]. Similarly the letter z in name zacharia is name-list[5][1]. A process to sort these names into alphabetical order would need to compare each name character by character to determine the appropriate ranking. It would not be sufficient simply to compare each first letter since the letters might be the same. In the above example james and janet can only be ordered on a comparison test when the third letters are compared. For instance, name-list[1][3] < name-list[2][3].

## Arrays of records: tables

An array of records can considered to be a two-dimensional table in which the rows represent the records and the columns the fields. See Figure 4.4.

| Field names | first name | last name | grade of post | job type |
|---|---|---|---|---|
| Records | John | Chang | a1 | engineer |
|  | Eric | Teo | a5 | computing |
|  | David | Smith | a4 | admin |
|  | Peter | Lee | a4 | writer |

**Figure 4.4**

To search or sort tables a key field is chosen. This array could be sorted on the key of the surnames – Figure 4.5.

| Field names | first name | last name | grade of post | job type |
|---|---|---|---|---|
| Records | John | Chang | a1 | engineer |
| | Peter | Lee | a4 | writer |
| | David | Smith | a4 | admin |
| | Eric | Teo | a5 | computing |

**Figure 4.5**

Figure 4.6 shows a data structure diagram of the above array of records.

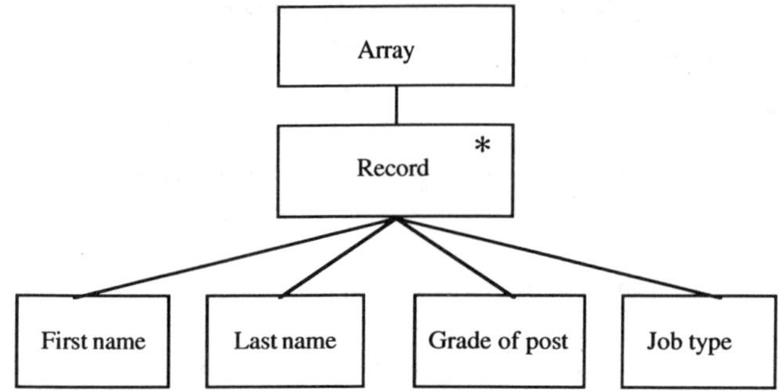


**Figure 4.6**   Data structure diagram for the array of records in Figure 4.5.

## Pseudo-code for the array data structure

The array is defined by writing the name and showing the upper and lower bounds followed by the data type, e.g.

*name: array[1, 10] of character*

Now let us consider two simple examples of programs using arrays.

## Example 4.7

A program to read in a set of 10 integer numbers to an array and output them in reverse order

*Program reverse*
*numbers: array[1, 10] of Integer*
*count,n: Integer*
*FOR(n=1, n< 10, n+1)*
*    DISPLAY "Enter a number"*
*    ACCEPT numbers[n]*
*ENDFOR*

```
DISPLAY "The numbers you entered in reverse order are"
FOR (count=10, count> 0, count-1)
   DISPLAY numbers[count]
ENDFOR
```

## Pseudo-code for the record data structure

The record will be given a name and each field of the record will be declared
with a name and data type. These will be referred to individually as in the following example. To declare a record called car with fields, make, size, and colour.

```
car = RECORD
        make: string
        size: integer
        colour: string
        ENDRECORD
```

To refer to each of the fields individually in pseudo-code we type

```
car.make to refer to the make field
car.size to refer to the size field
car.colour to refer to the colour field
```

## Example 4.8

A program to output the name of the student with the highest mark from a
series of names and marks entered at the keyboard and stored in an array of
records. There are 12 members of the class.

```
Program highest
student = RECORD
            name: String
            mark: Integer
ENDRECORD
classlist: array[1, 12] of student
n,highest: Integer
FOR (n=1, n<12, n+1)
   DISPLAY "enter student name"
   ACCEPT student[n].name
   DISPLAY "enter student mark"
   ACCEPT student[n].mark
ENDFOR
highest=1
FOR (n=2, n<12, n+1)
   IF student[n].mark > student[highest].mark
   highest:=n
ENDFOR
DISPLAY "The student with the highest marks was" student[highest].name
DISPLAY "The mark was" student[highest].mark
```

## Exercise 4.3

A company telephone directory is made up of entries of the form

| | |
|---|---|
| First name | 20 characters |
| Initials | 5 characters |
| Last name | 20 characters |
| Room number | 6 alphanumerical characters |
| Site | 7 characters |
| Telephone number | 4 digits |

**(a)** Define an appropriate record structure for the above information.
**(b)** Assuming the directory has no more than 100 entries, define a table which can hold all the information.
**(c)** Use pseudo-code to design a program fragment which inputs all the information from a file into the table which you have defined in **(b)**.
**(d)** Give a design for a procedure which prints the full names of all people on a particular site. (IDCS 1/94.)

## 4.7  Sorting

The techniques of external sorting will not be considered in this book. The following section deals with internal sorts, i.e. performed in the immediate access memory of the computer. There are many different algorithms for sorts and this section only gives three examples of the different types.

The algorithms for sorting will work just as well for arrays of tables as for one-dimensional arrays. The following examples of sorting strategies will be illustrated by the use of lists for presentational simplicity.

### Selection sorts

Consider the following example.

### *Example 4.9  A selection sort using two arrays*

The technique is to repeatedly look through the data array to find the lowest key (for a sort in ascending order). This element is written to the empty array in position one and the element in the data array marked by overwriting the key with a rogue value, i.e. one which is clearly identified as not belonging to the actual data. The search is repeated finding the next lowest key and writing this in position two in the second array and overwriting as before. The process continues until the sort is complete. See Figure 4.7.

| data array | empty array | pass 1 d.array | pass1 e.array | pass 2 d.a. | pass 2 e.a. | pass 3 d.a. | pass 3 e.a. |
|---|---|---|---|---|---|---|---|
| 205 | | 205 | 45 | 999 | 45 | 999 | 45 |
| 310 | | 310 | | 310 | 310 | 999 | 205 |
| 45 | | 999 | | 999 | | 999 | 310 |

**Figure 4.7**

## *Example 4.10*

The following description outlines an algorithm for a selection sort using an exchange of variables. This method avoids the use of the extra array needed in the last example.

In this selection sort the array is scanned to find the location of the smallest element. This element is exchanged with the first member of the array. The array is scanned again starting at the second member and the location of the smallest remaining member determined and the element at this location exchanged for the second member of the array. The process continues until all array elements have been scanned and placed in their correct position.

This algorithm is to sort an array of size n using a basic selection technique.

```
variables
numbers: array[1, n] of Integer
count,pass,lowest: integer
temp : array type
*temp must be of the same type as the array since it is to  be used for the exchange
of values in the array.*
FOR (pass=1, pass<=n, pass +1)
   count: = pass
   lowest: =pass
   WHILE count < n–1
      IF numbers[count+1] < numbers[lowest]
      lowest := count+1
   ENDWHILE
   temp:= numbers[pass]
   numbers[pass] := numbers[lowest]
   numbers[lowest] := temp
ENDFOR
```

## *An insertion sort*

The first two elements of the array are compared and arranged in order. The third element is compared with the first two and inserted into the correct position. The process is repeated until every element in the list has been placed in its correct position.

## *Example 4.11  Using a list of integers*

| initial array | first pass | second pass | third pass | fourth pass | fifth pass |
|---|---|---|---|---|---|
| 21 | 16 | 16 | 16 | 16 | 12 |
| 16 | 21 | 21 | 21 | 19 | 16 |
| 35 |    | 35 | 35 | 21 | 19 |
| 47 |    |    | 47 | 35 | 21 |
| 19 |    |    |    | 47 | 35 |
| 12 |    |    |    |    | 47 |

**Figure 4.8**  Using a list of integers.

The pseudo-code algorithm for the insertion process shown in Figure 4.8 (assuming the numbers are stored in the array 'show') is

```
variables.
show: array[1, 6] of Integer
position, pass, copy: Integer
note that copy is to be used to store the array element and must be of the same data
type.
FOR (pass = 2, pass < 5, pass+1)
   copy := show[pass]
   position := pass
   WHILE position > 0 AND show[position-1] > copy
      show[position]:=show[position-1]
      position:= position-1
   ENDWHILE
show[position] := copy
ENDFOR
```

## *The bubble sort*

This is so called because the smallest element rises to the top of the array and then the next smallest 'bubbles' up to the next position and so on. Of course the array could be sorted in descending order when the largest element would be the one 'bubbled' to the top. The algorithm is simple and effective, particularly so when none of the elements are far from their final position. On the first pass the first two members of the array are compared and exchanged if necessary. The process is repeated with the second and third elements and then the third and the fourth and so on until the smallest element arrives at the top. Now one element is in the correct position the process is repeated until every element has been sorted. This will happen as soon as no more exchanges have taken place or when the complete cycle of passes has ended.

The pseudo-code for a bubble sort of an array of integers of length size is as follows:

```
variables temp, exchange_count, pass, size, n: Integer
example array[1, size] of Integer
exchange-count :=1
pass:=1
REPEAT
exchange_count:= 0
FOR (n=1, n < size -pass, n+1)
   IF example[n] > example[n+1]
      temp:= example[n]
      example[n] := example[n+1]
      example[n+1] := temp
      exchange_count := exchange_count+1
   ENDIF
ENDFOR
pass:= pass+1
UNTIL exchange_count= 0
```

## 4.8 Searching

Finding one particular element in an array is simply a matter of looking through the array element by element until the required key is found. This can be done sequentially, i.e. starting from the first element and looking for a matching key at this or each succeeding element until a match is found. Since it probably is important to also determine if the particular key is present it may be necessary to search the entire array.

This method is clearly inefficient, although for small searches this may not matter. A more efficient method is to start by sorting the array on the key to be found. A test can then be included to stop the search when the key is matched or when the key reached is greater than the key to be found.

The pseudo-code algorithm for the search of the sorted array of 100 key names is as follows:

```
type key-name -- the type you choose for your program.
variables
key_array array [1, n] of key-name
```

*key-to-be found: key-name*
*count, n: integer*
*count:=1*
*found:= false*
*REPEAT*
*IF key-to-be-found = key-array[count] THEN found: = true*
*ELSE count:=count+1*
*UNTIL found = true OR count = array-size*

## The binary search

This method is used with sorted data and can substantially reduce searching times when dealing with larger arrays. There is more processing per comparison since a calculation is required, however the number of comparisons is less.

The technique is as follows. First find the centre of the array. Compare the key required with the key at this location. If the key required is less than the key found, the key we are looking for is in the first part of the array, otherwise it is in the second half of the array. This process can now be repeated with the appropriate section of the array, i.e. a new mid-point is found and the position of the key in the new position determined. This process is continued until the key is found. Of course, it is possible that the key may not be found at all and an allowance must be made for this event.

The pseudo-code for this algorithm is as follows: 'start' is used as the lower partition bound, 'end' is used as the higher partition bound. At the beginning of the search these are the first and last elements of the array.

*start:=1*
*found:= false*
*REPEAT*
*middle:= (end+start)/2*
*IF key-required = key-name[middle] THEN found:= true*
    *ELSE IF key required < key-name[middle] THEN end: = middle-1*
    *ELSE START:= middle+1*
*UNTIL found = true OR start > end*

## Exercise 4.4

(a) Describe fully a sort algorithm for a list of numbers stored in an array.
(b) Describe how you would create a file of employee records containing records with the following fields: employee number, name, address, date of birth.
(c) Describe how you would search the file for a record of a given employee.
    (ICDS 2/94.)

## 4.9 Recursion

Recursion is a method of problem solution that depends on successively restating the problem in a consistently similar manner, but in a simpler form until a position is reached where no more simplification can take place and the simplest case reaches a basic value. This fundamental solution can then be used to recycle through the decomposed problem elements thus reaching a solution.

We shall consider an example which is easy to describe and evaluate.

Multiplication can be considered in a recursive manner since it can be written as a repeated addition, each successive term being a smaller instance of the problem with the terminating condition occurring when the last term evaluates to zero

$$x * n = x * (n - 1) + x$$
$$x * n - 1 = x * (n - 2) + x$$
$$\text{until } x * 0 = 0$$

the function could be called multiply($x,n$); multiply($x,n$) can be decomposed until $n=0$.

Consider the multiplication of 5 * 3 and decompose it successively into 'smaller' instances

| | | |
|---|---|---|
| 5 * 3 | decomposes to | 5 * 2 + 5 |
| 5 * 2 | decomposes to | 5 * 1 + 5 |

that is

| | | |
|---|---|---|
| multiply(5,1) | decomposes to | 5 * 0 + 5 |
| multiply(5,0) | decomposes to | 0, i.e. the termination value |

recycling from this position the evaluation is

| | | |
|---|---|---|
| multiply(5,1) | becomes | 5,0 + 5, i.e. 5 |
| multiply(5,2) | becomes | 5,1 + 5, i.e. 10 |
| multiply(5,3) | becomes | 5,2 + 5, i.e. 15 |

i.e. multiply(5,3) evaluates as a recursive function to 15!

In computing terms the procedure or function is made to call itself until the final case is reached. The function calls are then recycled in reverse order to produce the solution.

Note that if there is not a basic case then disaster will occur since the recursion cannot conclude.

The above case would be written as in our pseudo-code as

```
FUNCTION multiply(x,n: Integer): Integer
variable temp: Integer
IF n=0 THEN RETURN 0
ELSE temp:=multiply(x,n – 1) + x
    RETURN temp
ENDFUNCTION
```

Consider the following example. The calculation of the exponent of a number can be written as a recursive function. The problem can be decomposed into successively smaller but similar instances of the same problem.

$$x^n = x^{(n-1)} * n$$

Writing this equation as a recursive expression

$$\text{exponent}\,(x, n) = \text{exponent}\,(x, n - 1) * x$$

There is a clear terminating condition since any number raised to the power 0 is 1. The function therefore becomes

```
FUNCTION exponent(x,n:Integer) Integer
variable temp: Integer
IF n= 0 THEN RETURN 1
ELSE temp:= exponent(x,n – 1) * x
    RETURN temp
ENDFUNCTION
```

## Example 4.12

This is one of the classic examples of recursion. The factorial of a number $n$ is

$$\text{factorial}\ n = n * (n - 1) * (n - 2) * (n - 3), \dots 1$$

This can clearly be expressed recursively as

$$\text{factorial}(n) = \text{factorial}(n - 1) * n$$

and the terminating condition happens at

$$\text{factorial}(1) = 1$$

A pseudo-code program using this function is as follows:

```
Program find-factorial
variable n: real
PROCEDURE MAIN
DISPLAY "enter number whose factorial you require"
ACCEPT n
```

```
DISPLAY "the factorial of the number" n "is" factorial(n)
ENDPROCEDURE
Function factorial(n:real):real
   IF n=0 then factorial := 1
   else factorial := factorial (n-1) * n
end function.
FUNCTION factorial (n: Integer): Integer
variable temp: Integer
IF n = 1 then RETURN 1
ELSE temp:= factorial(n − 1) * n
   RETURN temp
ENDFUNCTION
```

## Example 4.13

Since each element of an array has a successor (or a predecessor if you count the other way) which is a similar instance of the same type arrays can be processed recursively. The terminating condition can be the size of the array. In this example a recursive procedure is written in pseudo-code to allow a string of characters to be output in reverse order.

```
Program reverse
variable name ARRAY[1, 10] of character
PROCEDURE main
name:= "abcdefghij"
reverse (1)
ENDPROCEDURE
PROCEDURE reverse (position: Integer)
IF position <> 11 THEN
   reverse (position+1)
   DISPLAY name[position]
ENDIF
ENDPROCEDURE
```

# 5
# Software design tools

## Objectives

When you have finished this chapter, you will be able to:

❑ describe and use decision tables and Nassi–Schneiderman diagrams
❑ understand and use the standard system flow diagram symbols
❑ demonstrate an understanding of data dictionaries.

## 5.1 Decision tables

A decision table can be simply defined as a table showing the action(s) to be taken for different combinations of conditions.

For example, in a video rental shop, the registration of a new customer depends on various conditions. The customer needs to provide some type of identification and prove that he or she is not restricted from renting. A table showing whether an applicant is allow to become a new registered member of this particular video shop can be considered as a simple decision table.

There are four quadrants in a decision table, separated from each other by double lines as in Figure 5.1.

| Condition Stub | Condition Entries |
| --- | --- |
| Action Stub | Action Entries |

**Figure 5.1**   Layout of a decision table.

The right-hand quadrants contain the condition entries and action entries. Condition entries show whether the condition is true or false. Action entries indicate whether the action takes place or not. The most common convention is to use a cross and dash (X/–) for actions and a 'Y' and 'N' for conditions.

The rules are specified by defining all the combinations of conditions for which a particular action is to be taken.

The quadrants on the left-hand side contain the condition stub and the action stub. All possible conditions are noted first, each condition on a new line. Below these all possible actions are written out, using one line for each action.

Decision tables fall into two basic categories, depending on which conditions and actions are defined in the stub

❏ where conditions and actions are wholly specified in the stub, the table is called 'limited entry'. Entries can only be of two types: Y and N. All the conditions in them have to be phrased so that they can be answered in this way
❏ where conditions and actions are generally identified in the stub, with specific values shown in the entries, the table is called 'extended entry'.

Additionally some tables contain a mixture of limited entry and extended entry; these are called 'mixed entry'.

### 5.1.1 Limited entry decision tables

Each vertical line shows one possible combination of conditions and the corresponding set of actions. This specifies one 'rule'.

When there are two conditions, for each of two possible values of the second, the first can also have two states, e.g. if the second is 'Y', the first could be 'Y' or 'N'. Thus, we will have $2 \times 2$ possible combinations and will require four rules to specify all the actions.

When there are three conditions, for all the four states above, the third could have a value, 'N' and the same four could again be repeated with the value 'Y'. Thus the rules are twice as many.

After writing all the conditions and actions in the two left-side quadrants, the number of rules can be calculated from the number of conditions.

The right-hand side is divided into $2n$ columns, one for each rule. Now the condition entries are to be filled in.

On the first line set down half the number of columns with 'Y' then 'N'. For the next line the columns of 'Y's are halved and filled first with 'Y' then 'N'. Similarly, the columns of 'N's are filled with half 'Y' and half 'N'.

Repeat this procedure until all conditions entries are made. On the last line the values will alternate.

Now the corresponding actions can be entered in each column. 'X' means the action should be executed whilst '–' means it should not.

**Table 5.1**  Decision table for a video rental shop (registration of a new customer)

|                                    | 1 | 2 | 3 | 4 | 5 | 6 | 7 | 8 |
|------------------------------------|---|---|---|---|---|---|---|---|
| Customer already registered?       | Y | Y | Y | Y | N | N | N | N |
| Customer provide identification?   | Y | Y | N | N | Y | Y | N | N |
| Customer restricted from renting?  | Y | N | Y | N | Y | N | Y | N |
| Register customer                  | – | – | – | – | – | X | – | – |
| Do not register customer           | X | – | X | – | X | – | X | X |

Table 5.1 summarizes the main features of decision tables for the video shop example. There are three conditions which will decide whether the applicant can become a new member (in fact, there are more than three conditions but this example will be treated with only three conditions to make it easier to understand)

❑ is the customer already registered?
❑ is the customer providing adequate identification?
❑ is the customer restricted from renting?

Since there are three conditions, the right-hand side is divided in $2^3 = 8$ columns.

*Advantages of a decision table.* As the number of rules can be mathematically calculated a decision table, in its simplest form, is 'self-checking'. It can be checked for completeness and when filled in ensures that the specifications are unambiguous. As a document for communication with a user, it is easy to understand, and areas of uncertainty or bad communication are easily identified.

Users are often not aware of the complexities of a computer program and may fail to communicate all conditional actions completely. Putting them down in this manner eliminates the possibility of vagueness. If the user responds with a phrase like 'Yes, that's how it happens, mostly' an immediate follow-up is obviously required to identify other exceptional circumstances. When this happens, amending the table is done quite easily by adding more conditions or actions.

Using the dash rule (see Figure 5.2), Table 5.1 can be simplified as shown in Tables 5.2–5.4a. Using the else rule (also in Figure 5.2), Table 5.1 can be simplified as shown in Table 5.4b.

| Simplification of Tables |
|---|
| With 2n rules for n conditions, the tables can become very large and hence unmanageable. Just four conditions give rise to 16 rules, while 8 conditions generate $2^8 = 256$ rules! |

| Rule | Definition |
|---|---|
| The Dash Rule | For any two rules when the conditions are identical in all but one row and the actions are also identical, the two rules can be combined into one with the common condition replaced by a dash.<br>Thus, an entry can be 'Y', 'N' or '-'. The dash stands for a 'don't care' condition i.e. it does not matter whether the condition is true or false.<br><br>**Simple Rules** → Reduces TO → **Combined Rule**<br><br>Rule 1: Y Y N / - X - X    Rule 4: Y N N / - X - X    Combined: Y - N / - X - X |
| The Else Rule | The 'ELSE' rule can correspond to a default condition: 'When no other rules apply then use this one'.<br>When three or more rules in a table give rise to the same set of actions they can be combined using the single word 'ELSE' in place of the condition values. This can be written in the column or over the top.<br><br>

| | 1 | 3 | 3 | ELSE |
|---|---|---|---|---|
| Test A true ? | Y | N | N | |
| Test B true ? | Y | N | Y | |
| Test C true ? | N | N | Y | |
| Goto table A | X | - | - | - |
| Goto table B | - | X | - | - |
| Goto table C | - | - | X | - |
| Goto err. table | - | - | - | X |
|
| The Else Rule Alternative Form | Another way of writing the same table is shown in this visual. It introduces the 'extended entry table' where entries can be of more than just the simple two types - 'Yes' or 'No', Do or Don't do.<br><br>

| | 1 | 3 | 3 | ELSE |
|---|---|---|---|---|
| Test A true ? | Y | N | N | |
| Test B true ? | Y | N | Y | |
| Test C true ? | N | N | Y | |
| Goto table | A | B | C | ERR. |
|

**Figure 5.2**

**Table 5.2**  Decision table for columns 2 and 4 combined

|  | 2 | 4 |  |  |
|---|---|---|---|---|
| Customer already registered? | Y | Y | → | Y |
| Customer provide identification? | Y | N |  | – |
| Customer restricted from renting ? | N | N |  | N |
| Register customer | – | – | → | – |
| Do not register customer | – | – |  | – |

**Table 5.3**  Decision table for columns 1, 3, 5 and 7 combined

|  | 1 | 3 | 5 | 7 |  |  |
|---|---|---|---|---|---|---|
| Customer already registered? | Y | Y | N | N | → | – |
| Customer provide identification? | Y | N | Y | N |  | – |
| Customer restricted from renting? | Y | Y | Y | Y |  | Y |
| Register customer | – | – | – | – | → | – |
| Do not register customer | X | X | X | X |  | X |

**Table 5.4a**  Simplified decision table for a video rental shop (using the dash rule)

|  | Columns 1, 3, 5, 7 combined | Columns 2, 4 combined | 6 | 8 |
|---|---|---|---|---|
| Customer already registered? | — | Y | N | N |
| Customer provide identification? | – | – | Y | N |
| Customer restricted from renting? | Y | N | N | N |
| Register customer | – | – | X | – |
| Do not register customer | X | – | – | X |

**Table 5.4b**   Simplified decision table for a video rental shop (using the else rule)

|  | 2 | 4 | 6 | E |
|---|---|---|---|---|
| Customer already registered? | Y | Y | N | L |
| Customer provide identification? | Y | N | Y | S |
| Customer restricted from renting? | N | N | N | E |
| Register customer | – | – | X | – |
| Do not register customer | – | – | – | X |

## 5.1.2 Extended entry tables

Entries can be extended in two ways. The conditions can be stated so that fewer are required, or action entries can be extended. A table may have limited conditions and extended action entries or vice versa – or both condition and action entries could be extended.

Table 5.5 shows an extended entry table used to work out the annual registration fees to become a new member.

*Sequencing actions.* The sequence of actions is determined normally by the order in which they are listed. If for a particular rule the order of two actions is reversed, this may be taken care of by writing the same step twice.

*Hierarchical tables.* When there are more than three conditions, it is recommended that the table should be broken into a set of smaller tables, although it is possible to handle up to a maximum of 16 rules, or four conditions, in one table. The tables, then, would have a hierarchy with the one at the highest level being tested first and directing the control flow to one of the others.

**Table 5.5**   Decision table for annual registration fees in a video rental shop

|  | 1 | 2 | 3 | 4 |
|---|---|---|---|---|
| Is customer unemployed? | Y | Y | N | N |
| Is customer over 50 years old? | Y | N | Y | N |
| Annual registration fees | £20 | £30 | £30 | £50 |

The division of the conditions requires some thought, although it will usually be found that some conditions are more important in determining what needs to be done. These should be placed at the higher level.

Table 5.4a, which is the simplified decision table for a video shop used to register a new member, can be re-arranged as shown in Table 5.6 to link itself with Table 5.5, which the decision table for the annual registration fees to be charged.

**Table 5.6**   Simplified decision table for a video rental shop linked to Table 5.5

|  | Cols 1, 3, 5, 7 combined | Cols 2, 4 combined | 6 | 8 |
|---|---|---|---|---|
| Customer already registered? | – | Y | N | N |
| Customer provide identification? | – | – | Y | N |
| Customer restricted from renting? | Y | N | N | N |
| Register customer | – | – | Goto Table 5.5 | – |
| Do not register customer | X | – | – | X |

*Processing a decision table.* There are four methods of implementing a decision table. In addition to manual coding, there are software aids available. Computerizing the process is possible because the decision table is such a precise method for expressing designs.

(1)  Manual coding is done by inspecting and analysing the table. There are no simple rules for coding.
(2)  A preprocessor is software which converts a decision table into a source program. This can form the input to an existing compiler. The preprocessor would, of course, be language dependent.
(3)  An interpretive program may be used which interprets the table.
(4)  Special compilers exist which give the output in machine code directly without having to be further translated into any programming language.

## 5.2 Nassi–Schneiderman diagram

These diagrams were derived in 1973 by Nassi and Schneiderman in order to replace the traditional flow charts. They have had some success, but are often criticized as being suitable only for lower level specifications. Figure 5.3 shows diagrams commonly used to express sequence, loop, selection, etc.

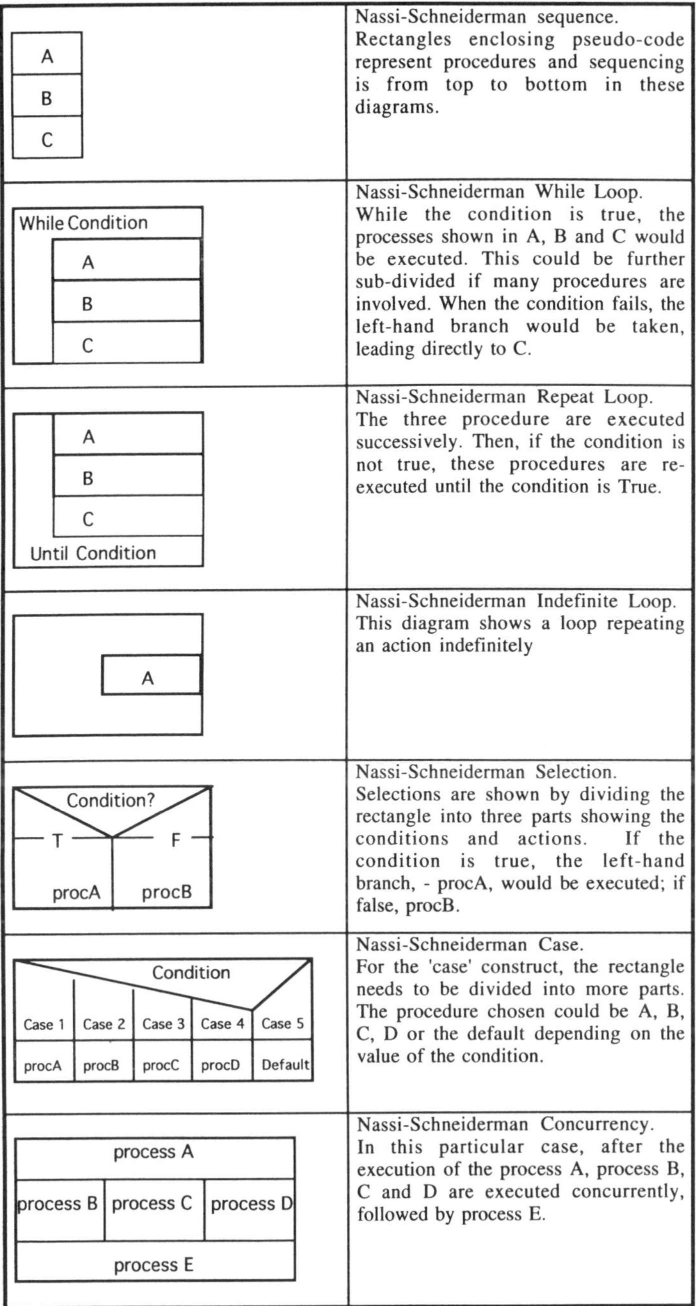

| | |
|---|---|
| | Nassi-Schneiderman sequence. Rectangles enclosing pseudo-code represent procedures and sequencing is from top to bottom in these diagrams. |
| | Nassi-Schneiderman While Loop. While the condition is true, the processes shown in A, B and C would be executed. This could be further sub-divided if many procedures are involved. When the condition fails, the left-hand branch would be taken, leading directly to C. |
| | Nassi-Schneiderman Repeat Loop. The three procedure are executed successively. Then, if the condition is not true, these procedures are re-executed until the condition is True. |
| | Nassi-Schneiderman Indefinite Loop. This diagram shows a loop repeating an action indefinitely |
| | Nassi-Schneiderman Selection. Selections are shown by dividing the rectangle into three parts showing the conditions and actions. If the condition is true, the left-hand branch, - procA, would be executed; if false, procB. |
| | Nassi-Schneiderman Case. For the 'case' construct, the rectangle needs to be divided into more parts. The procedure chosen could be A, B, C, D or the default depending on the value of the condition. |
| | Nassi-Schneiderman Concurrency. In this particular case, after the execution of the process A, process B, C and D are executed concurrently, followed by process E. |

**Figure 5.3**

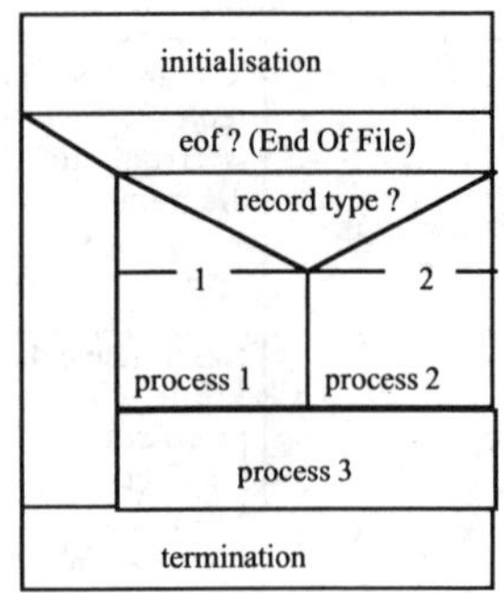



**Figure 5.4**  A full program.

A program design is shown in Figure 5.4 and can be described as follows:

1. the program starts with initialization
2. a test is made for end-of-file. If the condition is satisfied the termination routine is entered via the left-hand branch
3. if not, the record is tested to see if it is type 1 or 2
4. type 1 data goes through process 1, then process 3
5. type 2 data goes through process 2, then process 3
6. the iterative process is repeated until end-of-file, at which stage the termination routine is entered.

## 5.3  Flow diagrams

Events in a system – or part of a system – were traditionally represented diagrammatically by means of a system flow diagram. This is one of the end-products of the system design stage.

The system flow diagram shows three elements

❏ the programs
❏ the data (including their input and output)
❏ their interaction.

It is similar to a program run chart. Although still used by many analysts, it has disadvantages as an aid to the conceptualization of a system, especially for a user. It may therefore be created after the programs and other elements have been designed. System flow diagrams are now giving way to data flow diagrams (DFDs) at different levels, LDSs (logical data structures) and ELHs (entity life histories). These also may be used during the system design stage. The DFD illustrates the data movement in the system. It shows the flow of information to, from and within a system.

There is generally no provision for showing conditional actions within flow diagrams. All possible flows are shown while decisions are made within the processes themselves.

## 5.3.1 System flow diagrams

The set of symbols used are illustrated in Figure 5.5. Program or procedure names are written in rectangles, with the named inputs, outputs and backing storage elements being shown for each. The direction of data flow is shown by means of arrows. Each file is drawn only once and arrows are used to link it to those programs which use it either for input or for output. The sequence of execution of different programs is also shown by means of arrows.

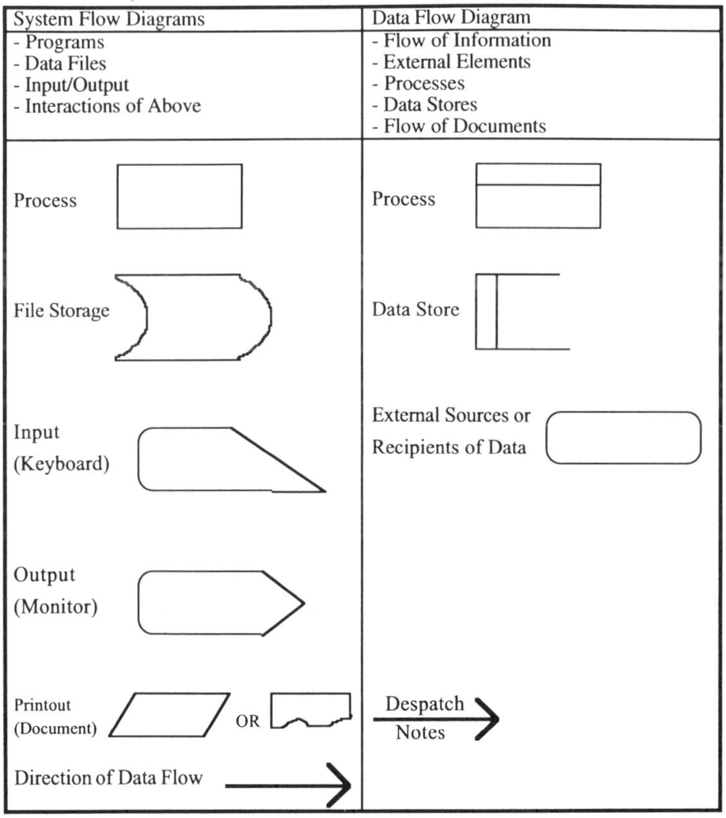

**Figure 5.5**  Flow diagrams.

A large system is broken down so that subunits of it can be presented on different pages. In this case, it may be necessary to show the same file or program more than once. Appropriate reference numbers and symbols must then be included for cross-referencing, as required.

## 5.3.2 *Data flow diagrams*

The emphasis is on the data and its flow within a system. It shows:

❑ how information enters and leaves the system
❑ what changes the information
❑ where information is stored.

They are an important technique of system analysis for various reasons.

❑ Boundary definition. The diagrams clearly shows the boundaries of the system represented.
❑ Completeness of analysis. the construction of the diagrams helps to ensure that all information flows, stores of information and activities within the system have been considered.
❑ Basis for program specification. DataFDs denote the major functional areas of the system.

The symbols used are shown in Figure 5.5.

In the structured systems analysis and design method (SSADM), DFDs may be used to represent a physical system or a logical abstraction of a system. It has a specific notation where elements from outside the system are shown by an oval, as shown in Figure 5.6.

**Figure 5.6**   Element from outside the system.

A process is represented by a rectangle with a division within it for cross-referencing and numbering the process. The location of the process is placed at the top of the box. This might be a physical location, but it is often used to denote the staff responsible for performing the process (see Figure 5.7).

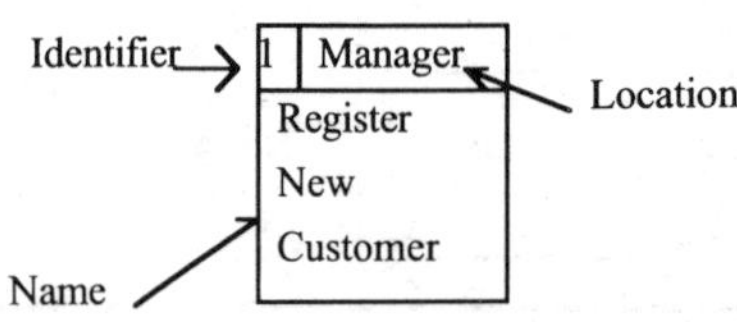


**Figure 5.7**   Process.

Three types of objects exist in a DFD, sometimes also known as a bubble diagram:

- ❑ input objects (files, terminal input)
- ❑ output objects (reports, messages)
- ❑ storage objects (temporary or permanent, e.g. arrays, records, tables).

In the diagram, objects are drawn as bubbles, actions as boxes. When the arrow is between an object and a processing action, the action reads the data object. Similarly, when the arrow is between an action and data object the action writes information into the data object.

## Examples

Figure 5.8 gives an example of a DFD for the registration of a new member in a video rental shop. Only one file is involved: the file containing information about the customer. The new applicant information which has been checked and accepted is stored in this file. This is then processed to create a membership card which is then returned to the customer.

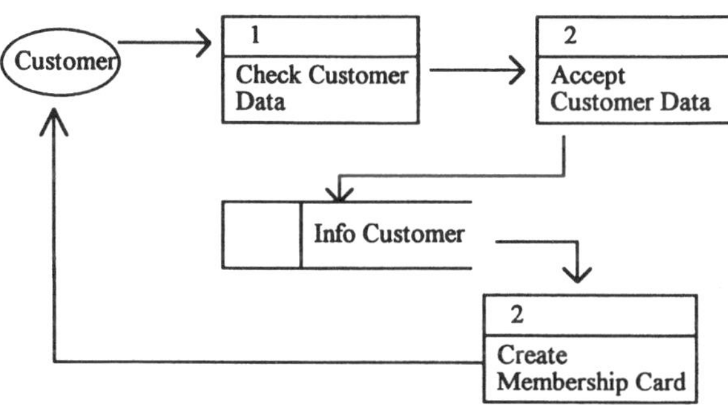


**Figure 5.8**  Example DFD.

The system flow diagram corresponding to the above system is shown in Figure 5.9 on the next page.

A part of the membership system is shown here. There are three programs and one file. The check data customer procedure accepts delivery details from the keyboard. After checking and accepting the customer information, it writes onto the information customer file. This file provides input to the create membership card procedure which then prints out the card.

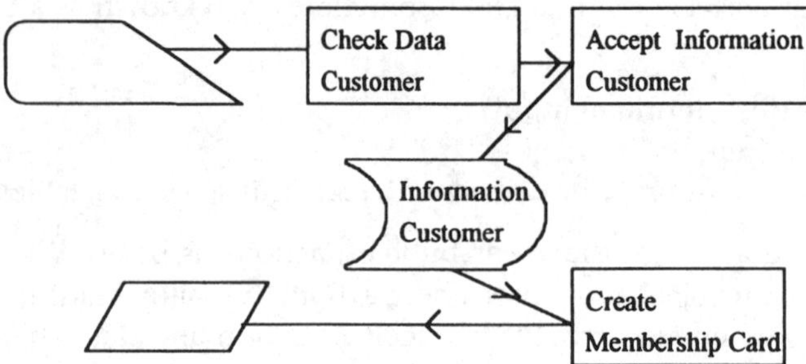



**Figure 5.9**   System flow diagram.

## 5.4 Data dictionary

Good documentation is needed for the software data components as well as program components. A data model and a data dictionary are used to document the data. The data model, preferably a canonical data model, is a graphic representation of the data identifying the inherent structure of the data and their dependencies. The data dictionary lists all the data items that are used, their definitions, how and where they are used, and who is responsible for them.

A data dictionary may include a large amount of information about each of the data elements. It should contain such entries as the data element names with explanations; the range of possible values with explanation, for example, F, M, U (female, male, unspecified); the data element type; data relationships; the source of the data; the use of the data; what security is needed; and whether the element is mandatory or optional and under what circumstances. Each variable would have an entry like the example in Figure 5.10.

| Data Name | Number_of _video_rented | Customer_name |
|---|---|---|
| Data Type | Integer | Characters |
| Meaning | This is the number of video that the customer has taken out and didn't return yet. | It is the name of the customer that is applying for membership or is already a member. |
| Input Format | | Maximum 35 Characters |
| Output Format | | Maximum 35 Characters |
| Range | 0 to 5 | None |
| Where Referred to | line 545 in CHECK_MAX_VI program | line 496 in CHECK_INFO program |
| Where Changed | Line 299 in INPUT_DATA | line 152 in INPUT_NEW_NAME program |

**Figure 5.10**   Illustration of data dictionary entities.

## Summary exercise

(a) Name the four components of a decision table.

(b) Explain why in some cases the use of a decision table is preferable to a flow chart.

(c) A business has decided to encourage early payment on its invoices by introducing the following payment procedures for its regular customers:

10% discount if the invoice is settled within 7 days
 7% discount if the invoice is settled within 14 days
 5% discount if the invoice is settled within 30 days

Other cases for discount must be referred to the manager. Construct a decision table for implementing the above procedure.

(d) Name at least two ways of converting a decision table into a program. (IDCS 1/92.)

# 6
# Testing

## Objectives

When you have finished this chapter, you will be able to:

❑ explain why the testing of a coded program is necessary
❑ know the difference between various types of testing
❑ understand the various components in test documentation
❑ debug a program
❑ write a test plan (with suitable test data) for a program including desk checking, dry running and the use of diagnostic aids
❑ appreciate program maintenance problems and techniques.

## 6.1  Introduction

Testing for reliable software is essential. Typically, a programmer will ask the question 'why do we need testing?'. It is not just to be sure that a program meets technical requirements, but also that it is economical and maintainable. Testing is used often as a means of determining quality and proving that software is fit for its purpose. While it can assist, it is almost impossible to check all the inputs for any program and we are forced to rely on a set of carefully selected data. However, in spite of these limitations, testing is a very necessary phase in the life cycle of a program and needs to be planned carefully.

## 6.2  The test plan

Throughout all phases in the development of a program, verification and validation (V&V) procedures are applied at the end of each stage. Verification attempts to find errors by executing a program in a tested or simulated environment while validation is the process of finding errors by executing a program in the real environment. The verification process checks that the work requirement specified at the beginning of any phase of work has been completed at the end. The validation process provides a global check that all the functional, safety and contractual requirements specified have been completed at the end of the project.

Experience shows that the majority of errors occur at the requirements specification stage of program development and that if they are not trapped early in the development of a program they create proportionately the greatest effort to correct.

Testing is an extension of V&V procedures, the basic difference being that it is done 'dynamically', i.e. with the compiled or interpreted program actually running. As we said earlier, testing has its limitations. It cannot improve a program, nor prove that it is correct, but there is currently no practical alternative. Testing is the only way of assessing whether a program meets the conditions and requirements laid down in the original program specification.

### 6.2.1 Documentation of tests

All tests must be described fully before they are carried out. Otherwise it is experimenting. It can be difficult to coordinate tests when a large number of people are involved in a development. This is why the test documentation is necessary. It is done by maintaining a file of test data throughout the life cycle of the system for audit purposes. This file specifies all aspects of the system, data and procedures which are to be tested (see Table 6.1 on the next page).

The type and range of test data, along with the other details can be drawn up as program modules are designed. Note that test data should be developed from the design, not the implementation, so that the consistency of the design is automatically rechecked.

### 6.2.2 Suitable data test

Choosing the most suitable values for test data does not always receive the attention it deserves. Successful testing is an integral part of program development and, sometimes, of program specification. In order to specify sensible test data, the exact purpose of the test must be properly understood. The two main aspects that are tested are the control structure and the computation.

Testing control structure requires that all selection and repetition constructs are understood and related to the data. For example, let us consider the following pseudo-code:

**Table 6.1**   A contents checklist (NCC DP documentation standards)

| | |
|---|---|
| Title page | Title and reference<br>Author and department; date |
| Contents | Main and sub-heading with chapter/sheet numbers |
| Testing philosophy | Describe the approach to testing of the system<br>Identify any distinct stages or timing considerations<br>If the testing involves the creation of complex conditions, explain how these may be set up<br>Emphasize any aspects of the test which are likely to be overlooked, or areas which may prove troublesome or critical |
| File creation | Test data for creation programs will be in the same form as the data for setting up the live master files. Files will be checked for validity of format and accuracy of data. Check record controls and file security |
| Program suite input | Data conversion<br>Data transmission/Remote Job Entry<br>Data control<br>Computer validation<br>Error routines and correction procedures |
| Program suite output | User acceptance of program output<br>Form design<br>Data control procedures<br>Data transmission |
| Input/output handling | Each procedure will be checked for accuracy and understanding, ambiguity, timing and staff confidence<br>Completion of input documents<br>Maintenance of clerical files<br>Checking of documents<br>Delivery of output and inspection<br>Distribution of output<br>Actioning and turn-round of documents<br>Error procedures<br>Contact with computer operations department |
| Test data | Test data listings and data preparation documents |

```
DO CASE OF choice
   CASE choice = 1
      Process_number_1
   CASE choice = 2
      Process_number_2
   OTHERWISE
      Default_process
```

Values 0, 1, 2 and 3 can be used to test this piece of code. There would be no point in trying any more. Also when testing repetition constructs, a test for zero repetitions of a loop should be included. Similarly to the test computation aspect, any formulae and equations used in the code need to be understood to appreciate the significance of data values. We can best illustrate this by considering a formula involving a multiplication operation. This is tested with values other than zero and one, since neither of these may show up errors in coding or typing.

Let us consider the mathematical formula $(1 - 3r)(1 + 2n)$, and compare the output of this formula with the output of a wrong version of this formula, using various value of $r$ and $n$ (see Table 6.2).

**Table 6.2**  Calculation of formulae with different parameters

| Value of $r$ | Value of $n$ | Result using the correct formula $(1 - 3r) \times (1 + 2n)$ | Result using a wrong formula $(1 + 3r) \times (1 + 2n)$ |
|---|---|---|---|
| 0 | 0 | $1 \times 1 = 1$ | $1 \times 1 = 1$ |
| 1 | $-1/2$ | $-2 \times 0 = 0$ | $4 \times 0 = 0$ |
| 0 | 10 | $1 \times 21 = 21$ | $1 \times 21 = 21$ |
| 1 | 1 | $-2 \times 3 = -6$ | $4 \times 3 = 12$ |

The first three rows show that the wrong version of the formula still gives a correct looking result and illustrates that data should be carefully chosen. When there is a formula with multiplication, it is better not to use the value zero or any other values that would make one of the factors equal to zero.

Similarly, terms involving exponentiation may give incorrect results if tested with inappropriate values. An odd combination of errors and values may give correct results and so the test must be carried out with more than one combination of values.

Try the formulae $(1 + 2r)^n$ and $(-1 - 2r)^n$ (you should find that they give the same result when $n$ is odd). Choose data that do not give the same result.

## 6.3  Stages of testing

In the development of a large system, testing involves several stages as shown in Figure 6.1. The first one is unit (module) testing. A program is generally composed of several modules which can be tested individually as a single program. These tests are implemented in a controlled environment whenever possible. A set of predetermined data is fed through the unit and the outputs are compared with the expected ones.

The next step is to ensure that these modules interface with the others as defined. This test is usually called the integration test. It can be described as the process of checking that the elements of a system interact as specified in the program design and system design specifications.

System testing involves testing the system as a whole to ensure that it meets the requirements specified at the beginning of the project. It assesses the system on its functionality, performance and validity. In small-scale systems, integration and system testing are frequently combined, especially if the smallest unit code being produced is a program.

The final two stages of testing a program are carried out with the customer. Acceptance testing checks that the system meets the customer's requirements description. When this has been completed, the accepted system is installed in the environment in which it will be used and a final installation test is performed to ensure that the system still functions satisfactorily.

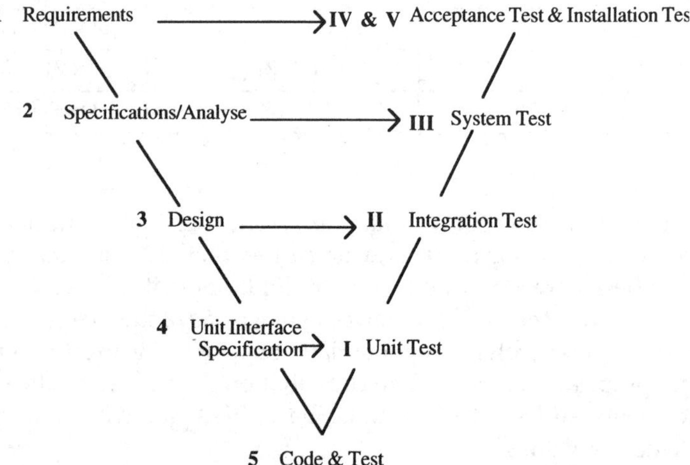


**Figure 6.1**  Idealized systems development life cycle.

## 6.3.1 *Unit testing*

This is the testing of small units of code, e.g. programs, modules or procedures, in order to ensure that they perform their intended functions. There are two types of testing strategy: black-box and white-box.

*Black-box testing strategy*. The black-box testing strategy (data-driven, or input/output-driven strategy) is shown in Figure 6.2. Code is treated as a box into which data is put and from which data (and messages) are output and checked for correctness.

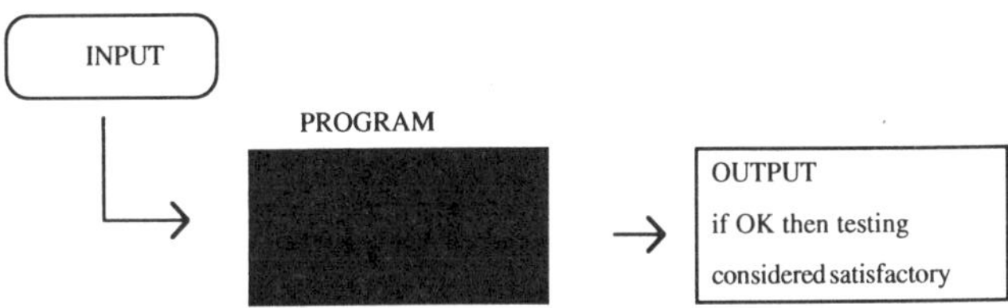


**Figure 6.2**   Black-box testing strategy.

This takes place after the code has been produced, but before any integration or system testing. The amount of testing required varies in proportion to the size and complexity of the module. However, even the simplest, such as lines of code, if defined sensibly, e.g. ignoring comment lines will give an indication of which modules are most likely to give trouble and therefore need to be tested more thoroughly.

It is usual to record the number of errors found during checking of the code for each module. This number, relative to the lines of code in the module will indicate which modules are error-prone and will need most testing.

Experience has shown that modules having a high number of errors per 1000 lines of code later prove to need disproportionate amounts of testing. (For modules which have less than 1000 lines the values should be calculated proportionately, e.g. four errors in 250 lines = 16 errors in 1000 lines.)

Unit testing is simplified by designing modules which have only one function. This makes it easier to identify errors and fewer tests are required.

The tester is not interested in what the contents of the box (the code) looks like nor whether all the lines of code have been executed. The test data to be used are extracted from the specification and as long as the coding behaves exactly as it should then to all intents and purposes the module has achieved the required level of correctness. We have seen that the achievement of absolute correctness is not practical, so this method of testing is limited in the level of correctness that can be achieved. Also it does not indicate what proportion of the code has actually been executed. In general it is estimated that only 60% of the lines of code are actually tested this way, which leaves a high proportion untested. Therefore there are likely to be routines in the code which are not activated during testing because only a sample of data values is input. Untested values may cause the module to fail after it has gone live.

*White-box testing strategy.* There is also the white-box testing strategy (logic-driven strategy) shown is Figure 6.3. This method involves ensuring that every part of the program has been activated during testing so that no 'logic bombs' are left.

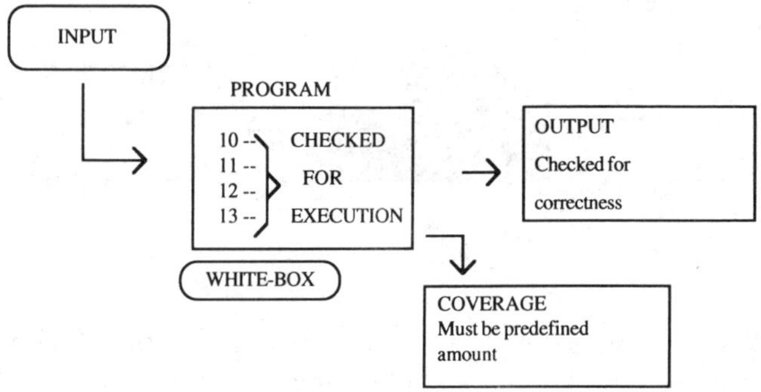


**Figure 6.3**   White-box testing strategy.

The module is divided into units (either lines of code or logical paths) which are monitored during testing to discover if they have been executed.

As with black-box testing, it is not possible to test every line or path; e.g. a simple 16-line COBOL module might have a million possible logical paths. Testing each line once would be an inadequate sample and leave some statement options, e.g. IF-THEN-ELSE constructs, unchecked. However, it would be impractical to test all possible paths.

One measure of test effectiveness is the percentage of statements executed. A minimum acceptable level is 85%. This is because an approximation of the amount of code likely to be executable (comments and abnormal end routines for instance may not be actionable). Confirmation of what code has been tested is usually achieved by 'instrumenting' it. This is simply adding statements which display a message when activated, such as 'print block 50 executed'.

## 6.3.2 *Integration testing*

Integration testing follows on from unit testing and is concerned with testing how modules interface, rather than with the modules themselves. It is therefore extremely important when modules have been written by different programmers.

Integration testing is used to identify situations such as:

❏ data being lost between modules
❏ one module creating a fault in another module
❏ creating a major undesirable side-effect when combining several modules.

Integration testing might include some retesting of modules already unit tested. When a requirement detail can only be met by combining more than one program unit, it cannot be tested until those units are integrated (e.g. parameter passing, etc.).

The requirement for integration testing depends on the prior level of unit testing that has been done. Ideally, all unit testing is completed before integration begins so that integration starts with units that contain no known faults. Each module's interfaces will have been tested in isolation in unit testing, but now they should be checked to ensure that all the incoming calls and messages are expected and in the correct format, and that all outgoing messages and calls are in the right format and are being sent to the correct destination.

There are several options for controlling the way that modules are combined for integration testing. Consider the system modules shown in Figure 6.4 to illustrate the several options that can be followed.

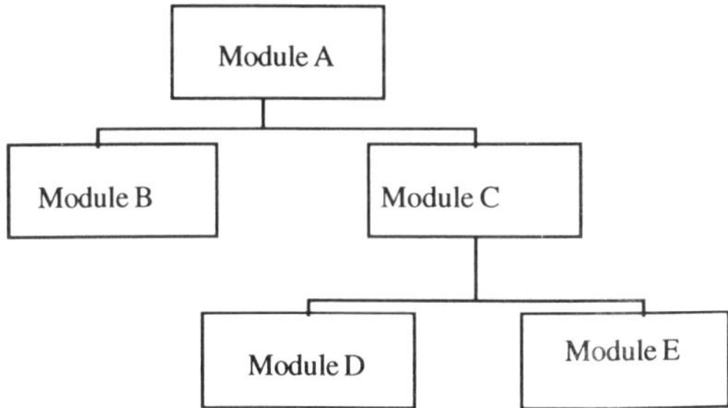


**Figure 6.4**   Sample modular hierarchy.

The first of these is the number of units that will be combined at one time. There are three possible alternatives:

❑ big-bang – where all modules are integrated at once. This approach is usually a desperate measure, when a project is running late, as it relies on hope for the best approach

❑ phased – where modules are integrated according to their level in the design structure, usually several at once

❑ incremental – where modules are added one at a time. This approach enables new errors revealed in testing to be identified easily. It is the most successful method. It does need more individual integration steps however, and if saving time is essential then phased testing may be more suitable.

Figure 6.5 shows how modules are integrated using the big-bang alternatives on our example. Whatever errors are revealed are often difficult to associate with any particular module, especially in a large system, since all the modules are merged at once. Therefore, interface errors and modules error cannot be easily distinguished. Although this strategy is not practical for large systems, it is sometimes used for small systems, but it is not recommended.

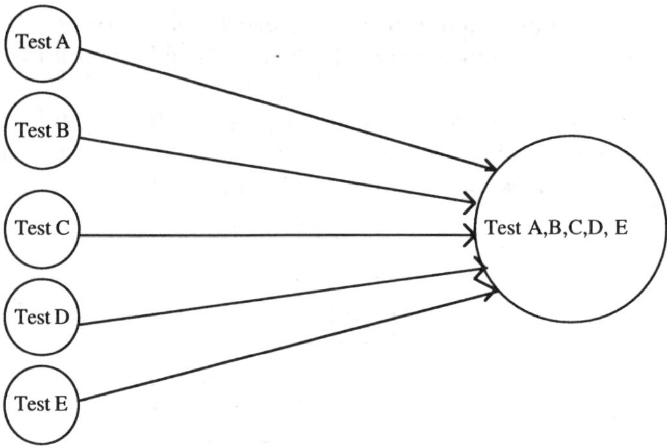


**Figure 6.5**   Big-bang testing strategy.

The second factor is the order in which the units are to be combined. This can be:

❑ top-down
❑ bottom-up
❑ sandwich integration.

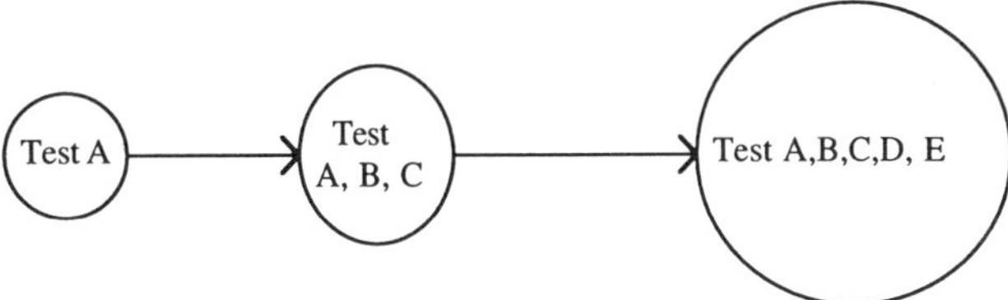

**Figure 6.6**   Top-down testing strategy.

A top-down approach begins at the top level and adds modules from the levels immediately below, either a group at a time (phased) or one at a time (incremental). Figure 6.6 demonstrates how top-down testing the phased alternative works. First the top module (module A) is tested alone and then it is combined with modules from the next level (modules B and C) and so on.

The top-down approach needs 'stubs' to be added to represent calls to, and replies from, those modules which have not yet been integrated. A disadvantage to this testing technique is the possibility that a very large number of stubs may be required (as can happen when the lowest level of the system contains many general-purpose routines). This problem can be solved by using the incremental alternative, which gives the modified top-down testing strategy shown in Figure 6.7. Each level's modules are individually tested before they can be merged.

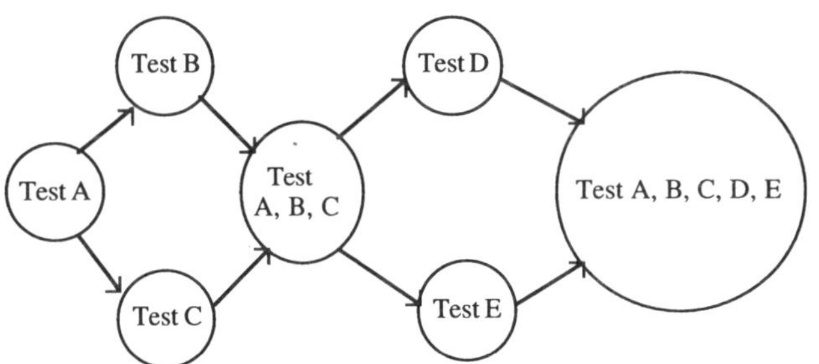

**Figure 6.7**   Modified top-down testing strategy.

Bottom-up testing begins with the lowest level modules and adds new modules from successively higher levels. Bottom-up testing is usually done using a phased approach rather than an incremental one. It needs 'drivers' to execute the low-level modules, since the modules which will drive them will not yet have been integrated. A driver can be as simple as a program to call the module being tested, and print any output, or a full test harness simulating input, messages, etc.

Using the same system modules example from Figure 6.4, the test starts with the lowest level modules which are D and E. Then the tester moves to the next higher level where the modules have not yet been tested. They combine with the modules that they call and have already been tested. In this particular example, D and E are combined with C. This routines carries on until it reaches the highest level. Figure 6.8 illustrates the various steps of this strategy.

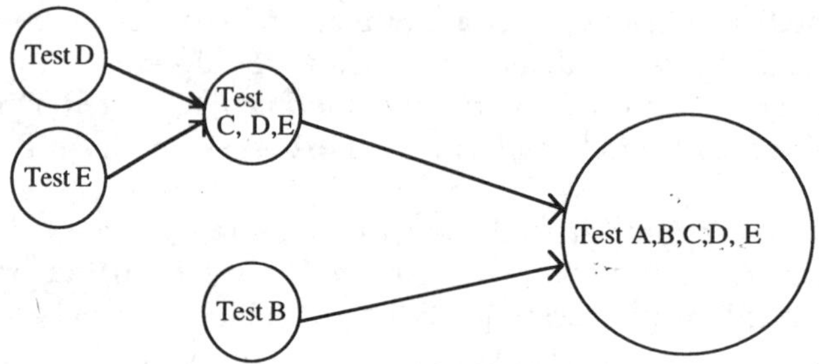


**Figure 6.8**   Bottom-up testing strategy.

Since both top-down and bottom-up testing have advantages and disadvantages, a sandwich approach is often adopted as an alternative, especially for very large systems. With this method top-down integration is started at the top level at the same time as bottom-up integration is started from the bottom. Somewhere in the middle the bottom-up units are integrated into the top-down units as one unit. Both stubs and drivers are needed for the higher and lower level units respectively, but no modules require both and at the middle level the last units integrated need neither.

Figure 6.9 shows the sandwich testing strategy using the phased alternative. However, it does not test all individual modules thoroughly before integration. In this particular case, module C is not individually tested. The incremental alternative allows upper level modules to be tested individually before merging them with others for testing. This procedure is described as the modified sandwich testing strategy (Figure 6.10).

The choice of method used depends on which method's advantages are considered to be most important. Some programmers prefer to develop their code one way and integrate the opposite way. The sandwich method avoids a choice having to be made.

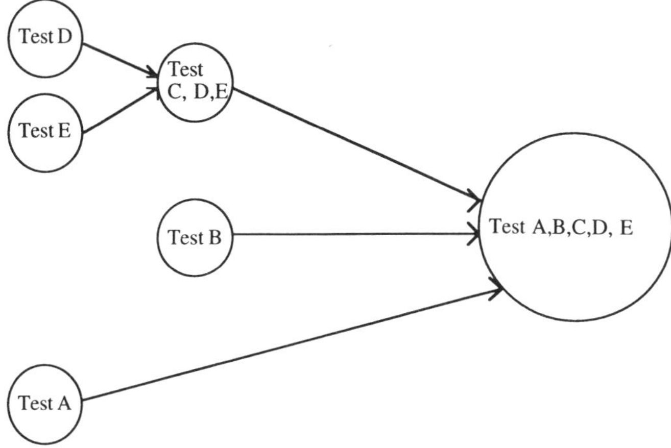


**Figure 6.9**  Sandwich testing strategy.

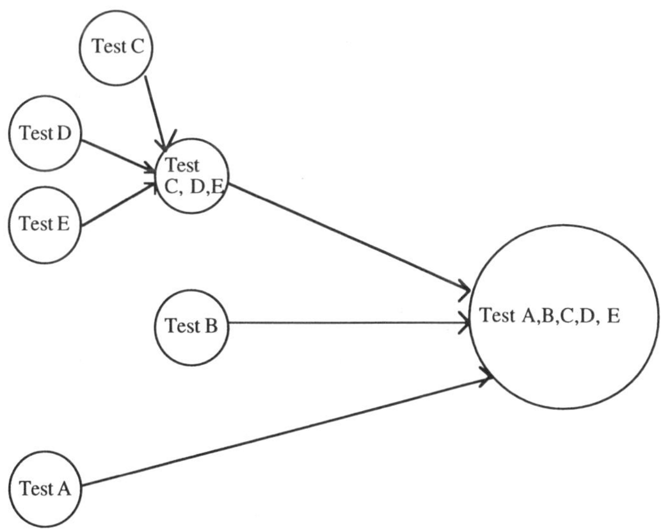


**Figure 6.10**  Modified sandwich testing strategy.

### 6.3.3 *System testing*

System testing aims to check that new programs operate together as a working system and conform to the requirements specification. It is implemented as a large black-box with examples of actual data and transactions being used to check that all the functions and features conform to the specification. In addition to the functional and stress tests described earlier, system testing should also include various features as shown in Table 6.3.

The objective is to ensure that the system meets the defined level of quality, and that as many errors as possible are uncovered before the system goes live. The work involved in writing and running system test suites and in scheduling and controlling them can be considerable.

**Table 6.3**   Various features for system testing

| Feature | Description |
|---|---|
| Facility | Checking that each facility mentioned in the objectives are actually implemented. It can normally be performed without the use of a computer. It is sometimes sufficient to compare the objectives with the user documentation. |
| Volume | Testing the program with heavy volumes of data. It is basically to demonstrate that the program can handle the volume of data specified in its objectives. |
| Performance | Testing under pre-specified conditions to assess whether system performance can be improved. These can uncover situations which will lead to degradation and possible system failure. |
| User interface | Checking that program interfaces comply with the details laid down in the user documentation and the original specification. |
| Security | Checking that all protection mechanisms guard the system from accidental or unauthorized penetration. Companies are increasingly concerned about privacy since many programs have specific security objectives. |
| Recovery | Forcing the system to fail in various ways to check that a proper recovery can be performed. |
| Error exit | Checking that each system error message is correct and that when an exit takes place, the system is left in a tidy state. |
| Help information | Ensuring that the system help is adequate for a new user. |

## 6.3.4 *Acceptance testing*

This is the process of comparing the program to its initial requirements and the current needs of its end users. The description of this test is defined in the initial requirements and it includes the form, the quantity and the quality of what is to be delivered. Up to this point, only the programmers have been involved with testing. Now, at this level, the customer leads testing and defines the cases to be tested. The acceptance testing can be carried out in three different ways as described in Table 6.4.

**Table 6.4**   Different ways for carrying out acceptance testing

| Name | When are they used? | How are they used? |
| --- | --- | --- |
| Benchmark test | Commonly used when the user has special requirements. | The user prepares a set of data that will be typically used when the system operates on the user's site. These tests are performed with the actual users or a special test team which is familiar with the user's requirements and able to evaluate the actual performance of the system. |
| Pilot tests | This test is much less formal and structured than the previous one because it relies on the everyday working of the system to test all functions, rather than on a set of special data or cases. | A pilot test installs the system on an experimental basis. It can be performed by users from the company and then by a selected group of customers when systems are intended for a wider variety of customers. |
| Parallel testing | This is used when the system developed is a replacement for a previous one. | The new system runs in parallel with the old version and the users gradually become accustomed to the new system. Such a method allows the customer to compare and contrast the new system with the old one and to approve the new features of the updated version. |

The acceptance test is determined by the type of system developed and the preferences of the customer. In fact, a combination of the tests can be more appropriate for the user and the designer. If the customer is satisfied, the system is then accepted as stated in the contract.

### 6.3.5  Installation testing

The purpose of the test is not to find software errors but installation errors. Since errors can occur during this operation, it is important to locate and correct any errors made during this installation process.

When a new system is installed the following are among the required tasks:

❑ configuration of the system to the user environment
❑ connection of the proper type of devices to the main processor
❑ set up of the communication process with other systems
❑ allocation of files
❑ accessibility to appropriate functions and data.

The last tests assure the user that the system is complete and that all necessary files and devices are present. They are normally performed by the company which developed the system but are performed, in some cases, by the users at their sites. If acceptance tests have been carried out on site, then these tests are not necessary.

## 6.4  Desk checking and dry running

### 6.4.1  Desk checking a program design

This is the process whereby programmers read their own programs before they are tested. It is however, not recommended that programmers should do this themselves – it being generally accepted that programmers are not very effective at testing their own programs. It is much more difficult to find errors in one's own code than in someone else's! For this reason, desk checking is best performed by a person other than the author of the program (e.g. two programmers might swap programs rather than desk check their own). This task is checking the action or process of a program and should be carried out according to the guidelines given in Table 6.5.

### 6.4.2  Dry running the corresponding code

This is the next step after the desk checking of a program design. Again, it is useful to have a different person to test the code. This activity can be consider-ed as the lower level of desk checking where the reader pays more attention

**Table 6.5**  Guidelines for desk checking a program design

| Checking points | Examples |
| --- | --- |
| Subroutines, functions | Each call should be made to a subroutine or function that exists and the parameters should be in the right order, the right number and of right type. |
| Variables list | All variables should be checked in order to find undeclared and incorrect variables. |
| Constant | For all constants the value (e.g. $\pi = 3.1415$), the type (e.g. integer, real) and format (e.g. octal, decimal). |
| Equation of variables | When two variables are equated, the reader should check the type consistency.<br>For example in C, the formula to calculate a volume of a sphere is: V = (4/3)*PI*R*R*R where V is declared as an integer and R a real.<br>This equation will not give the correct result since 4 and 3 are declared as integers. In C, the division of two integers gives an integer. so for this example, 4/3 =1 !!!<br>Therefore, the formula should be as follows:<br>V = (4.0/3.0)*PI*R*R*R with V declared as a real. |

to the code itself, i.e. it is read, rather than merely scanned it. Each instruction is examined to find out if it is sensible. Dry running a program segment involves the execution of the segment with the programmer acting as a computer. The success of the technique depends upon the ability to simulate a computer's action without making any assumptions at all.

First, a table is drawn with one column for each data variable in the program, including any indices or loop counters. The initial values are then filled in, exactly as defined. The design code is then work through, one command at a time, simulating its effect by entering new values for variables as they occur.

A major pitfall is anticipating an affect, particularly in the case of loops and conditions. Values of conditions must be carefully worked out and the actions and indices in loops need to be traced step by step, especially when at the beginning or close to the end of the loop. This technique can be very time-consuming especially when the logic is very complicated, but yields the best results where independent checking is not possible.

*Example*

Let us consider the following code segment used to find the average of marks entered by the user.

```
Number_mark := 0
Count := 1
Sum := 0
Mark := 0
Average : = 0
DISPLAY "How many marks?";
ACCEPT Number_mark;
FOR (Count = 1, Count <= Number_mark, Count + 1)
    DISPLAY "Input mark please";
    ACCEPT Mark;
    Sum := Sum + Mark;
ENDFOR
Average := Sum / Number_mark;
DISPLAY "The average is :"
PRINT Average;
```

Dry running this section of code gives Table 6.6 with a set of four marks (50, 70, 20, 60).

Table 6.6   Desk checking a program

| Input | Number_mark | Mark | Count | Sum | Average | Output |
|---|---|---|---|---|---|---|
| – | – | 0 | 1 | 0 | 0 | How many marks? |
| 4 | 4 | 0 | 1 | 0 | 0 | Input mark please |
| 50 | 4 | 50 | 1 | 50 | 0 | Input mark please |
| 70 | 4 | 70 | 2 | 120 | 0 | Input mark please |
| 20 | 4 | 20 | 3 | 140 | 0 | Input mark please |
| 60 | 4 | 90 | 4 | 200 | 50 | The average is 50 |

## 6.5 The diagnostic aids generated during compilation or runtime

So that programmers may more readily detect the cause of a program's failure, they must be able to make effective use of all the clues provided. Additionally they must be able to take the necessary steps to obtain as many clues as possible. The operating system offers a number of utilities which are useful for trying to debug a program. While testing a program which generates or changes the contents of a file, the programmer must be able to examine the contents. Similarly, it helps to be able to examine the contents of selected memory variables while the program is running or at the point where it fails.

Earlier utilities offered the facility to 'dump' the contents of the file and memory in an octal or hexadecimal format, i.e. the characters would be printed out without any effort being made to interpret them. The programmer had to painstakingly trace through all this code trying to derive the required information. By referring to compiler and linker listings, and using octal or hexadecimal arithmetic, it was possible to determine the addresses of the required locations. The data could then be interpreted.

## 6.6 Typical facilities available during interactive debugging

Nowadays there are a number of symbolic debuggers and program tracers which reduce considerably the effort required. One which is often available is a file examination utility which prints or displays serially a file using a general code such as ASCII.

The trace package, offered by most compilers and interpreters allows one to **watch** program execution by displaying the name of the module or the number of the statement under execution. Some packages also allow the programmer to specify certain variables, which are then displayed whenever their values change.

A debugger package accepts built-in checkpoints where the program execution halts (with the program memory left intact) and allows memory examination. The memory addresses corresponding to each variable can be determined using a cross-reference table provided. The name of the variable, of course, is not understood outside the program.

Most batch operating systems automatically record major events taking place on the computer onto a system log file. Such information as to which files have been opened and/or closed, and the number of file transfers, can be found here. Some systems can even log the number of instructions executed, together with a list of the last $N$ (typically 16) instructions. This sort of information can be very useful when trying to reconstruct the sequence of events which has led to program failure.

Today's fourth generation languages (4GLs) generally provide many more facilities for debugging. Along with trace packages, there is a facility for single stepping through the program, i.e. executing the program one step at a time, examining memory variables as required.

A facility called animation displays source code at runtime, highlighting the current instruction as it is executed. This facility can be combined with single stepping to get single step with animation.

4GLs generally allow the variables to be accessible by name after program execution halts. Not only is the memory saved, but the variable names can be made to retain their meaning when outside the program.

Perhaps the greatest danger involved with interactive debugging is that of the unrecorded fix. There is a great temptation, having made the program work, to forget to update the documentation.

All that is required is adequate self-discipline – easy to say, but not so easy to achieve! When in an interactive environment it is important to save the latest working version of any program that is changed and to destroy all out-of-date versions. Also, when editing source programs, it is important that the version number is recorded correctly in the source.

## 6.7 The problems and the techniques of program maintenance

All programs require maintenance. This is because they need updating or errors have been found. Errors are of two types: logic and coding.

*Logic errors.* Logic errors should be trapped and corrected before the program is encoded and tested. If a test fails because of a logic error, then the programmer must re-examine the logic at the highest possible level in order to effect a correction. Representative data values are used to check the program modules. Most of the errors in a module can be caught by careful desk checking. The common logical errors are failure to initialize a variable, type errors, off-by-one loop control and omitting one or more of the possibilities when setting up branching.

Although it may appear to be easier to 'juggle the code' to correct the problem, this must be avoided as it does not solve the problem, it merely evades it. Care must be taken to ensure that any alteration to the logic of the program is properly documented, and that adequate checks are made to guard against the introduction of new errors by the inconsistent use of data items.

*Coding errors.* Coding errors are rarer if a systematic approach is adopted. When they do occur, coding errors are almost invariably due to a misuse of the language facilities. This is usually due to an inadequate understanding of, or familiarity with, the programming language being used. Programmers need to understand all aspects of a language, not just use an inappropriate subset.

The technique for problem-solving is a four-stage process.

### 6.7.1 Understanding the problem/identifying the fault

The worst mistake that can be made is not identifying and understanding the problem thoroughly and correctly. Understanding the problem involves the following:

❑ studying the available facts
❑ investigating what is not known
❑ deciding whether more information is needed
❑ identifying any information that is contradictory.

There may be a lot to sift through, but the aim is to get a grasp of what is going on overall.

It is useful to think of the thing being wrong, e.g. a printout value, as an error, and the cause in the software, as a fault. Identifying the fault is the most important part of debugging; if it is not done correctly then all the rest of the debugging process is wasted. This in fact often happens. If you have approached testing systematically however, proving probable correctness, unit by unit, then any error is most likely to be in a new, hitherto untested, part. A second person's idea can help here, just as with checking a design.

When test data produce incorrect output it is necessary to trace through the logic to determine how and where the program has failed. The values in memory variables can be examined by introducing additional; 'print' or 'display' statements at selected points. Some variation of the dry-run method can then be used to trace through the code and see how these values are being produced.

Statements added for debugging purposes must be removed however, after the error has been corrected.

While inspecting the code a few pointers may be helpful:

(1) It is important to be able to approach the code with a fresh and open mind, even when looking at it for the *n*th time. Never believe even yourself; it is surprising how easy it is to make assumptions. The code must be seen from the viewpoint of an obedient and 'dumb' (highly literal) computer.

(2) Only the output of a program is relevant while analysing a failure. The error in the output is a direct indication of what has failed, and however impossible it may seem at first (or even second) glance, the fault must exist at a related point in the code.

(3) In case of an elusive error, one must keep in mind that an error can escalate and show up at a point distant from where it was caused. The total picture has, therefore, to be re-examined at such times.

(4) It sometimes helps to be able to 'image' the problem, especially when connected with one of the input or output devices or with a file transfer. While considering each statement, one should try to imagine exactly what would be happening in the computer.

### 6.7.2 Devise a plan/find the cause

Before starting to effect a solution, the aim should be decided. Next, alternative methods of achieving the aim should be considered and the best one chosen. Past experience is often a useful guide, e.g. has a similar problem occurred before? Could this help in devising a solution to the whole or part of this problem?

This stage is to put together a theory for the cause of the fault. All the evidence about the fault must be gathered together and analysed in order to account for all of the things seen. The aim is to verify that what is thought to be at fault is actually at fault.

### 6.7.3 Carry out the plan/devise a solution

Stick to the plan, and check at each step that the problem is being solved as planned.

This stage is to devise a solution. If stages 6.7.1 and 6.7.2 have been done thoroughly then the solution will probably have become obvious by this time anyway. However, the solution still has to be verified, otherwise new errors will be introduced whilst trying to fix the old ones; another thing which often happens.

Use test data to dry-test the proposed solution, both the standard test data and the data that caused the error to show: this should now become part of the standard test data for the unit. As far as is reasonably possible ensure that there are no side-effects from the change; if you have any suspicions about side-effects it will save time to check them out now rather than later.

### 6.7.4 Review the solution/carry out changes

The solution should be tested to ensure that it solves the problem. If not, then it should be checked to assess whether all the relevant facts have been used; if it does then details should be kept in case it is useful for solving another problem in the future. This stage carries out the change to the software. This consists of three steps, but again a methodical approach is essential, otherwise more trouble will follow later. The three steps are:

❑ putting in the change
❑ testing
❑ implementing the change.

*Putting in the change.* Ensuring that the previous versions of the source and object code are safe (in case anything goes wrong!), the source code can be edited, checked and compiled until correct. Any time needed for testing should be scheduled at this stage.

*Testing.* The original data which caused the error to be noticed should now work. Next the standard unit tests should be run, which should also work. If either test fails then go back to stage 6.7.1 and re-think. If the software is still in the unit-testing phase then this type of testing is enough. If, however, the testing has reached the integration stage or beyond, then additional 'regression', i.e. doing the ones already done, testing at the subsystem or system level may be needed.

*Implementing the change.* This should be accomplished using standard in-house company procedures, these will vary, but one thing to remember is to update all the relevant documentation. This is especially important for the additional test cases that have been added.

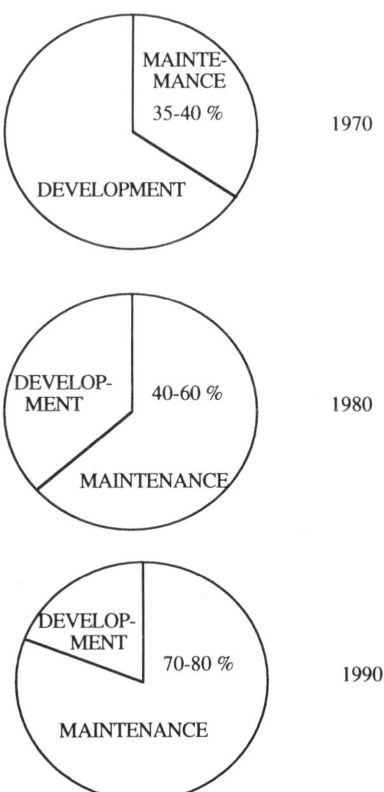


**Figure 6.11**   Escalating maintenance costs.

## 6.8 The need for robust and reliable software

The main reason for developing robust and reliable software is to reduce the time spent on maintenance when the program is installed. Software maintenance dominates the software life cycle in terms of effort and cost. For a company this activity is not profitable since it is taking valuable and scarce resources away from new development efforts. Additionally, the need to change programs and the difficulties of doing so are difficult to estimate – this activity can be very time-consuming. Figure 6.11 (Zelkowitz, 1978) on the previous page shows that now only one-third of the money spent on a system is used for developing it. The remaining two-thirds of it is spent on modification.

It is easier to test a program when it is robust and well structured. So the testing process is carried out more rapidly and therefore more economically. It is important to understand that this phase in the software life cycle of a program does not add any value to it since the developer is supposed to provide an error-free program.

Finally, a software house needs to have regard to its public image and its effect on future business. Only by producing robust and reliable software, will they be able to promote the image of the company.

## Reference

Zelkowitz, M. V. (1978) Perspectives on software engineering. *ACM Computing Surveys*, June.

## *Exercise 6.1*

The following pseudo-code attempts to find the 'largest' and 'smallest' values in a set of 20 numbers (held in an array called NUMBERS subscripted by COUNT from 1 to 20). There are a number of errors in the design.

Identify the errors, explaining in each case what is wrong. (IDCS 6/87.)
Pseudo-code, with errors.

```
1 Largest := 0
2 Smallest := 0
3 Count := 0
4 WHILE Count < 20
5   IF Numbers(Count) > Largest
      THEN
6      Largest := Count
      ENDIF
```

```
7   If Number(Count) < Smallest
       THEN
8       Smallest := Count
       ENDIF
ENDWHILE
9 Count := Count + 1
10 DISPLAY Largest and Smallest
```

## Exercise 6.2

Dry-run the following section of code using the stated input data. Take care to document clearly **all** data items in the code and to show execution of each numbered statement.

Use the input data: ONE TEST. (IDCS 2/90.)

```
1  x :=10;
2  READ ch;
3  WHILE ch <> "."
4     IF ch <> " "
          THEN
5         Word(x) := ch;
6         x := x – 1;
          ENDIF;
7     READ ch;
ENDWHILE;

8  x := x + 1
REPEAT
9     WRITE(word(X))
10    x := x + 1
UNTIL x = 10
```

# 7
# Working with people

## Objectives

When you have finished this chapter, you will be able to:

- [ ] understand the process of collaboration between computer staff and the users, particularly the programmers' place in a development team and the need for agreement on users' requirements
- [ ] describe the roles and contributions of team members
- [ ] explain why standards in development methodology and documentation lead to maintainable systems
- [ ] describe the systems cycle
- [ ] recognize user-friendly and user-defined systems
- [ ] understand the need for documentation and coding standards
- [ ] state the attributes of good documentation
- [ ] be able to understand and use the various tools and techniques used to document a program

## 7.1 Communication between people

### 7.1.1 Collaboration between users and computer staff

Most expensive errors are caused by not understanding the user, therefore good relations between users, analysts and programmers are essential. Users must be interviewed conscientiously, which may require considerable patience and the ability to communicate on both sides. In many cases, it is this stage that goes wrong. This can be caused by the following:

❏ lack of users' involvement
❏ lack of analysts' involvement
❏ possible users (or future users) left out from the interview's process.

There might be a lack of users' involvement in the system development because they are too busy themselves. Sometimes, they just want the analysts to write down their requirements and get on with it. Basically they cut off the communication lines at the end of the user request phase of development and then, at installation time, the user receives a system that may be a complete surprise in terms of performance, accuracy, quality or other factors.

The users may well need assistance to express their needs in data processing terms. The analysts will have to educate the users about the power of the computer. The process of educating the users is sometimes neglected since the analysts or programmers want to start work on programming as soon as possible. A claim that is often made by some development teams is that the users do not know what they want or that they are not aware of their own needs. This policy normally leads to a failure of the project since it does not match with the users' initial requests.

It is important for the development team to be able to interview all the users who are going to use the system. For example, a company might require a software system for the secretaries to type letters and invoices, laboratory technicians to keep records of their readings and the researchers to develop new formulae.

All information collected from these interviews must be analysed for consistency, completeness and sufficient detail. Once this phase is completed, the development team examines the feasibility of the project. Whenever requirements conflict they must be reconciled and trade-offs are usually based on priorities which should be discussed with the clients.

## 7.1.2 Contributions of the members of a system project team

Three groups of personnel are usually involved in a system project:

❏ user group staff
❏ technical staff
❏ management group.

The size of the user group staff depends on the importance of the system to be developed. It could involve a number of users from different departments within the company, particularly in large systems. In smaller systems, the user may be a single individual or department.

The technical group consists of system analysts, programmers, support/ maintenance technicians. The system analysts, in cooperation with the user group staff, collect and analyse functional requirements. Communication skills are essential and they should be able to determine how computer equipment, business procedures, and people can best solve the users' problems and accomplish improvements. The programmers carry out the actual implementation of the design. Their role is to check the program logic in the design, code and test the programs, and to develop documentation relating to the programs. The support/maintenance technicians are involved with training the users to their new system and maintaining it. Their task is sometimes underestimated but they are carrying out a major part of the software life cycle in terms of effort and cost.

The management involvement in systems development is important for supporting the effort underway and controlling progress. Individual stages can have separate stage managers who have specific responsibility for completing the stage. Then, there are overall project managers responsible for the complete life cycle of the system.

### 7.1.3 User-driven and user-friendly systems

Once developed, conventional computer programs are difficult to change to respond to a different external environment. The users cannot modify the system themselves and they need to go through a lengthy procedure, that is the system cycle, for modifications.

User-driven systems allow the users to modify the system they acquired, quickly and easily. The application development time is days or at most weeks. The system is self-documenting or interactive documentation is created when the application is created.

User-driven computing needs fourth generation languages (4GLs). They are intended for interactive on-line operation. Commands and messages are in simple English sentences and many of them offer a facility for menu-driven operations. Thus, they may be called 'user-friendly'.

**User-friendly** is a term which tends to be used rather too often. It implies a high degree of **usability** (i.e. the ease with which a system can be learnt or used; or a figure of merit or qualitative judgement of ease of use or learning), but often, in practice it is used to denote systems that have appealing screen designs. A discussion of **user-friendliness** must consider all aspects of a system which impinge on users' needs and their ability to perform tasks easily.

Historically, the **user interface** has described the physical aspects of a computer system (e.g. layout of controls, screen design, system feedback, input/output devices and the dialogue structures). The term **human–computer interaction** is a broader term which encompasses the physical aspects, but also involves psychological aspects (e.g. users' abilities to perform tasks), organizational aspects (e.g. training, workplace organization) and environmental aspects (e.g. safety and health considerations).

## 7.2 The need for documentation and coding standards

Good documentation depends on the availability and use of comprehensive and proven standards. The purpose of standards is to enforce a rigorous set of guidelines on the development, production, testing and documentation of a product and its subsequent monitoring and maintenance. The NCC published a manual, *Data Processing Documentation Standards*, which has been compiled by leading experts, using contributions from the very wide range of users of NCC standards and incorporating the latest international proposals.

During the various stages of a project development such as fact-finding, system design, programming, testing, implementation and maintenance, the need arises to pass on information. Sometimes, this may be done verbally, but verbal communication serves only the short-term need, and information passed in this way can easily be misunderstood or forgotten. To meet the longer-term need information must be documented, but unless there are rules to define the documentation, it may still not be fully effective. There can be ambiguity, duplication, omission and contradiction.

There must be standards governing the ways in which documentation is prepared and maintained so that it becomes a language for passing information about systems and programs to all levels of user, be they analysts, programmers, operators, managers or end users. They can be considered as a common language. One that is less precise than mathematics, but more reliable and economical than normal everyday language. Good standards provide a framework in which to work. They are not rigid, constraining rules.

The importance of documentation cannot be over-emphasized. It is required at all stages in the development of a project. However, some people tend to neglect this task because it is tedious and they do not always think of the four main functions it performs:

- communication between personnel
- assessing the product in its development
- improvements and modification to an existing system
- documentation for the user.


### 7.2.1 Communication between personnel

It is essential that good communication between personnel is maintained in the development of software. If this is not the case, the initial specifications may be distorted as they go from one department to another, without any standard form and consistency. For example, there might be a misunderstanding between the systems analyst and the programmer which will result in a final product that does not match with the initial specifications. The systems analyst might not state clearly and explicitly some essential points in his or her documentation and therefore the programmer will not be able to implement them correctly.

As emphasized earlier in this chapter, communication with management is important for supporting the effort underway and controlling progress. This is normally carried out with three documents

❏ study proposal
❏ system proposal
❏ system audit report.

The study proposal is concerned only with primary investigations of the users' problems or needs. The information given must be the minimum necessary to enable management to make an informed decision. The main features that will emerge from this document are cost and timescale without presupposing the outcome of the study. Table 7.1 shows a contents checklist of such a document.

If the result of the study proposal study is positive (i.e. the management team agree with the feasibility of the project), then the next step is a formal system proposal. The purpose of this proposal is to describe the details of a proposed system. It emphasizes the effects and implications of the proposal, anticipated costs, savings and other benefits. The system audit report is used as a basis for a review of system performance and a comparison with the planned performance.

In the software industry there is often a high turnover of technical personnel. Newly employed programmers will carry on the work of their predecessors. This task will be easier if there is already a standard documentation to help to understand what has been done so far. At the extreme, with no documentation, a project would have to start from the beginning!

### 7.2.2  *Assessing the project in its development*

During the development of a project, it is necessary to supervise it and to ensure that it meets all the specified requirements. Before the coding, the only way to assess a project and control its quality is through its documentation. Further, the documentation provides a current assessment of the amount of development work in progress. It is indispensable that each step of the program is described clearly to establish the design and performance criteria to be met during subsequent phases of project work.

### 7.2.3  *Improvements and modification to an existing system*

On the software market, products are out of date relatively quickly because of the competition (e.g. another company producing better software) or

**Table 7.1** Contents checklist for the study proposal (NCC, *Data Processing Documentation Standards*)

| Title page | Report title and reference<br>Author and department<br>Month and year of publication<br>Space for authorization<br>Distribution list |
|---|---|
| Summary | Brief description of the nature of the proposal<br>Origination of the proposal<br>Cost of the study<br>Anticipated completion date for the study<br>(The summary should not extend beyond one typewritten page) |
| Proposed terms of reference | Description of the problem(s) or other requirement<br>The purpose and scope of the study<br>Constraints on the study in terms of cost, timescale, resources<br>Constraints to be placed on the outcome of the study<br>Reporting mechanisms: method, timing, to whom<br>Planning: method, including progress control |
| Resource requirements | Manpower required for the study<br>Department directly or indirectly involved in the study<br>Additional resources anticipated,<br>e.g. consultancy, computer time<br>Support services required, e.g. accommodation, typing |
| Timetable for the study | |
| Organization and membership of the study team | |

hardware development (e.g. programs running faster and therefore requiring a different approach in their conceptions). This is why programmers need to update existing products regularly. However, this can be time consuming and frustrating if they cannot understand part or all of a program that already exists. Obviously, accurate documentation is essential for this task.

## 7.2.4 Documentation for the user

When the project is finally completed, there is still a need for documentation. Software is often used by non-specialists and they need to know its capabilities. This documentation or manual can be seen as an instructional device. It must be available to users in a comprehensive form before introduction of the system (see Table 7.2 opposite).

## 7.3 The attributes and elements of good documentation

Good documentation requires time and effort. The first attribute of good documentation is that it must be complete and up-to-date. It is annoying for a programmer to study, and make changes to, someone else's work on the basis of the information given in the documentation and then to find that some prior changes have not been documented, thus invalidating the new changes.

Good documentation should be well structured, with neither too much information nor too little. For this, the writer should have the ability to construct clear and concise technical prose. For example, if too much information is provided for users, it will confuse rather than help.

The number and the size of software produced increases continuously. For this reason, it is necessary to index documents to allow users to find the information that they require. The information should be presented in a standard format so that it is easier to locate. For example, if there are different styles of information presentation, the users will have to assimilate each of them before finding what they want.

## 7.3.1 A full documentation

All large software systems, irrespective of applications have a prodigious amount of documentation associated with them. This documentation can be classed as either user documentation or system documentation. User documentation describes the functions of the system, without reference to how they are implemented. System documentation includes all aspects of the system design, implementation and testing.

However, these two classes are very broad and cannot be described as an entity on their own. For this reason, documentation can be categorized further into four distinct application areas which will make it easier to explain each step of software development and the documentation associated with it:

- ❏ the user request
- ❏ the system design
- ❏ the coding
- ❏ the manuals and guides.

**Table 7.2** Contents checklist for the user manual (NCC, *Data Processing Documentation Standards*)

| | |
|---|---|
| Title page | Title, author and author's department<br>Month and year of publication<br>Name, department and telephone number of contact(s) in the event of problems during the operation of the system and for general enquiries concerning use of the system |
| Contents list | Main and sub-heading with section/sheet numbers |
| System summary | As brief as possible, and explained non-technically. It should not extend beyond one typewritten page |
| Clerical and terminal input procedures | System flow chart and description of the whole system, including options, part-runs, etc.<br>System flow chart and procedure description for each department involved or, for smaller systems, for each function involved<br>Batching, controls, error detection and correction<br>Timetable for any time-critical activities |
| Computer input documentation | Completed example of each document/display facing a page of description and supported as necessary by a clerical document specification or display specification<br>Conversion tables, codes<br>Handling of incorrect/incomplete documents<br>Error correction |
| Computer output documentation | Sample of each output and explanation of contents<br>Distribution of output<br>Description of possible error reports<br>Handling of errors |
| Non-computer documentation | Completed example of each document facing a page of description and supported by a Clerical Document Specification<br>Handling of faulty documents<br>Error correction |
| Glossary of terms | Explanation of any technical terms which the user may required to understand. This may includes the program names |
| Amendment list | Record of the amendment made to any of the documents within a documentation file or communication document |

**Table 7.3**   Objectives of the user request stage

| Objectives | Details of these objectives |
|---|---|
| State the problem | This is the first formal approach to initiate a project. The users/clients with the assistance of a systems analyst in some cases, will provide all the required information. That is details of the company, definition of the problem and available studies or back-up material of known or potential value to the system analysts |
| Evaluate the feasibility | This is a description of a proposed approach to the project which states the objectives and parameters of the project. The users will then be able to agree to and approve the proposed changes |
| Plan and schedule for implementation | This is a timetable which contain instructions and priorities for subsequent development work. It will also state an approximate date of completion for the project |

The user request is the starting point of every software project and it is crucial to get it right from the beginning. Principally, it is a written and approved statement of the nature and objectives of the project as described in Table 7.3.

In general, these specifications are not written either by programmers or by systems analysts, but by the specialist in various fields (banking, insurance, engineering or whatever). They are able to understand and talk to the clients in their own jargon so that they clearly define the problems and their solution.

System design documentation is performed by the systems analyst who interfaces between the user and the programmer. It requires the production of subset specifications which can be seen in Table 7.4.

Program documentation needs to be organized in a hierarchical form so that the documentation for individual modules can be accesses quickly. Table 7.5 overleaf gives an overview of this documentation.

**Table 7.4**  Specification for system design documentation

| Objectives | Details of these objectives |
|---|---|
| Overall systems specifications | This is a general description of the complete system which gives a non-technical description of the proposed system. It also shows how the requirements are decomposed into a set of interacting programs. This is not required when the system is implemented using only a single program |
| Input/output specifications | It describes all the input and output of the system. This includes the format, the values (min, max), the purpose, the frequency and the volume of information coming in and out of the program |
| Program specification | It details the hierarchical structure of the programs, the data flow between programs and program interfaces. It also includes internal program design such as choice of algorithms and flow charts or pseudo-code |
| Systems test plan | It described how each program unit is to be tested and also the testing of all units/program is to be carried out |

A simple program documentation is shown in Table 7.6 on page 127. This is a program written in pseudo-code which is used to find the average of marks entered by the user.

Manuals and guides are written by technical specialists with input from the systems analyst and the programmer. They will produce three types of document, one for each of the people who are going to use them after completion: the operator, the user and the maintainer. Users, unless they do set-ups themselves, do not need to know detailed set-up procedures, but operators do. Maintainers need detailed design knowledge, users do not (see Table 7.7 on page 128).

**Table 7.5**  Various elements of the program documentation

| Documentation | Definition |
| --- | --- |
| Tables of contents | All the modules should be listed with a brief description of its functions. This should serve as the index. |
| Module documentation | This is the lowest level of documentation outside the source code itself and it will be the most useful when the program needs to be maintained or improved later on. The amount of documentation will depend mainly on whether it is an internal module, requiring only a few lines of code, or a module implemented as external procedures. In this case, more documentation is required since its function is more complex. The description of each module should be functional and contain only the necessary information. It should include :<br>– name of the module which would preferably related to its function<br>– function of the module<br>– list of routines called<br>– input data with their type, format and range of values. This consists of an external data dictionary<br>– local variable used. This is called an internal data dictionary and includes flags, calculation results, tables and other temporary variables<br>– description of algorithm if an algorithm has been used and is not a well-known one<br>– identification of internal functions/procedures with any access of global variables listed<br>– data and program flowcharts<br>– error handling which is basically a list of types of errors detected and the action taken<br>– and finally the test performed on the module and their results. |
| Source code documentation. | This internal documentation should be kept to a minimum and written in such a way so that it does disturb the reader or break the flow of the code. Above all it should be accurate. |

**Table 7.6**   Documentation of a pseudo-code program

**Table of content**

This code segment is used to find the average of marks entered by the user. The user starts by entering the number of mark that he/she wants to average and then inputs the marks one after the other

Module name: Average_mark
Routines called: None
Input data:      Number_mark, integer. Number of marks to be input. Default = 0
                 Input_mark, integer. Variable holding the mark input. Default = 0
Local variable: Count, integer. Variable used to increment the loop index.
                 Sum, integer. Variable used to add up the mark input.
                 Average, real. This is the average of all the marks input.

```
/* initialization of all the local variable*/
Number_mark := 0
Count := 1
Sum := 0
Mark := 0
Average : = 0
DISPLAY "How many marks ?";
ACCEPT Number_mark;
FOR (Count = 1, Count <= Number_mark, Count + 1)
   DISPLAY "Input mark please";
   ACCEPT Mark;
   Sum := Sum + Mark;
ENDFOR
Average := Sum / Number_mark;
DISPLAY "The average is :"
PRINT Average;
```

**Table 7.7** Various manuals

| Manual | Content |
|---|---|
| Operator's manual | This document, which is intended for technical persons, explains how to install the system and tailor it for particular hardware configurations ( e.g. it should describe the minimal hardware configuration required to run the system and any permanent files that need to be created). However, most of the software applications have a set-up file nowadays which is setting up the system, configuring the computer automatically so that it can be done by almost anybody. |
| User's manual | Mainly, this manual should provide fast access to information and be accurate since very few users are willing to read a manual from cover to cover. Depending on the size of the system, this document may be provided as two separate manuals or bound together. The first part or manual is for novice users and it describes how to get started on the system and how the user might make use of the common system facilities. It should include examples that the user can easily follow step by step, and information on how to recover from mistakes that inevitably beginners do. The second part or manual is more technical and intended for experienced users. This is the definitive document on system usage and therefore should be complete. For example it should describe error  reports generated by the system and have a comprehensive index. The best application systems have on line help, and probably a work through tutorial. the manual itself is produced as a resource for those wishing to use specific commands or options in the systems. If the system is at all complex, there will probably be a blow by blow account of the use of the system, with a set of worked examples, and some examples of finished products which are placed in the documentation to assist the user up the sometimes steep initial curve. |
| System maintenance manual | This document is needed for a thorough understanding of the data organization, program functions, an explanation of all error messages and recommended actions. It could also give details information about hardware intervention if necessary (e.g. changing a printer ribbon). |

## 7.4 Techniques of documentation

### 7.4.1 Flow charts

Flow charts have been used to describe systems design and to indicate the organization of a program. It is a visual tool, so the program/system structure should appear immediately to the reader. The symbols and their interpretation are in accordance with British Standard BS4058:73 and are shown in Table 7.8.

Program or procedure names are written in rectangles, with the named inputs, outputs and backing storage elements being shown for each. The general direction of flow is for horizontal flow, left to right, and for vertical flow, top to bottom. It is shown by means of arrows. Each file is drawn only once and arrows are used to link it to those programs which use it either for input or for output. Decisions are written in diamond-shaped boxes and are used to indicate conditional changes.

**Table 7.8**   Symbols and their interpretation for flow charts

| Symbols | Type of Chart | | |
|---|---|---|---|
| | System Flowchart Interactive System Flowchart and Clerical Procedure Flow chart | Computer Run Chart | Computer Procedure Flowchart |
| ▭ | All operations or procedures | | |
| ◇ | All decisions | | |
| (storage symbol) | Storage media, permanent or temporary | Computer Backing Storage | Not Used |
| ◯ | Documents, Cards, paper tape, displays, etc. | Data passing between computer and non-computer parts of the system | Not used |
| (connector symbol) | Connector, showing continuity between symbols where it is not possible to join them by a flowline | | |
| ▽▷ | Data moving from one location to another | Not used | |

## 7.4.2 HIPO charts

A HIPO chart (which stands for hierarchical and input–process–output) conveys much of the same information as the structure chart (Nassi–Scheiderman chart), but does not indicate module interfaces or any procedural details. HIPO charts appear at that phase of the system design when the analyst is ready to start on the data design and program design. They are used to identify the major functions of each program and the major elements of the data without implying any particular data organization or program – subprogram hierarchy or choice of algorithm. However, this can be seen as a drawback since these charts have no mechanisms for handling non-functional requirements (e.g. reliability, performance and other constraints).

**Table 7.9**  Table of contents for a storage system

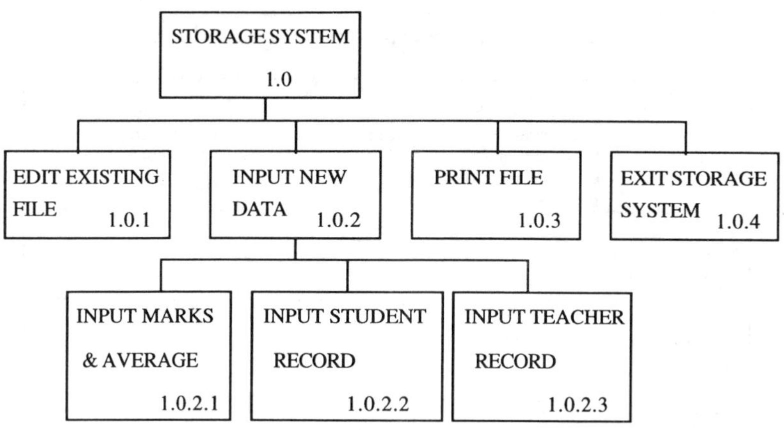

**Table 7.10**  Input–process–output for box 1.0.2.1

INPUT MARKS & AVERAGE

| INPUT | PROCESS | OUTPUT |
|---|---|---|
| From keyboard<br>  Marks<br>  Number of marks<br><br>From library<br>  Student record | REPEAT<br>  ACCEPT Marks<br>  STORE marks<br><br>UNTIL no more marks-<br>  DISPLAY average | To screen<br>  Average<br><br>To library<br>  Student record<br>  updated |

Table 7.9 is an example of a table of contents for a storage system. The name of the function is indicated in the box, along with a reference number. Associated with each functional box in the table of contents is a diagram to show what acts as input to the function, what process is involved in the function, and what are the outputs of the function. Thus, the table of contents shows the 'H' (hierarchy), while the corresponding diagrams detail the 'IPO' (input–process–output) of the functions. Table 7.10 is a diagram for box 1.0.2.1 of the hierarchy shown in Table 7.9.

### 7.4.3 Warnier–Orr diagrams

Another technique for writing functional requirements for a system or a program is by using Warnier–Orr diagrams. They are good visual representation of data structuring and refinement process (e.g. activity structure for a given system). It is also possible to code directly from a Warnier–Orr diagram depending on the level of detail.

## Exercise 7.1

The documentation of a program includes parts which aid the use of the program and parts which help in program maintenance.

Name and describe, with examples, three items you would find in program documentation making clear whether or not they would be useful for a user or maintenance programmer. (IDCS 2/94.)

## Exercise 7.2

Give features that should be used to make a program code easy to read (self-documenting). (IDCS 2/94.)

## Exercise 7.3

List five elements which should be included in program documentation. (IDCS 3/94.)

## Exercise 7.4

Briefly describe the purpose of program documentation. (IDCS 3/94.)

# 8
# Programming languages

## Objectives

On completion of this chapter you should be able to:

❏ identify the attributes of a number of different types of language including machine code, assembly languages, functional languages, logic languages and object-oriented languages
❏ evaluate the input, output and file handling capabilities of two different languages.

## 8.1 Introduction

There are many programming languages used throughout the world for scientific, business and research applications. The main purpose of this chapter is to introduce you to some of the major concepts associated with the programming languages used in many of the world's applications.

The second part of this chapter provides an introduction to the input and output capabilities of two different classes of programming language. The first example shown is the C programming language which takes a simplistic but efficient approach to input and output. The second illustration is of an object-oriented language called Smalltalk.

## 8.2 Assumptions

For this chapter you are expected to have an understanding of:

❏ a structured programming language, such as Pascal, C or Modula2
❏ binary number representations
❏ the fundamentals of recursion.


## 8.3 Machine code and assembly languages

At the end of this section you should have an understanding of:

❏ machine code and how it relates to the actual computer hardware
❏ assembly languages, how they are constructed and how they relate to the
  machine code
❏ the different sorts of assembly languages
❏ the applications that these languages are suited to.


### 8.3.1 Machine code

At the heart of all computer systems is the computer hardware, which basically
consists of four components:

❏ a store to hold information
❏ a processor to manipulate that information
❏ registers to hold temporary information
❏ registers to hold status information.

A simple example of the architecture of a computer system is shown in Figure
8.1.

   The store holds all the computer's data plus the commands associated with
a computer program. The central processing unit (CPU) carries out all the
arithmetic (for example add, multiply and divide) and logical (for example
AND, OR, NOT) operations. The memory address register (MAR) and
program counter (PC) are status registers and the accumulator (ACC) holds
intermediate results from the CPU. This simple architecture has three data
highways A, B and C.

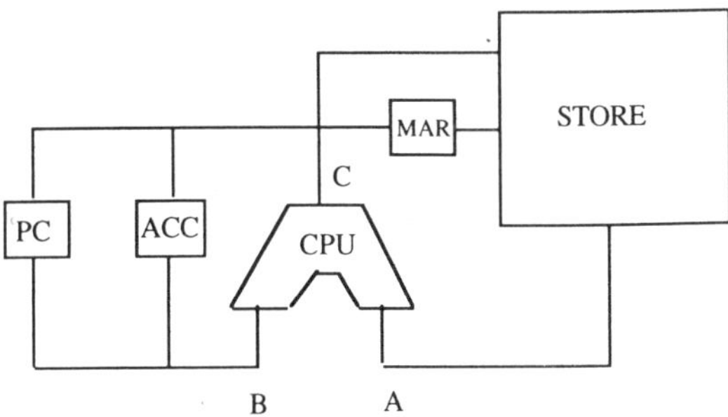


**Figure 8.1**   The architecture of a simple computer.

The only values understood by a piece of computer hardware are one and zero, i.e. binary. These binary digits (or bits) are converted into electrical signals that pass around the computer hardware and tell the computer what to do.

The instructions understood by computers are made up from different binary values. For example, suppose a computer has four instructions – LOAD, ADD, STORE, STOP – these could be represented by the binary values:

❑ 00: LOAD; place contents of store onto highway A, pass through the CPU, onto highway C, into the ACC and onto highway B
❑ 01: ADD; place contents onto highway A, use CPU to add contents of highway B, place result on highway C, pass into the ACC and onto highway B
❑ 10: STORE; place contents of ACC onto highway B, pass through the CPU, onto highway C and into the STORE
❑ 11: STOP; terminate execution of program.

This is a very simple example. A more realistic computer may have 16 instructions which are represented by the binary values 0000 to 1111 inclusive. Figure 8.2 shows the machine code instructions for such a computer.

The second part of any machine code instruction represents the value to manipulate. This is usually a store location or address but may represent a register or a constant value. For example suppose we want to load store location 32 in our simple computer. This would be represented as:

| | |
|---|---|
| 0000 : LDA | load contents of store into accumulator |
| 0001 : LDC | load constant value into accumulator |
| 0010 : STO | store contents of accumulator |
| 0011 : INC | increment contents of accumulator (add 1) |
| 0100 : DEC | decrement contents of accumulator (subtract 1) |
| 0101 : CLR | set contents of accumulator to zero |
| 0110 : ADD | add store to contents of accumulator |
| 0111 : SUB | subtract store from contents of accumulator |
| 1000 : MUL | multiply accumulator by contents of store |
| 1001 : DIV | divide accumulator by contents of store |
| 1010 : BR | unconditional branch |
| 1011 : BEQ | branch if contents of accumulator is zero |
| 1100 : BNE | branch if contents of accumulator is not zero |
| 1101 : BLT | branch if contents of accumulator is less than zero |
| 1110 : BGT | branch if contents of accumulator is greater than zero |
| 1111 : STP | stop execution |

**Figure 8.2** Instruction set of an imaginary computer.

00 100000

and add location 17 would be represented as:

01 010001

It is all very well being able to load data from store, manipulate it in some way and return it to store, but it is often necessary to be able to move to parts of your machine code program. In order to achieve this the machine codes of all computers include branching instructions. A branch instruction has two parts; the branch command and the location to branch to.

We will now extend our simple machine code with three new instructions:

❑ branch: always branch
❑ branch if zero: branch if the contents of the processor are zero
❑ branch if greater than zero: branch if the contents of the processor are greater than zero.

## Exercise 8.1

**(a)** Devise a simple instruction set for a computer with the following eight instructions: load, add, subtract, store, stop, load a constant, branch and branch if greater than zero. How many bits do you need for the instruction? In an eight-bit computer how many would be left for the address?

**(b)** Relate this to the simple computer architecture in Figure 8.1 and explain what happens for five of your instructions. Do not explain your branch instructions or the stop instruction.

**(c)** If you were to extend your instruction set to 16 instructions, how many bits would you need? Suggest the sort of instructions you might include, such as increment (add one), decrement (subtract one), multiply and divide.

### 8.3.2  Assembly language

Since binary is difficult to read all computers have an assembly language. These are usually a mnemonic representation of the machine code instructions. So for our simple computer we may have the assembly language instructions:

    LDA – load
    ADD – add
    STO – store
    STP – stop.

Similarly, the values to be manipulated can be represented by names (for simplicity we will use single character names). So we have:

```
LDA A
ADD B
STO C
STP
```

This loads the value of the store location associated with the variable A into the processor, adds the contents of the store location associated with the variable B, stores the result in the location associated with the variable C.

This is similar to the pseudo-code instructions:

```
C := A + B
END
```

Sometimes it is necessary to store constant values and this could be achieved by including a 'load constant' instruction, e.g. LDC:

```
LDC #12
STO A
```

which would put the value 12 in the store location associated with the name A. This is similar to the pseudo-code instruction:

```
A := 12
```

### Exercise 8.2

(a) Convert your simple machine code, from Exercise 8.1, into an assembly language.
(b) Write a simple program using your assembly language to multiply two numbers by repeated addition and explain what is happening?

### 8.3.3  Additional learning points

There are currently two schools of thought in the design of computer hardware and the associated assembly languages. The first advocates a reduced instruction set computer (RISC) where all instructions are small and simple, and the second advocates a complex instruction set computer where some instructions are complex.

It is important to note that all computers have their own instruction sets and consequently their own machine code and assembly language.

Assembly languages and machine code are largely used where the performance of a computer is of paramount importance or the storage capacity is severely limited.

Finally, it is important to note that the result of all compilations of a higher level language is assembly language or machine code.

## 8.4  Functional languages

At the end of this section you should have an understanding of:

❏  what a functional language looks like
❏  how functional languages differ from other languages
❏  the benefits and drawbacks of functional languages
❏  the applications that functional languages are suited to.

### 8.4.1  What are functional languages?

Languages, such as Pascal and C, allow programmers to express algorithms which are accurate descriptions of **how** to solve problems. These languages are called imperative languages.

An alternative approach is for the programmer to specify **what** has to be computed rather than **how** the computation will take place. Languages that try to meet this goal include both functional and logic languages and are called declarative languages.

Functional languages, are declarative languages where all programs are written as a series of functions.

In imperative languages, such as Pascal or C, it is possible to define functions to perform specific tasks. For example the following fragment of C code defines a function with two parameters $i$ and $j$ that returns, as its result, the multiplication of $i$ and $j$:

```
int mult (int i, j)
{
   return i * j ;
}
```

It is now possible to write statements, such as

```
x = mult (2, 3) + mult (4, 5);
```

where $x$ will finish with the value $(2 * 3) + (4 * 5)$, which is 26, or even

$y = \text{mult} (2, \text{mult} (4, 5));$

where $y$ will finish with the value $2 * (4 * 5)$, which is 40.

It is also possible to include functions inside functions, so a function to double a number could be defined as:

```
int double (int x)
{
  return mult (2, x);
}
```

So, if we can do this in imperative languages why bother with functional languages?

The problem with imperative languages is that it is possible to build side-effects into the functions, for example we would want the expression

$x = 2 * \text{mult} (2, 3);$

to be equivalent to the expression

$x = \text{mult} (2, 3) + \text{mult} (2, 3),$

which would be for our definition of mult, but there is nothing to stop us defining mult as

```
int mult (int i,j )
{
   print (i,j) ;
   return i * j ;
}
```

Now in the first case we have the side-effect of printing $i$ and $j$ once, whereas in the second case it prints $i$ and $j$ twice.

In pure functional languages, there are no side-effects in the functions. This property is known as referential transparency and is the most important criteria of functional languages.

The other important feature of functional languages is that there is no notion of global variables.

Functions in functional languages tend to have a slightly different structure to functions in an imperative language. For example, the following represents the declaration of a function:

$\text{mult} \quad :: \text{integer} \times \text{integer} \rightarrow \text{integer}$

This defines the mult function to have two integer parameters and return an integer result. This represents the function's interface to the outside world.

The following represents the definition of the function and states that the result of the function is the multiplication of its two parameters.

$$mult(i\ j) = i * j$$

Note that the use of brackets around the parameters is usually optional.

The final property of all functions is the ability to specify recursion, where functions call themselves or other functions. For this there is usually, and importantly, a terminating condition and a general condition. A popular example is a recursive definition of the factorial function. The factorial function or fac for short is defined thus:

$$fac(0) = 1.$$

$$fac(x) = x * fac(x - 1);\ \text{where } x \text{ is any integer greater than zero.}$$

So, fac(1) is 1 * fac(0) which is 1, fac(2) is 2 * facl(1) which is 2 and fac(3) is 3 * fac(2) which is 6 and so on. Note that factorials of negative integers do not exist.

Using the format described above, factorial can be expressed as

```
fac  :: integer → integer          || declaration

fac(x) = 1, if x == 0              || fac(0) = 1, terminating condition

fac(x) = x * fac (x − 1), otherwise || fac(x) = x * fac (x − 1), general condition
```

An illustration of how fac(2) and fac(3) are evaluated is shown in Figure 8.3.

It is possible, of course, to express factorial using functions in an imperative language and by iteration using loops.


## Exercise 8.3

**(a)** Illustrate your understanding of how the factorial function works by showing the evaluation of fac(4).

**(b)** What is the effect of doing fac(−1)? How can this be fixed? How can the number of recursive calls be reduced?

**(c)** Illustrate in pseudo-code; **(i)** an imperative version of this recursive function, **(ii)** an iterative version.

```
Evaluation of the factorial of two.

fac(2)
    fac(2) = 1, if 2 == 0 : FALSE
    fac(2) = 2 * fac(1)
                        fac(1) = 1, if 1 == 0 : FALSE
                        fac(1) = 1 * fac(0)
                                        fac(0) = 1, if 0 == 0 : TRUE
                        fac(1) = 1 * 1
    fac(2) = 2 * 1 * 1
fac(2) = 2.


Evaluation of the factorial of three.

fac(3)
    fac(3) = 1, if 3 == 0 : FALSE
    fac(3) = 3 * fac(2)
                        fac(2) = 1, if 2 == 0 : FALSE
                        fac(2) = 2 * fac(1)
                                        fac(1) = 1, if 1 == 0 : FALSE
                                        fac(1) = 1 * fac(0)
                                                        fac(0) = 1, if 0 == 0 : TRUE
                                        fac(1) = 1 * 1
                        fac(2) = 2 * 1 * 1
    fac(3) = 3 * 2 * 1 * 1
fac(3) = 6.
```

**Figure 8.3**   Evaluation of fac(2) and fac(3).

## 8.4.2  *Additional learning points*

Functional languages are great for building prototypes of applications where **what** the system does is more important than **how** it does it. These prototypes are used by the application developers to check that the application is going to do what is expected of it before building the real application. The prototype is usually developed in a very short space of time whereas the real application will take much longer.

Applications developed using functional languages will be slower than applications developed using other languages, such as C.

## 8.5  Logic languages

At the end of this section you will have an understanding of:

❑ what logic languages look like
❑ how logic languages differ from structured languages
❑ the benefits and drawbacks of logic languages
❑ the applications that logic languages are suited to.

### 8.5.1 *What are logic languages?*

In essence logic languages, such as Prolog, are very simple, and have two main components: **(1)** a relational database, consisting of all the facts know about a system, and **(2)** a logic language, based on Boolean algebra, that allows the facts to be manipulated. There is no need to declare the types of any variables that you are going to use and with functional languages they belong to the set of declarative languages.

The simplest way to explain the concepts of a logic language is by example.

The language used in this chapter has the following characteristics: all names starting with a lower-case letter are facts or data and all names starting with an upper-case letter are variables. The following are the symbols for the three logical operators:

, means logical **and**
; means logical **or**
~ means logical **not**

### 8.5.2 *A worked example*

Our example is about an imaginary railway network with a number of uni-directional tracks from one place to another as shown in Figure 8.4.

This railway network can be shown as a two-entry table called track with five entries, as shown below:

| track : | From | To |
|---|---|---|
| | a | b |
| | b | c |
| | a | d |
| | d | e |
| | b | e |

Using a logic language this table can be 'built' by stating the following facts:

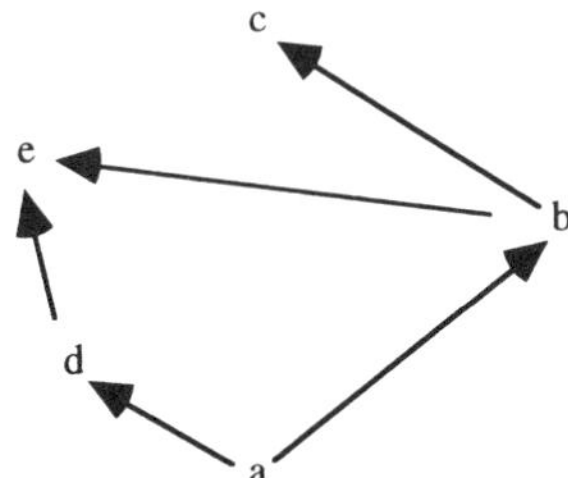

**Figure 8.4**  Network of tracks.

```
track(a,b).      || states that there is a track from a to b
track(b,c).      || states that there is a track from b to c
track(a,d).      || states that there is a track from a to d
track(d,e).      || states that there is a track from d to e
track(b,e).      || states that there is a track from b to e
```

The table can now be interrogated with questions such as:

track(a,b). – this will return yes, because there is a track from a to b.

but

track(x,y). – will return no, because there is no track from x to y.

We can further investigate the table by using variable names:

track(X,b) – will return all the tracks to b, namely X = a.
track(b,Y) – will return all the tracks from b, namely Y = c and Y = e.

Finally:

track(X,Y); will return all the rows in the track table.

Complicated expressions can be built up using the **and, or** and **not** constructs. Some examples of more complex expressions include:

track (a,b), track (a,d) – is there a track from a to b and from a to d?

The answer is yes.

track (a,SOMEWHERE), track (SOMEWHERE,e) – is there a track from a to SOMEWHERE from SOMEWHERE to e?

The answer is SOMEWHERE = b.

track (a,SOMEWHERE); track (SOMEWHERE,d) – is there a track from a to SOMEWHERE or from SOMEWHERE to d?

The answer is SOMEWHERE = b or SOMEWHERE = a.

~track(ANYWHERE,a) – there is no track from ANYWHERE to a?

The answer is yes.

It is possible to write more complex rules to interrogate the track table. For example, the following will find possible paths between all the locations

```
you_can_get_from(HERE,HERE).
```

```
you_can_get_from(HERE,THERE) :-
   track(HERE,SOMEWHERE),
   you_can_get_from(SOMEWHERE,THERE).
```

The first part of the rule ensures that if two values are the same you can always get from somewhere to itself. This stops us having to add

track(a,a), track(b,b), track(c,c), track(d,d), track(e,e).

to the table.

The second rule determines whether it is possible to get from one place to another. This produces a search of the table that expands until a route is found or until all possibilities have been explored. For example, Figure 8.5 shows the search for:

you_can_get_from(a,e),

which says, can you get from point a to point e? Whilst Figure 8.6 illustrates the various searches made.

```
you_can_get_from(a,e) :-
    track(a,b),                    YES : selects first track from a.
    you_can_get_from(b,e).

you_can_get_from(b,e) :-
    track(b,c),                    YES : selects first track from b.
    you_can_get_from(c,e).

you_can_get_from(c,e) :-
    track(c,X),                    NO : no tracks from c.
    you_can_get_from(X,e).

you_can_get_from(b,e) :-
    track(b,e),                    YES : selects second track from b.
    you_can_get_from(e,e).         YES : using
                                   you_can_get_from(HERE,HERE).

Success!

you_can_get_from(a,e) :-
    track(a,d),                    YES : selects second track from a.
    you_can_get_from(d,e).

you_can_get_from(d,e) :-
    track(d,e),                    YES : selects first track from d.
    you_can_get_from(e,e).         YES : using
                                   you_can_get_from(HERE,HERE).

Success!
```

**Figure 8.5**   Expansion of you_can_get-from(a,e).

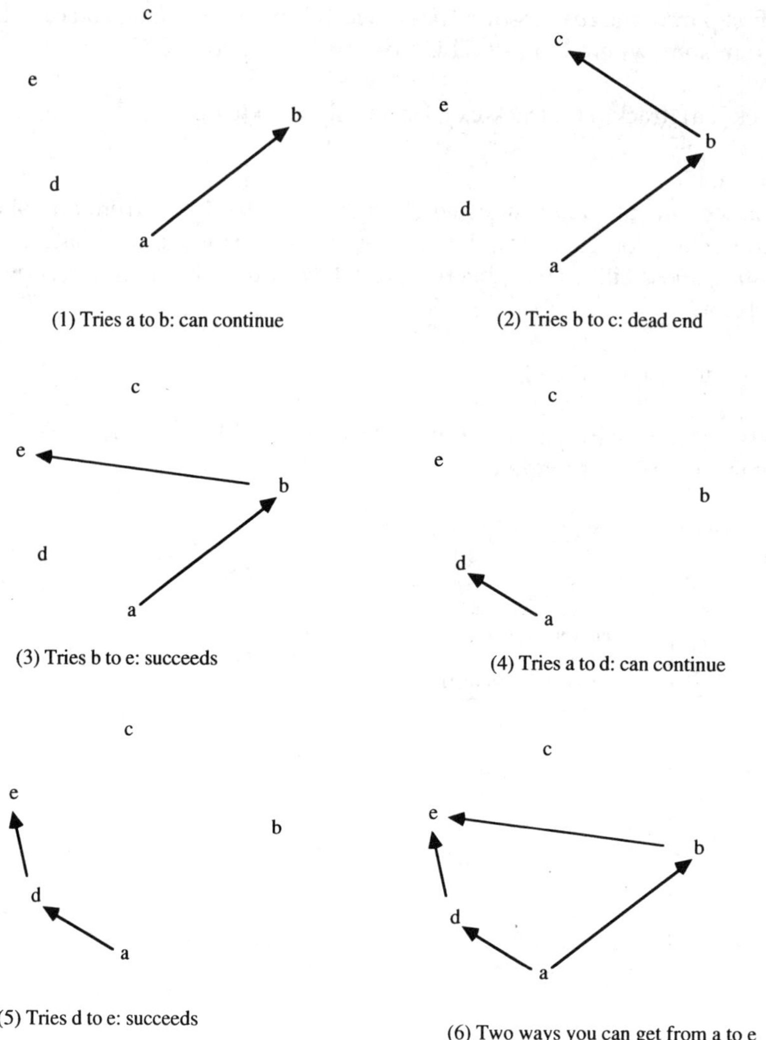



**Figure 8.6**   The searches made of the network.

## *Exercise 8.4*

**(1)** Show the full expansion of the following, as demonstrated in Figure 8.5:
    **(a)** you_can_get_from(a,c).
    **(b)** you_can_get_from(d,a).
    **(c)** you_can_get_from(b,e).
    **(d)** you_can_get_from(b,d).

**(2)** One problem with the imaginary railway network is that there is nothing
to stop us from asking:

> you_can_get_from(g,h).

where g and h don't actually exist in our network. Show how you can add
a new table called station which contains just our five stations, so that:

> station(g).

would give no!

**(3)** A popular use of logic languages is to define a family tree and develop
some rules about it, such as grandparent_of, uncle_of and sister_of.
Define a table which contains only parent_of relationships and whether
a person is male or female, and then write some rules for six other
relationships, such as brother_of, sister_of, father_of and mother_of.

### 8.5.3 Additional learning points

All processing, as with functional languages, is done by recursion. The system
maintains a search tree of those nodes that have been investigated and those
that have not.

Logic languages, such as the one described in this section, are mainly used
to develop knowledge-based systems and artificial intelligence systems where
computers are taught how to 'think'.

They are also ideal for developing prototypes of computer systems where
you want to experiment with a system's behaviour but are not concerned
about the performance or store use. They tend to produce very slow systems
that use a lot of computer memory.

## 8.6 Object-oriented languages

At the end of this section you should have an understanding of:

❑ what object-oriented languages look like
❑ how object-oriented languages differ from structured languages
❑ the benefits and drawbacks of object-oriented languages
❑ the applications that object-oriented languages are suited to.

### 8.6.1 What are object-oriented languages?

Object-oriented programming languages are based around the following
concepts:

❑ an object – where data and code are encapsulated
❑ the class – where each object is an instance of a class

❏ inheritance – where an object inherits properties from another object
❏ polymorphism – where the same operation can be applied to different objects but results in different behaviour
❏ abstract data types – where a type is defined by its data structure and the operations performed on it.

An additional concept that is not discussed is the ability to reuse what has already been defined and, more importantly, already been used. All object-oriented languages, such as Smalltalk, C++ and Eiffel, support these concepts.

## 8.6.2  What is an object?

An object consists of both code and data which are encapsulated in a package. The data represent the current state of the object. The code has all the mechanisms for enquiring about and modifying the data associated with the object. Some code is private to the object (i.e. the outside world cannot see it) or public (the outside world can both see and use it). The most important fact is that the data can only be manipulated and enquired about through its public mechanisms (often called methods).

This can be viewed as an extension of the concept of modules in structured programming.

The diagram in Figure 8.7 represents a view of an object containing a single integer and its public mechanisms (operations that can be performed on the integer).

This object has no private mechanisms and the only ways to access and manipulate the data are via the three mechanisms: print, set, increment (increase value by one). This enables the structure of the data to be changed provided that the interface to the outside world remains consistent.

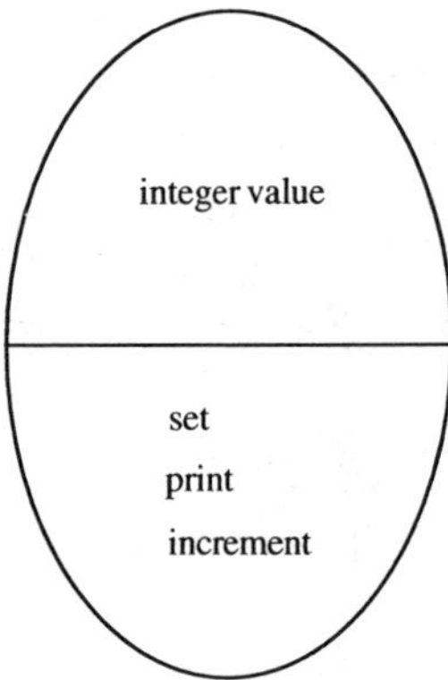


**Figure 8.7**   An integer object.

### 8.6.3 Classes

In all computers systems there will be many instances of each object; for example, there will be many integer values (see Figure 8.8). Note that there can be two or more objects with the same data value, for example two integers with the same value (see Figure 8.9). So, in object-oriented languages, object instances are not defined by their data values but by an identifier, as shown in Figure 8.10.

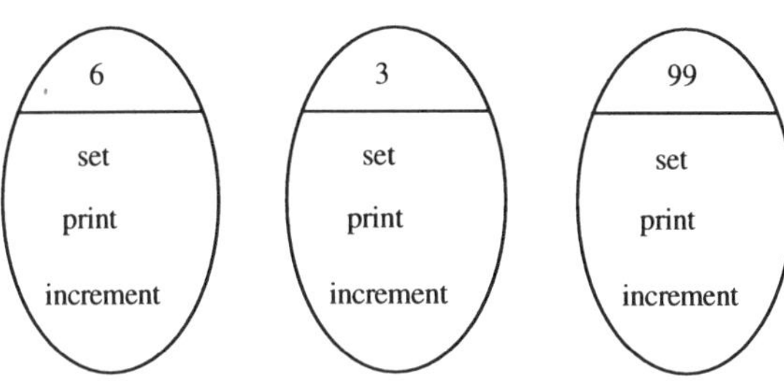

**Figure 8.8**  An example of three integer objects.

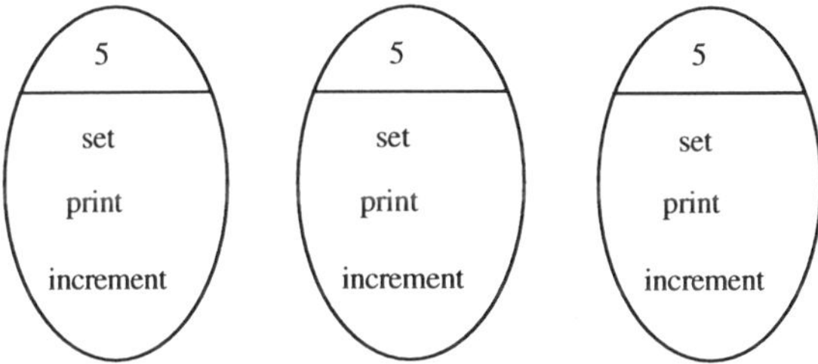

**Figure 8.9**  An example of three integer objects with the same values.

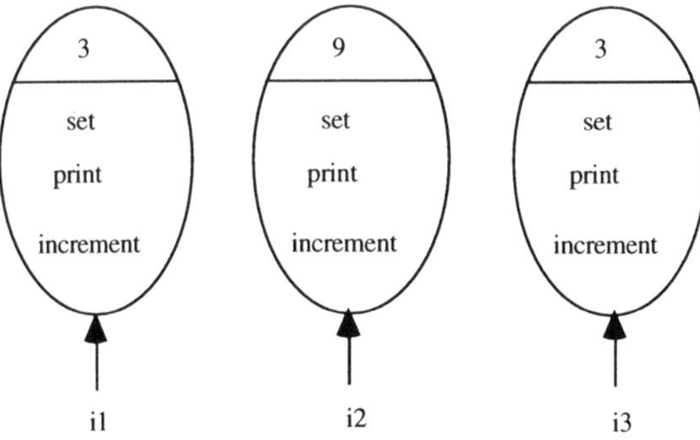

**Figure 8.10**  Three integer objects and associated object identifiers.

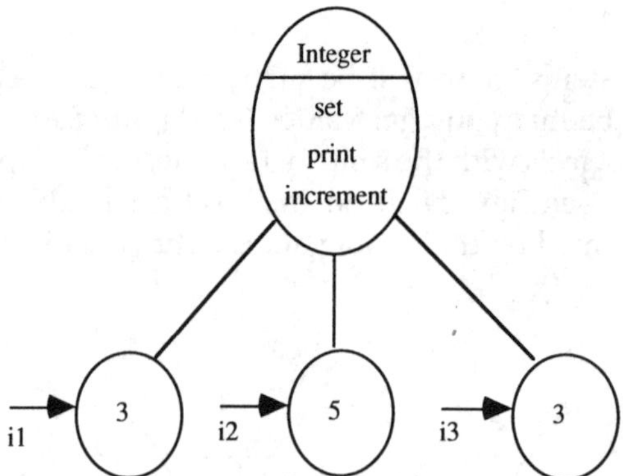


**Figure 8.11**   The integer class and three instances.

However, it would not be efficient to have copies of all code associated with each instance, so the concept of a class exists. The class represents the definition of an object including its code and its data and an object instance represents the different values.

For example, there could be many instances of the above integer class, as shown in Figure 8.11. Here i1, i2, i3 are all instances of the same class.

## *Example*

The following is one class definition for the desks in a classroom.

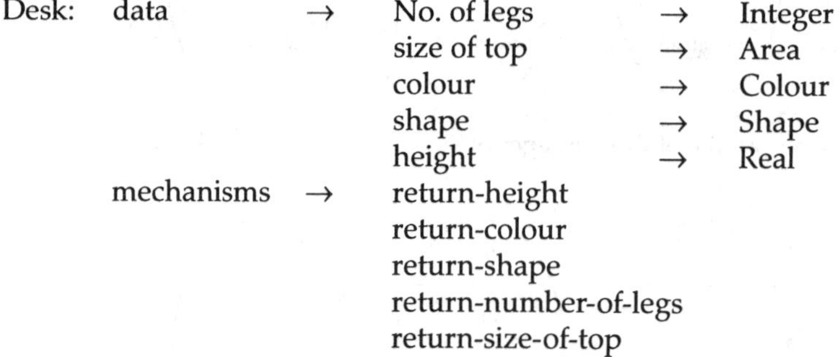

| Desk: | data | $\rightarrow$ | No. of legs | $\rightarrow$ | Integer |
| | | | size of top | $\rightarrow$ | Area |
| | | | colour | $\rightarrow$ | Colour |
| | | | shape | $\rightarrow$ | Shape |
| | | | height | $\rightarrow$ | Real |
| | mechanisms | $\rightarrow$ | return-height | | |
| | | | return-colour | | |
| | | | return-shape | | |
| | | | return-number-of-legs | | |
| | | | return-size-of-top | | |

## *Exercise 8.5*

(1) Using some of the objects in your classroom, such as chairs, desks and windows, describe the difference between a class and an instance.
(2) Develop class definitions for the following objects with data and mechanisms
   (a) a chair
   (b) a window.

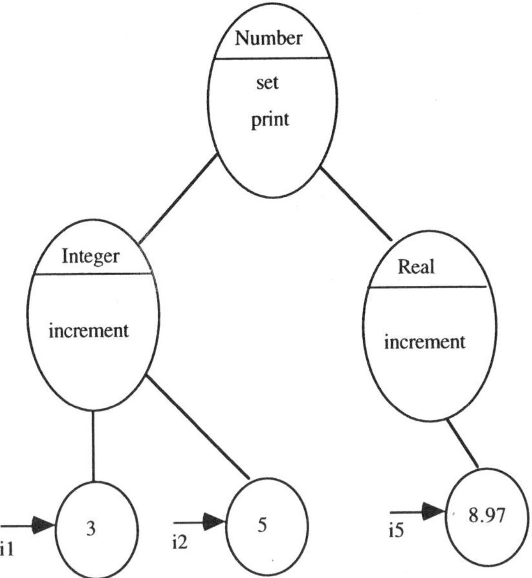


**Figure 8.12**  A small class hierarchy.

## 8.6.4 Inheritance

In many cases, the classes of objects have similar (but not identical) properties. In order to avoid duplication of common behaviour (mechanisms and data), inheritance is used. For inheritance a class inherits behaviour from a superclass. A superclass can have more than one subclass and a superclass can itself inherit from a further superclass. In fact the class hierarchy is a tree structure where all classes except the root inherit from the classes above it in the hierarchy, see Figure 8.12.

Often, when common behaviour is put into a superclass, the resulting class ends up being an abstract class. Such classes do not represent real things but abstract concepts and there can be no instances of such classes. For example, the number class in Figure 8.12 is an abstract class.

## Exercise 8.6

**(a)** Develop a hierarchy for an abstract class called shape. Some of the classes in the hierarchy could be circle, rectangle, square and oval. Look out for abstract classes between shape and the classes like circle and square by thinking of the different types of shapes.

**(b)** Develop a hierarchy for an abstract class called furniture. Some of the classes in the hierarchy could be table, chairs, desks and beds. Look out for abstract classes between furniture and the classes like table and chair by thinking of the different types of furniture.

### 8.6.5   Polymorphism

In many programming languages certain operators are defined to be polymorphic. This means that they can operate on values of different types. For example, the add (+), subtract (−), multiply (∗) and divide (/) operators are often defined to work on both integer (e.g. 4) and real values (e.g. 6.4356) but not character and string values.

In object-oriented programming languages, the same mechanism name, e.g. increment, can be used to change the values of instances of different classes, as illustrated in Figure 8.12. The mechanism increment may be used to increase the value of an integer and a real. In order for this to take place, the classes integer and real must have a mechanism called increment. The behaviour of the increment mechanism is not exactly the same in each case as it is operating on different types. Where the behaviour is the same, the mechanism is often placed in the class's superclass, as for set and print.

### Exercise 8.7

**(a)** What polymorphic mechanisms could be devised for the shape hierarchy that you developed in the previous exercise? Which of these mechanisms could be implemented in the abstract class?

**(b)** What polymorphic mechanisms could be devised for the furniture hierarchy that you developed in the previous exercise? Which of these mechanisms could be implemented in the abstract class?

### 8.6.6   Abstract data types

Abstract data types (ADT) represent an abstract concept with some associated data (although the structure of the data is hidden) and the operations that can be performed on the ADT.

Most typed computer languages, such as Pascal and C, have a default set of abstract data types in the language, such a strings, reals, integers and characters. Associated with each data type is a set of operations and functions that can be performed on the data type.

For example, in most languages there is a multiply operator for reals and integers but you cannot multiply two characters or two strings. Similarly, there may be an operator to join two strings but not two reals.

Some classic abstract data types include:

- ❑ stack – with the operations of push and pop and its LIFO property (last in first out)
- ❑ queue – with the operations add and remove and its FIFO property (first in first out)
- ❑ graph – with a number of operations and its links between nodes
- ❑ tree – with a number of operations and its tree structure (subclass of graph)
- ❑ binary tree – with each node having at most two children (subclass of tree).

These abstract data types can be implemented using the class notion in object-oriented languages as shown in Figure 8.13.

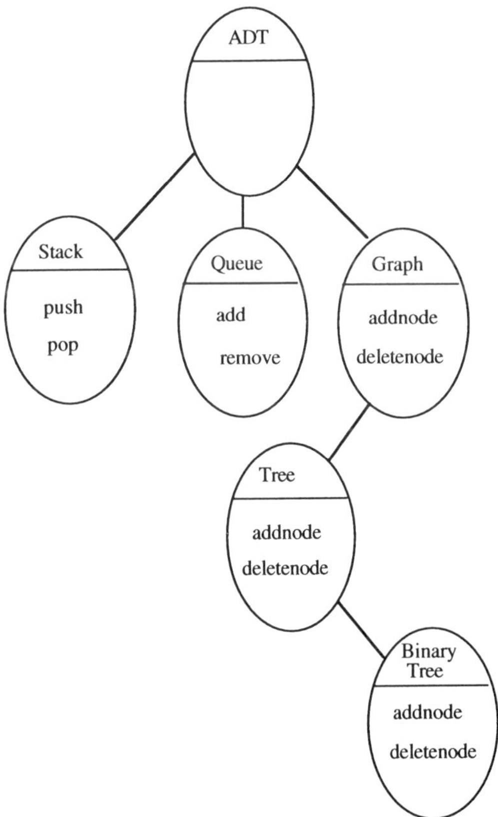


**Figure 8.13**   Class hierarchy for abstract data types.

*Example*

A family tree is a subclass of the ADT, tree, and could have the following data and mechanisms:

| | | | |
|---|---|---|---|
| FamilyTree | data | $\rightarrow$ | top-of-tree |
| | | | nodes-in-tree |
| | mechanisms | $\rightarrow$ | add-person |
| | | | remove-person |

## Exercise 8.8

**(1)** Develop some classes to represent the following real-life concepts, include data and mechanisms:
   **(a)** a pile of plates in a self-service restaurant
   **(b)** a line of people at a bank counter
   **(c)** a railway network.
**(2)** To which Abstract Data Type do they belong?
**(3)** Extend the hierarchy of Figure 8.13 by adding your classes to the appropriate abstract class, for example a family tree would be added to the tree class.

### 8.6.7 Additional learning points

The benefits of object-oriented programming can be summed up by the following slogans:

❑ small changes in a problem should require small changes in the solution
❑ everything should be done at most once
❑ if they behave the same they are the same
❑ object-oriented programming is the active process of not writing code.

Object-oriented languages have been used to develop applications in all areas of computing including finance systems, graphical-user interfaces and databases. In addition they have been used to develop prototypes of systems.

## 8.7 Input and output capabilities of languages

At the end of this section you should have an understanding that:

❑ different sorts of languages handle input and output differently
❑ file handling is different in language implementations.

## 8.7.1 What is input and ouput?

In simple terms input and output represent a computer system's mechanism for either communicating with the outside world or for storing and retrieving long-term data. A computer system may take input from a computer keyboard, from a screen using a mouse, from a file or from a database. Similarly, it may present output as text or graphics on a screen, produce a file or update a database.

There are many languages in the world and they all treat input and output differently. Some languages take a straightforward and simple view of input and output while others are more complex.

There are growing number of 'languages' available to support graphical input and output and a similar number of languages to support access to databases. These are not programming languages but provide 'extensions' to programming languages to make it easier for the programmer to interface to different input and output media.

## 8.7.2 Input and output in C

The most important point to learn about input and output in C (with the exception of database and graphical) is that everything is a file and all files are treated as a sequence of bytes (eight-bits).

By default, the keyboard is a special 'read-only' file called stdin (standard input) and the screen is a special 'write-only' file called stdout (standard output). There is another special file called stderr (standard error) where error messages can be sent and, by default, this is also the screen.

All other files are accessed through a pointer to a special file structure. The details of the file structure is beyond the scope of this book. These file pointers can be declared thus:

```
FILE *filein, *fileout;
```

which has defined two new file pointers to add to our default set of stdin, stdout and stderr. A file can be opened using the following function:

```
FILE * fopen(const char * filename, const char * mode)
```

for example

```
filein = fopen("myfilein", "r");
```

which allocates the file pointer filein to the file called myfilein with read-only access. Other access modes are "w" creating and writing, and "a" for appending.

For example

    fileout = fopen("myfileout", "w");

Once a file is open and a file pointer allocated to it, there are a number of functions that can be used to read and write information to and from the file. Table 8.1 is an incomplete list. Note, the 'unusual' use of the type integers for the characters. Although C does have a char type, it is simply an eight-bit integer and it is a lot safer in C to return an int to represent a character than a char. We will not discuss the reasons for this here.

The following are some examples of reading and writing standard input and output.

    ch = getchar();

**Table 8.1**

| C function | Explanation |
|---|---|
| int getc(FILE *f) | get next character from a file |
| int getchar(void) | get next character from standard input |
| int fscanf(FILE *f, const char *format, ...) | get different types of values, according to the format, from a file |
| int scanf(const char *format, ...) | get different types of values, according to the format, from standard input |
| char *fgets(char *str, int n, FILE *f) | gets a line of n − 1 characters from a file |
| char *gets(char *str) | gets a line from standard input |
| int putc(int c, FILE *f) | put character c to a file |
| int putchar(int c) | put character c to standard input |
| int fprintf(FILE *f, const char *format, ...) | print different types of values, according to the format, to a file |
| int printf(const char *format, ...) | print different types of values, according to the format to standard input |
| int fputs(const char *str, FILE *f) | puts a string to a file |
| int puts(const char *str) | puts a string to standard input |

ch becomes equal to the next character,

    putchar(ch);

puts the character to the screen,

    scanf("Hello World, I am %s \n", &str);

reads from the keyboard a string and places the final part of the string in the variable str. The & simply ensures that the value is returned to the string. The \n is a newline character and the %s indicates where in the format the string str is expected. For example, if you type

    Hello World, I am Tan

the value in str will be Tan.

    str = "Taletha";
    printf("Hello World, I am %s \n", str);

prints to the screen the string Hello World, I am Taletha.
    A file can be closed in C using the function:

    int fclose(FILE *f)

for example,

    fclose(myfilein);
    fclose(myfileout);

## Exercise 8.9

**(a)** Repeat the examples above but reading and writing from our two files myfilein and myfileout.
**(b)** Give some examples of using gets, fgets, puts and fputs.

### 8.7.3 Input and output in Smalltalk

Smalltalk is an object-oriented language and consequently takes a completely different view of input and output from C. Recall from the section on object-oriented languages that everything is an object and that an object has both code and data. All input and output in Smalltalk is achieved by calling an input–output object's mechanisms.

In Smalltalk there is a special class called a Transcript which accepts the values that need to be printed. Unfortunately, the Transcript can only output strings, so everything has to be converted to a string before it can be output. For this a special mechanism called printString exists to convert everything to a string. For example

Transcript tab; 23 printString; cr.

will print a tab character followed by the value 23 (as a string) followed by a carriage return to a special transcript window on your screen. The Transcript receives three commands; tab (print tab character), "23" (print 23 as string) and cr (print carriage return character).

As Smalltalk has its own graphical-user interface, all input from the keyboard is handled by the user interface.

More generally Smalltalk provides a stream class with a hierarchy, as shown in Figure 8.14.

The ReadStream class provides read only capability, the WriteStream class provides write only capability and the ReadWriteStream class provides read

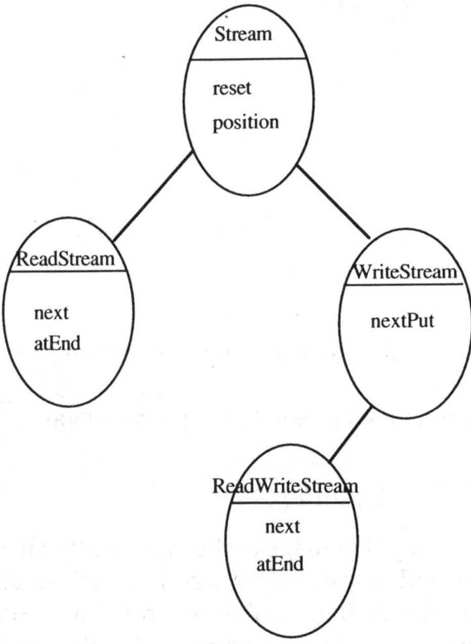


**Figure 8.14** The Stream class.

and write capability. As can be seen from the hierarchy the Stream class provides a reset mechanism to reset to the start of the stream and a position mechanism to set or return the current position.

The ReadStream class provides a next mechanism to return the next object on the input and an atEnd mechanism to test if we have reached the end of the stream.

The WriteStream class provides a nextPut mechanism to put the next object onto the output and the ReadWriteStream class (which inherits from the WriteStream class) provides all three.

File input and output in Smalltalk is handled using the FileStream class. Note that this class will vary according to the implementation. The FileStream class inherits from the Stream class and has two subclasses; ReadFileStream and WriteFileStream as illustrated in Figure 8.15.

The following segments of code open a file for three different purposes; the objects aReadFile, appendWriteFile and emptyWriteFile are similar to the file pointers in C.

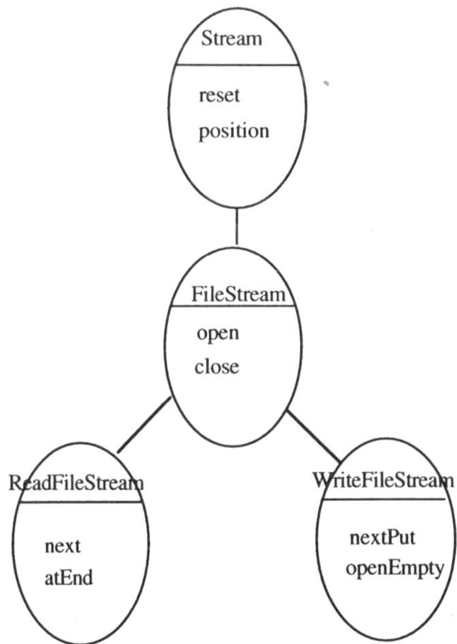


**Figure 8.15**   The FileStream class.

    aReadFile := ReadFileStream open: 'myreadfile.txt'.

This opens the file 'myreadfile.txt. for reading only.

    appendWriteFile := WriteFileStream open: 'mywritefile.txt'.

This opens the file 'mywritefile.txt' so that information can be appended to
the end of it.

    emptyWriteFile := WriteFileStream openEmpty : 'myemptyfile.txt'.

This opens the file 'myemptyfile.txt' as an empty file. If the file already existed,
its contents are discarded.
    A file can be close using the close mechanism, for example

    aReadFile close.

For an object of class ReadFileStream the mechanism **next** can be used to
read the next object from the file and for an object of class WriteFileStream
the mechanism **nextPut** can be used to write the next object to the file. For
example

    ch := aReadFile next.

will read the next character in the file into the Character object ch and

    emptyWriteFile nextPut: #a; nextPut: cr.

will write the character 'a' followed by a carriage return to the file.
    In Smalltalk all input and output to files is done either as characters or as
bytes and it is possible to interchange between the two.

## Exercise 8.10

**(a)** Write the Smalltalk to open a new file called 'myname.txt' for writing. Write
the Smalltalk to write your name to the file followed by a carriage return.
Now close the file.
**(b)** Write the Smalltalk to open the file called 'myname.txt' for reading and
read the first letter of your name and close the file.

### 8.7.4  *Review of input and ouput*

All languages handle input and output in a different manner. Even C++
which is supposed to be an improved version of C with object-oriented
features treats input and output differently from C.

Different languages provide a varying set of functions and procedures to handle input and output. For example, Pascal only provides four procedures write, writeln, read and readln. All input and output must be achieved with these procedures. While C, provides a wide range of functions that allows different types of data to be read and written.

Different languages handle input and output in different ways. As we have seen, C treats all input and output as a sequence of bytes (eight-bits) whilst Smalltalk treats input and output to the screen as strings and input and output to files are streams of bytes or characters. Alternatively, Pascal takes a completely different view and you can either view input and output as a sequence of characters or as binary values.

All applications have to use input and output in order to:

❏ communicate with the user
❏ interact with other applications
❏ read data from and write data to files
❏ read data from and write data to databases.

Consequently, it is important that you understanding the input and output capabilities of all the programming languages you use.


## 8.8 Refresher

This section summarizes the main uses of each of the different programming languages we have looked at in this chapter.

Assembly languages and machine code are largely used where the performance of a computer is of paramount importance or the storage capacity is severely limited. Remember, the result of all compilations of a higher level language is assembly language or machine code, because this is the language that computers understand.

Functional languages are great for building prototypes of systems where **what** the system does is more important than **how** it does it, but there are a number of drawbacks to functional languages. The main one is the problem of efficient implementation which is currently being addressed by developments in parallel computer architectures.

Logic languages, such as the one described in this section, are mainly used to develop knowledge-based systems and artificial intelligence systems where computers are taught how to 'think'. They are also ideal for developing prototypes of computer systems where you want to experiment with a system's behaviour but are not concerned about the performance or store use. They tend to produce very slow systems that use a lot of memory.

Object-oriented languages have been used to develop applications in all areas of computing including finance systems, graphical-user interfaces and databases. In addition they have been used to develop prototypes of systems.

## 8.9 Summary

If you have read this chapter thoroughly and completed all the exercises, you should have an understanding of:

❑ the attributes of a number of different types of language including machine code, assembly languages, functional languages, logic languages and object-oriented languages
❑ the input, output and file handling capabilities of two languages.

# 9
# Further data structures

## Objectives

On completion of this chapter you should:

❏ be able to choose and manipulate data structures to represent information in an application
❏ understand the difference between a data structure and a data storage mechanism.

## 9.1 Introduction

In Chapter 2 we discussed data structures. We now take a further look at the different types of data structures used to support data representation in many of the world's computer applications. Designing an appropriate data structure is often crucial in ensuring satisfactory performance from an application.

## 9.2 Assumptions

For this chapter you are expected to have a basic understanding of:

❏ the data structures
❏ the data storage mechanisms arrays and linked-lists
❏ pseudo-code.

## 9.3 Data storage mechanisms: linked-lists and arrays

At the end of this section you should have an understanding of:

❑ the difference between arrays and linked-lists
❑ when to use the different types of storage mechanism
❑ that these are implementation mechanisms not classic data structures.

### 9.3.1 What are linked-lists and arrays?

The first point to note is that arrays and linked-lists are not data structures. They represent two different storage mechanisms that allow classic data structures, such as trees and graphs (see later), to be held within a computer application.

The second point to note is that it is possible to represent any classic data structure as either a linked-list or an array.

### 9.3.2 Arrays

An array represents a fixed size area of store that can be indexed using an integer value. In some languages the lower bound is zero and in others the lower bound is one. We will assume for simplicity that the lower bound is one. Note that in some languages the upper and lower bound can be defined.

The following declares an array of 10 integers:

arr10 : array[10] of integer;

as illustrated in Figure 9.1.

The size of the array and the amount of memory required is allocated when a program is compiled. This means that if your program tried to store 11 integers it would, in some way, fail! This is known as static storage allocation and the amount of memory allocated is fixed throughout the life of an application.

Each element in the array can be accessed through its integer index, e.g. arr10[7] would access the seventh element. In the example in Figure 9.1, the value of this would be 92.

It is possible to have arrays of any type, e.g.

arr6x10 : array[6] of array[10] of character;

as illustrated in Figure 9.2.

| 1 | 2 | 3 | 4 | 5 | 6 | 7 | 8 | 9 | 10 |
|----|----|----|----|----|----|----|----|----|----|
| 12 | 45 | 73 | 65 | 31 | 87 | 92 | 27 | 53 | 34 |

**Figure 9.1**  An example of an array of 10 integers.

|   | 1 | 2 | 3 | 4 | 5 | 6 | 7 | 8 | 9 | 10 |
|---|---|---|---|---|---|---|---|---|---|----|
| 1 | a | s | d | f | g | d | h | j | k | p |
| 2 | a | s | d | f | g | d | h | j | k | p |
| 3 | a | s | d | f | g | d | h | j | k | p |
| 4 | a | s | d | f | g | d | h | j | k | p |
| 5 | a | s | d | f | g | d | h | j | k | p |
| 6 | a | s | d | f | g | d | h | j | k | p |

**Figure 9.2**   A two-dimensional array of characters.

This defines a two-dimensional array with six rows of 10 characters in each row. Each element can be accessed by providing two integer indices, e.g. arr6x10[5][4] would access the fourth character in the fifth row.

It is best to use an array where the maximum size of the data item to be stored is known, or where fast access to the data can be achieved through an index. In general, the elements of an array are held in consecutive locations in memory.

## *Exercise 9.1*

**(a)** Define arrays to represent some games, such as a chess board, a Rubic's cube or a draughts board.

**(b)** Your teacher wants to analyse the marks out of 100 that your class scores in an examination and present it as a graph. Define an array to store the information and explain how it could be used. Write a pseudo-code program to find the most popular mark and the average mark.

### *9.3.3 Linked-lists*

Linked-lists differ from arrays in that they provide the ability to dynamically allocate store as a program executes, rather than fixing the size of the store during compilation.

The basic concepts behind linked-lists, as illustrated in Figure 9.3, are that each element in a list always contains a pointer to the next element in the list

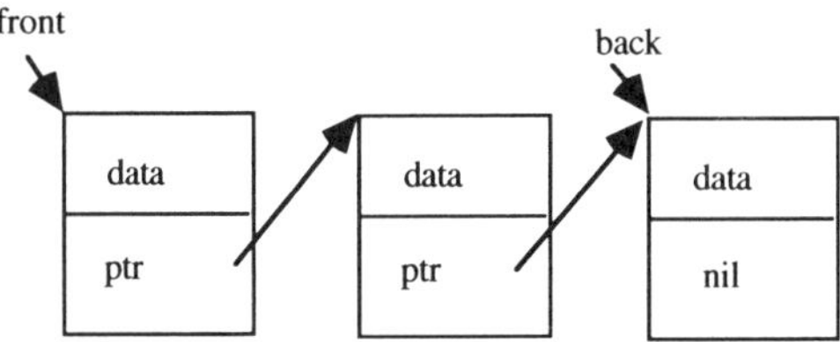


**Figure 9.3**   Linked-list concepts.

and there is always a set of pointers to the various elements in a list.

An element in a linked-list is usually defined as a record or structure, e.g.

```
Element =  RECORD
               data  : DataType
               ptr   : ElementPtr
           ENDRECORD
```

where the element pointer is defined to be a pointer to an element, thus

```
ElementPtr =  ^ Element
```

The record consists of some data, which can be of any type and may even be a pointer to some other linked-list or element. There are usually three pointers associated with a linked-list. These are:

front – a pointer to the first element in the linked-list
back – a pointer to the last element in the linked-list
current – a pointer to the current element of interest

as shown in Figure 9.4.

Note that there is a special value for all pointers which is **nil** or **null** and this means that the pointer points at nothing. This is used to terminate linked-lists.

There are two basic operations that can be performed on a linked-list:

add – adds an element to a linked-list
delete – deletes an element from a linked-list.

Linked-lists can be used to manipulate any type of complex data structure and the size of the information stored is limited by the size of memory available to an application.

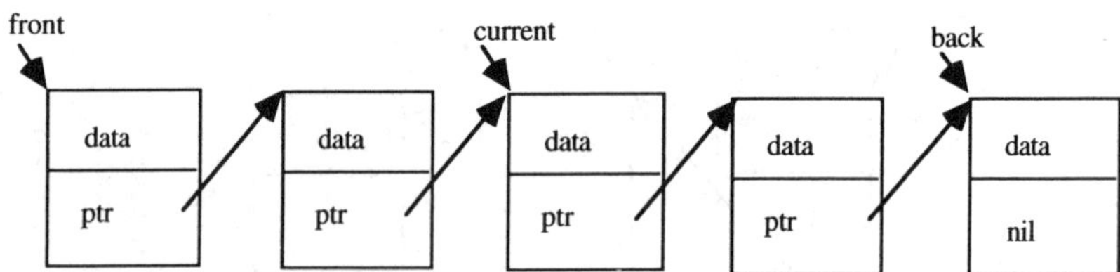


**Figure 9.4**   A basic linked-list.

### 9.3.4 Example

We want to keep a linked-list of integers, where the integers in the list are in ascending order. The numbers to be added to the linked-list are:

7, 3, 9, 2, 4

The following element has been defined for our linked-list:

```
Element =  RECORD
               int   : Integer
               ptr   : ElementPtr
           ENDRECORD

ElementPtr =  ^ Element
```

and the following pointers have been defined:

```
front    : ElementPtr;
current  : ElementPtr;
```

The following functions have been defined:

initialize(ElementPtr ptr) – sets a pointer to nil
firstelement(ElementPtr ptr, Element elem) – adds the first element to the linked-list
addelementbefore(ElementPtr ptr, Element elem) – adds an element before the pointer ptr
addelementafter(ElementPtr ptr, Element elem) – adds an element after the pointer ptr
createelement (Element Elem, integer i) – creates an element record

The sequence of diagrams in Figure 9.5 illustrates how the linked-list is built up as we add each integer.

### Exercise 9.2

**(a)** Develop the pseudo-code to perform the necessary searches and additions to the linked-list in order to maintain the list in ascending order.
**(b)** What changes would you need to make to store the list in descending order?

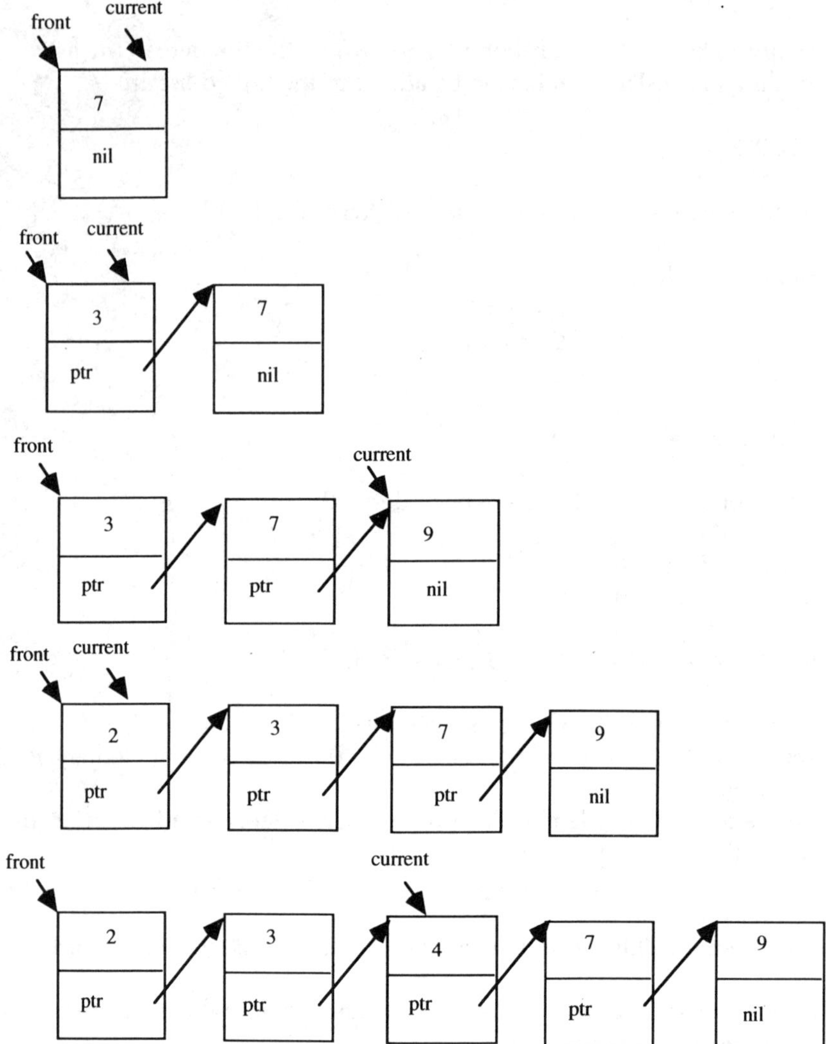

**Figure 9.5**  Addition of integers to a linked-list.

## 9.3.5  *Additional learning points*

The choice of storage mechanism for implementing a data structure can be critical to the performance of a computer application. In many cases the size of the data to be manipulated is unknown and hence, a linked-list must be used. However, if the maximum size of the data is known, or can be determined at the start of the program, an array can often represent a more efficient storage mechanism.

Many languages, such as FORTRAN and COBOL, do not support dynamic data storage mechanisms, such as linked-lists. In these languages the implementation of data structures must be done in arrays and it is the programmer's responsibility to manage the size of the array.

## 9.4 Classic data structures: queues and stacks

At the end of this section you should have an understanding of:

❏ the difference between a queue and a stack
❏ how to implement a queue and a stack using linked-lists and arrays
❏ when to use these abstract data structures.

### 9.4.1 What are queues and stacks?

A queue is a classic data structure where the first element added to the queue is the first element to be removed from the queue, for example, a line of people at a bus stop. It is often referred to as a FIFO (first in first out) list. The only operations that can be performed are to add elements to the back of the queue and remove elements from the front of the queue, as shown in Figure 9.6.

A stack is a classic data structure where the last element added to the stack is the first element to be removed from the stack, for example a pile of plates to be washed. It is often referred to as a LIFO (last in first out) list. The only operations that can be performed are to push elements onto the top of the stack and pop elements from the top of the stack (as shown in Figure 9.7).

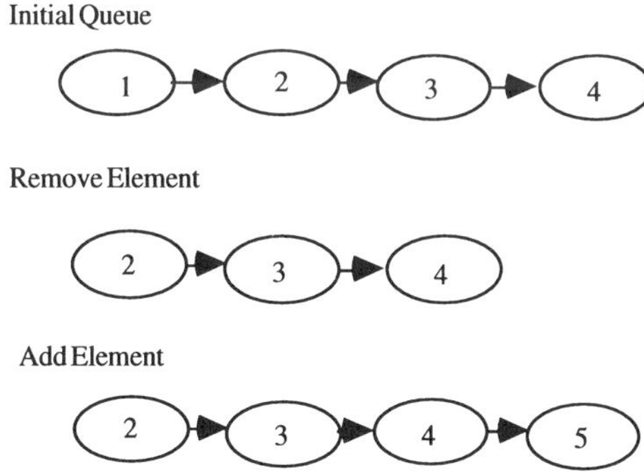


**Figure 9.6**   A queue.

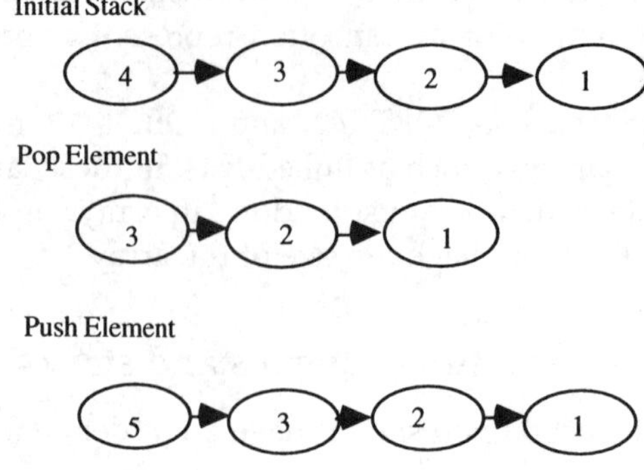



**Figure 9.7**   A stack.

## 9.4.2 Queues

This data structure is used whenever the processing of elements must happen in the order that they arrive. For example, processing the people queuing in a shop or at a bus stop. Queues can be implemented as arrays provided that the absolute maximum size of the queue is known or elements can be stopped from entering the queue until a space is available. One way to implement this is to have two variables; one to point to the index representing the first element in the queue and one to point at the index representing the last element in the queue. If an element is removed from the queue, the first variable is incremented and if an element is added to end of the queue the second variable is incremented. If either variable reaches the end of the array it is sent back to the beginning (this is known as a cyclic representation).

A queue is considered full when the pointer to the front of the queue is within one of the pointer to the back of the queue. The diagram in Figure 9.8 shows various states of an array implementation of a queue of integers.

For a linked-list representation, again two variables are needed. One for the front of the queue and one for the back. When an element is removed from the queue the front pointer is moved to the next element and when an element is added to the back, a new element is created and linked into the list. The diagram in Figure 9.9 shows a queue of integers implemented using linked-lists.

## Exercise 9.3

(a) Using pseudo-code define and describe a set of functions to manipulate a queue implemented as an array.

(b) Using pseudo-code define and describe a set of functions to manipulate a queue implemented as a linked-list.

Current State: front = 1;  back = 4

| 1 | 2 | 3 | 4 | 5 | 6 | 7 | 8 | 9 | 10 |
|---|---|---|---|---|---|---|---|---|----|
| 12 | 45 | 73 | 65 |  |  |  |  |  |  |

Remove Element State: front = 2;  back = 4

| 1 | 2 | 3 | 4 | 5 | 6 | 7 | 8 | 9 | 10 |
|---|---|---|---|---|---|---|---|---|----|
|  | 45 | 73 | 65 |  |  |  |  |  |  |

Add Element State: front = 2;  back = 5

| 1 | 2 | 3 | 4 | 5 | 6 | 7 | 8 | 9 | 10 |
|---|---|---|---|---|---|---|---|---|----|
|  | 45 | 73 | 65 | 77 |  |  |  |  |  |

**Figure 9.8**   An array implementation of a queue of integers.

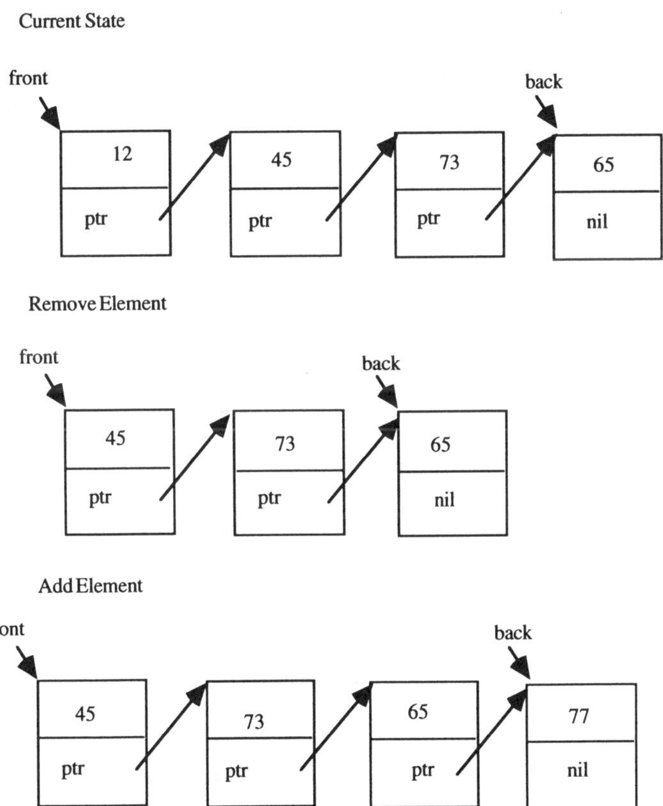


**Figure 9.9**   A linked-list implementation of a queue of integers.

### 9.4.3 *Stacks*

This data structure is used whenever the processing of elements must happen in the reverse to the order they arrive. For example, a pile of plates (the top plate is always used first) or a stack of examination papers (top one marked first).

Stacks can be implemented as arrays provided that the absolute maximum size of the stack is known or elements can be stopped from entering the stack until a space is available.

This can be implemented using arrays with a single variable to point at the index representing the top of the stack.

If an element is 'popped' from the stack the variable is decremented and if an element is 'pushed' onto the stack the variable is incremented. If the variable reaches the end of the array the stack is full.

The diagram in Figure 9.10 shows an array implementation of a stack of integers.

For a linked-list representation, again one variable is needed to represent the top of the stack. When an element is 'popped' from the top of the stack the front pointer is moved to the next element and when an element is 'pushed' onto the stack a new element is created and added to the top of the stack. The diagram in Figure 9.11 illustrates a linked-list implementation of a stack of integers.

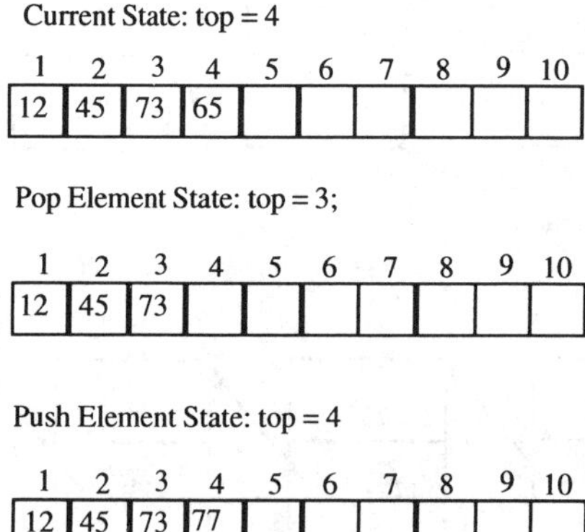


**Figure 9.10** An array implementation of a stack of integers.

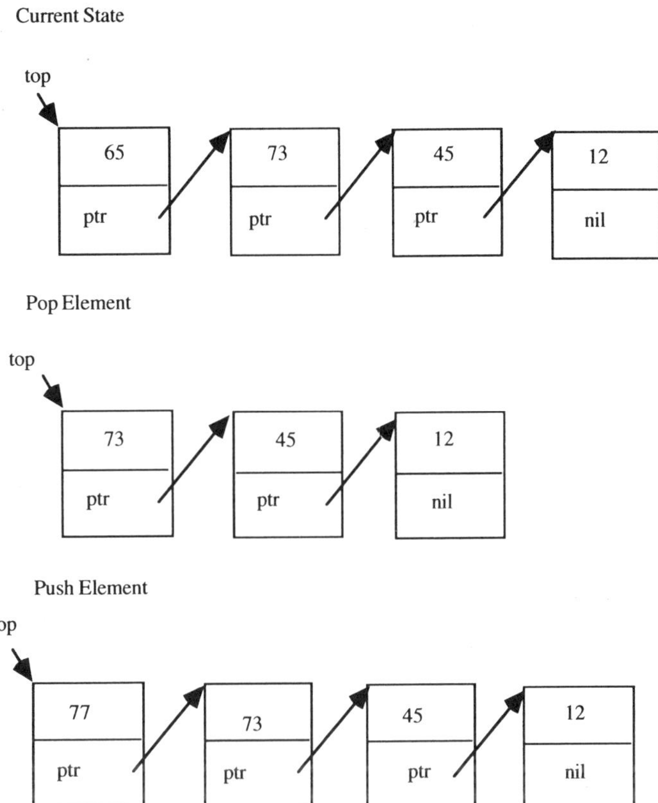


**Figure 9.11**   A linked-list implementation of a stack of integers.

## Exercise 9.4

**(a)** Using pseudo-code define and describe a set of functions to manipulate a stack implemented as an array.

**(b)** Using pseudo-code define and describe a set of functions to manipulate a stack implemented as a linked-list.

### 9.4.4  Additional learning points

Both queues and stacks are used in a wide range of software. Although implemented in different ways these data structures appear in everything from a computer's operating system to sophisticated computer graphics. In general these data structures are implemented using dynamic storage allocation and linked-lists because it is usually impossible to predict the amount of memory required. But, in languages such as FORTRAN and COBOL that cannot dynamically allocate storage, a very large fixed-sized array has to be used and the programmer has to manage the allocation of memory.

## 9.5  Classic data structures: graphs and trees

At the end of this section you should have an understanding of:

❑ the difference between a graph and a tree
❑ how to implement a graph and a tree using linked-lists and arrays
❑ when to use these abstract data structures.

### 9.5.1  What are graphs and trees?

A graph represents a multiconnected network of elements where each node has a link to one of more elements, for example a network of railway tracks between stations. Graphs can either be acyclic (no cycles), see Figure 9.12, or cyclic (containing cycles), see Figure 9.13.

Trees are a special subset of graphs where there is a single root element, each element has a set of children and each element has a single unique parent, see Figure 9.14. These sorts of trees are often called *n*-ary trees, where the *n* refers to the number of children associated with each node, for example a family tree.

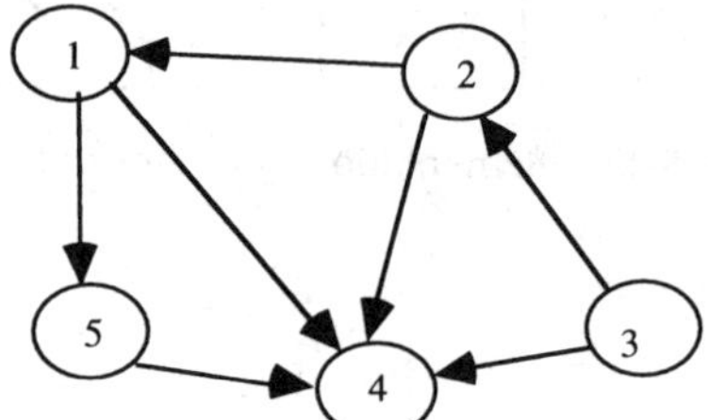

**Figure 9.12**   An acyclic graph.

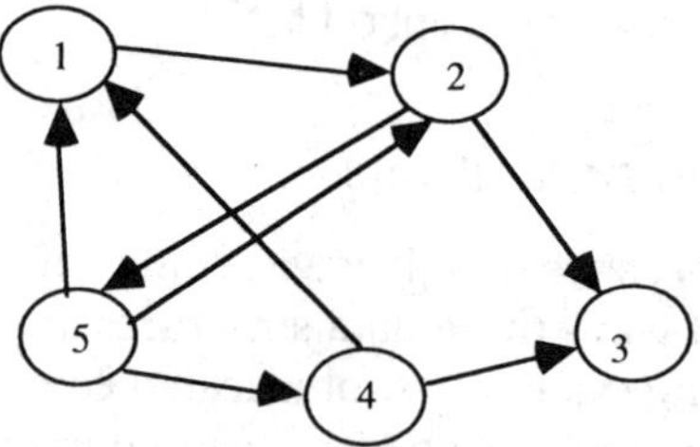

**Figure 9.13**   A cyclic graph.

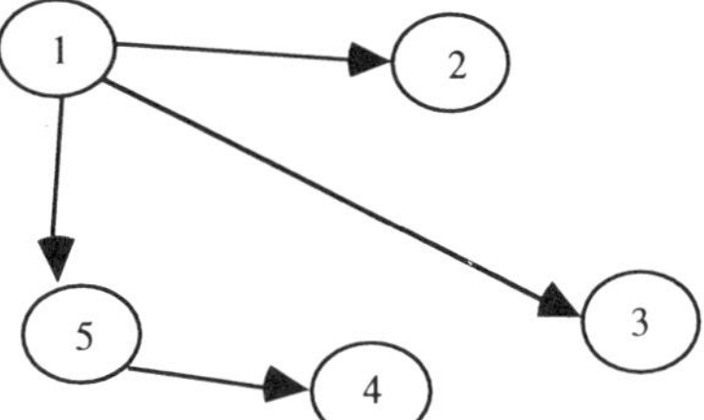

**Figure 9.14**   An *N*-ary tree.

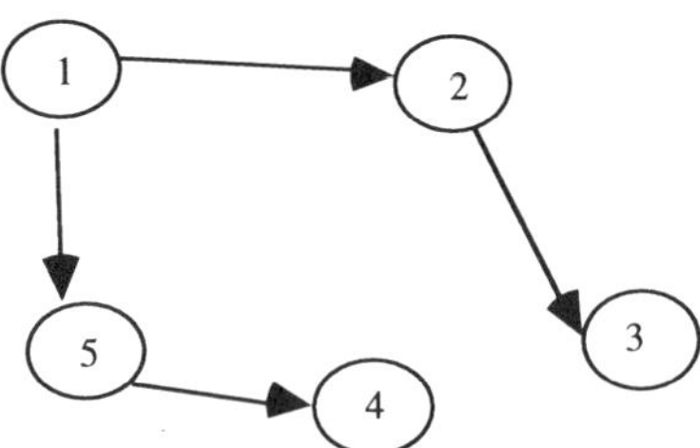

**Figure 9.15**   A binary tree.

A special case of trees is a binary tree where all elements have only two child elements, see Figure 9.15.

It is possible to represent all trees by a binary tree with a special structure where the left branch is the elements children and the right branch is the elements brothers and sisters. The tree in Figure 9.14 is shown in this form in Figure 9.16.

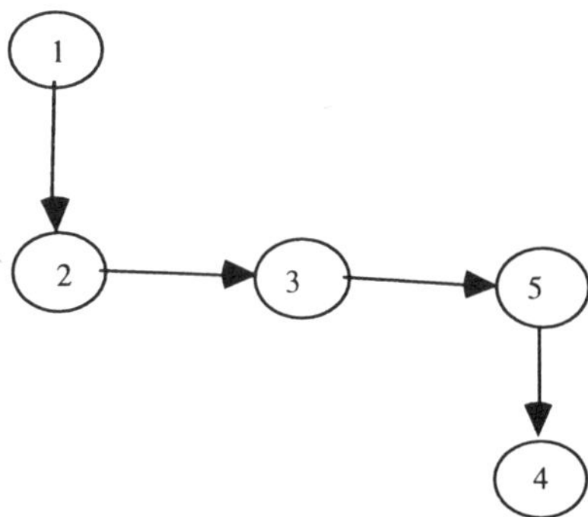

**Figure 9.16**   A binary representation of an *N*-ary tree.

## 9.5.2 Graphs

These are a general data structure of which trees and binary trees are subsets with specific properties. A generalized graph is a complex data structure to manage and has a number of difficulties:

❏ the number of children associated with each node is unlimited, in fact, each node may have a list of pointers to other nodes
❏ manipulation of the graph is complex, as the number of children associated with each node could be unknown
❏ and, for the same reason, traversing the graph is non-trivial.

It is possible to represent a graph as a two-dimensional array where the elements in the graph are on the $x$ and $y$ axis and the $(x,y)$ position is filled in if the elements are connected. The graph in Figure 9.12 is illustrated as an array in Figure 9.17. A graph can be presented as a linked-list with the appropriate list of links for each element. The graph in Figure 9.12 is illustrated as a linked-list in Figure 9.18.

|   | 1 | 2 | 3 | 4 | 5 |
|---|---|---|---|---|---|
| 1 | o | x |   |   |   |
| 2 |   | o | x |   | x |
| 3 |   |   | o |   |   |
| 4 | x |   | x | o |   |
| 5 | x | x |   | x | o |

**Figure 9.17** An array representation of a graph.

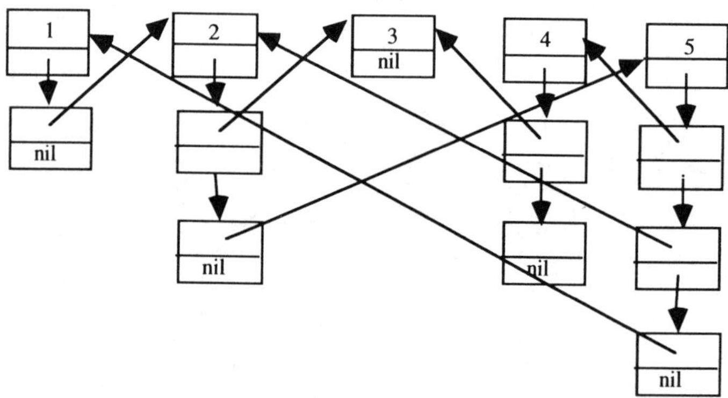

**Figure 9.18** A linked-list representation of a graph.

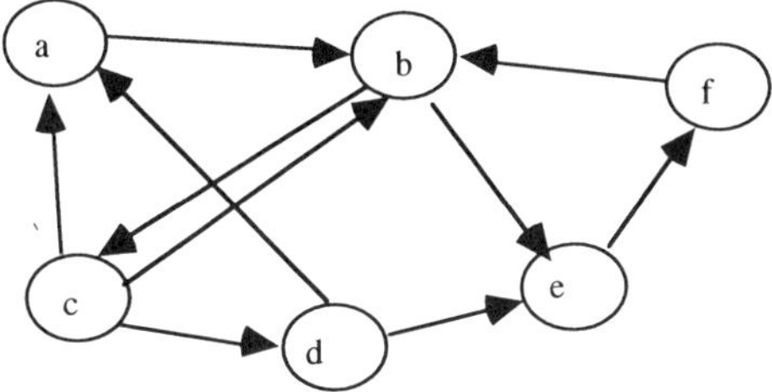

**Figure 9.19**  A railway network

## *Exercise 9.5*

A graph can be used to represent a railway network. The diagram in Figure 9.19 represents a railway network with six stations showing the various tracks and their directions between each station.

**(1)** Define a linked-list data structure to represent a network of this type and the pseudo-code functions you would need to:

    **(a)** add a new station

    **(b)** add a new track.

**(2)** Show how you would represent the network as an array.

## *9.5.3 Trees*

It is possible to represent a binary tree as an array provided that the total number of elements in the tree is known. The algorithm for access is, given a node at index **ind**, its left branch node is at index **2*ind** and its right branch node is at index **2*ind + 1**. The root is always at index 1. The binary tree in Figure 9.15 is shown as an array in Figure 9.20. Since it is possible to represent all trees as a binary tree, any tree can be represented using an array. However, it is worth noting that the processing of such a tree is non-trivial.

Any tree can be represented by a linked-list of nodes with either two or more pointers to its children. Note, it is easier to model all trees as binary trees so that each element only needs a left branch and a right branch pointer. The trees in Figures 9.14–9.16 are illustrated as linked-lists in Figures 9.21–9.23, respectively.

| 1 | 2 | 3 | 4 | 5 | 6 | 7 | 8 | 9 | 10 |
|---|---|---|---|---|---|---|---|---|----|
| 1 | 2 | 5 | 3 |   |   | 4 |   |   |    |

**Figure 9.20**  An array representation of a binary tree.

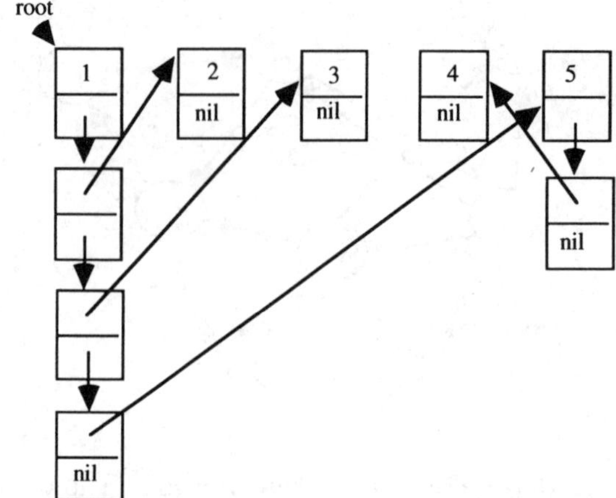

**Figure 9.21**   An linked-list representation of an *N*-ary tree.

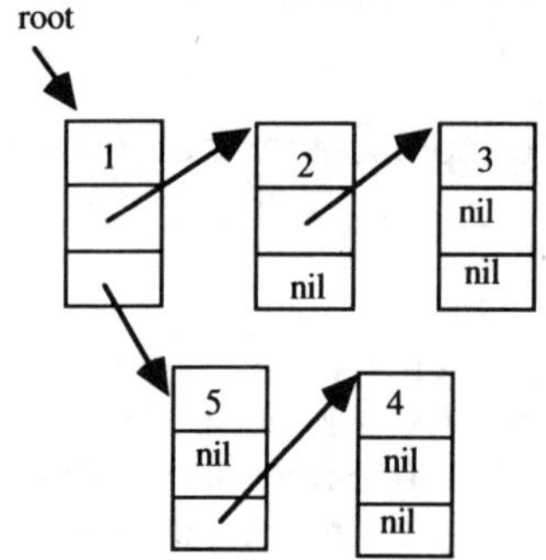

**Figure 9.22**   A linked-list representation of a binary tree.

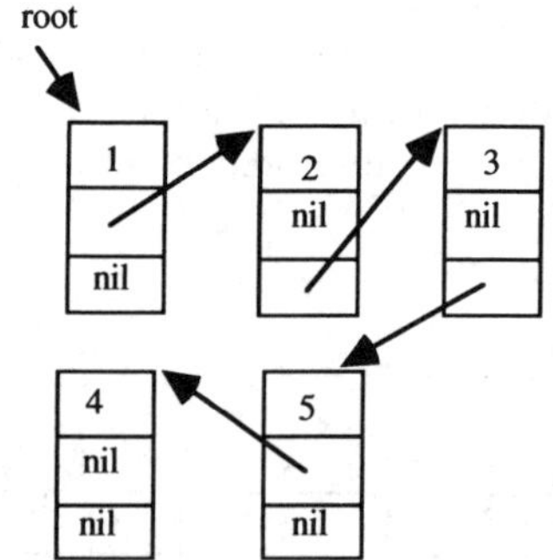

**Figure 9.23**   A linked-list representation of a binary tree version of an *N*-ary tree.

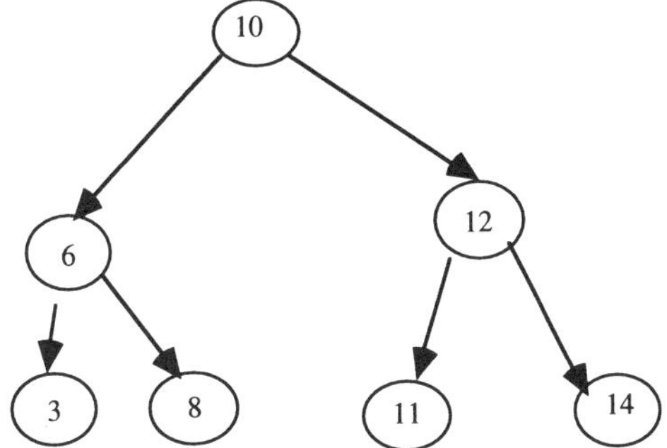

**Figure 9.24**   A binary tree of integers.

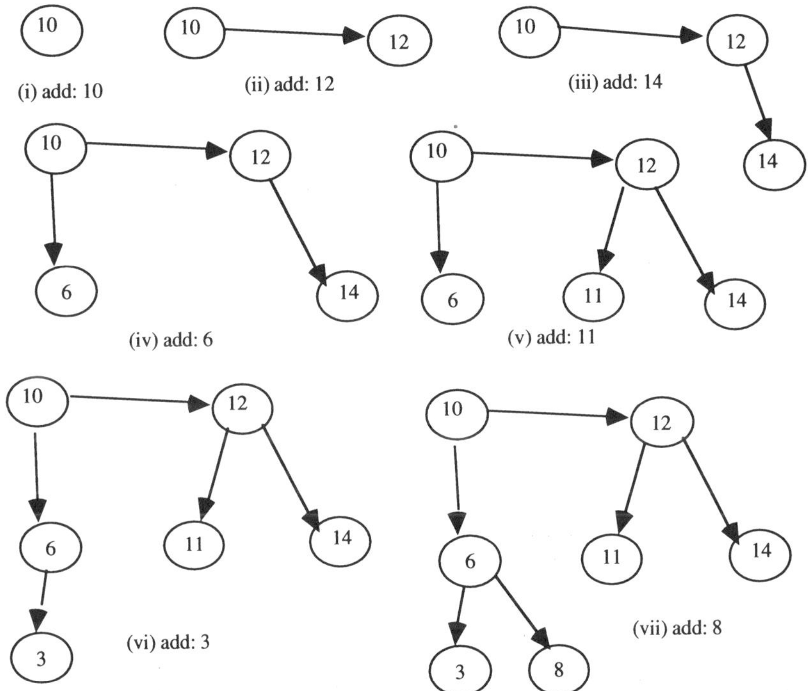

**Figure 9.25**   Building a binary tree of integers.

## *Exercise 9.6*

A binary tree can be used as a mechanism for sorting information. For example, given a random set of integer values, these can be stored in a binary tree. The tree is then processed to print the numbers in ascending or descending order.

Figure 9.24 illustrates how a set of integers may be stored in a binary tree.

As each number is read, if it is less or equal to the current node in the tree it goes to the left and if it is greater than it goes to the right. Figure 9.25 shows how the tree is built up as each integer is processed.

**(a)**  Define a linked-list representation of the tree.

**(b)**  Write a pseudo-code program to build the tree. You will have to define some functions.

**(c)**  Write a pseudo-code procedure to process the tree and print the integers in ascending order.

**(d)**  Show how you would change this program to print the integers in descending order.

### 9.5.4  Additional learning points

Both graphs and trees are used in a wide range of applications. Graphs are very useful for modelling a generalized data structure where there is no easily defined relationship between all the nodes of data in a system, such as modelling a railway.

Trees are often used in applications where searching and sorting is required, such as a dictionary in a word processor. One obvious application of a tree is to model the family tree structure.

## 9.6  Review

Arrays and linked-lists are data storage mechanisms that represent how data structures, such as queues, stacks, graphs and trees, can be stored within a computer application. They are not classic data structures. Arrays allow computer memory to be allocated at compile time, whilst linked-list support the dynamic allocation of memory as your application executes.

All data structures can be stored using either of the data storage mechanisms. If the maximum size of data to be stored is known, programs will often run faster if arrays are used instead of linked-lists. However some data structures, such as general trees and graphs are very hard to implement using arrays.

Some programming languages, such as FORTRAN and COBOL, do not provide linked-list capability and therefore arrays have to be used.

Queues and stacks are singly linked data structures with similar but different characteristics. Queues (also known as FIFO lists) allow items to be added to the end and taken off the front. Stacks (also known as LIFO lists) allow items to be pushed onto the top and popped off the top. No other actions are possible on queues and stacks.

Graphs and trees are multilinked data structures with very different characteristics. Graphs have a general structure where any node in the graph can be linked to any number of other nodes in the graph. A tree has a fixed structure where each node has a single parent and any number of children. There is a single root to the tree (a node with no parent). A special case of a tree is a binary tree where the node has a single parent and at most two children. All trees can be represented as binary trees.

## 9.7 Summary

If you have read this chapter thoroughly and completed all the exercises, you should know:

❑ the difference between a data structure and a data storage mechanism
❑ the properties of four different types of data structure, queues, stacks, graphs and trees
❑ how to implement the data structures using the data storage mechanisms
❑ the relationship between the different data structures used to represent information in an application.

# 10
# Alternative methods

## Objectives

At the end of this chapter you will be able to:

- ❑ explain the facilities provided by, and the advantages of using, commonly available commercial packages, particularly spreadsheets, word processors, database management systems and graphics/drawing systems
- ❑ use a commercially available word processor; spreadsheet, graphics package, a database management system and its associated database query language
- ❑ explain the features of an application program generator and the benefits of the use of one
- ❑ explain the client/server solution.

## 10.1 Introduction

Many readers will already be familiar with the different types of commercially available applications packages such as word processors, spreadsheets, graphics packages and database management systems. The purpose of this chapter is to relate the use of such packages to the development of solutions for users' problems. All students should therefore be able to use such packages, and appreciate that they all have similar features and are used in similar situations.

## 10.2 Applications software

At the end of this section you will be able to:

❑ describe what applications software is
❑ categorize the main types of applications software
❑ explain how to evaluate applications software to meet users' requirements.

As an alternative to developing programs specifically to meet users' needs, commercially available software can be purchased off-the-shelf. Computer magazines carry many advertisements for this type of software and many of you will be familiar with the types of software on offer. All this software is known as applications software because it is designed to serve a particular purpose. The most common categories are:

**(1)** General-purpose such as spreadsheets, word processors, database and graphics/drawing systems. This software is used by most computer users, each of whom will make use of it according to their own needs.
**(2)** General business management software for carrying out such functions as accounting, personnel management, office administration, and so on.
**(3)** Personal or home management (which could also be categorized as educational or recreational) and includes games, music, software for different hobbies, organizing video or compact disk (CD) libraries, and very many other purposes.
**(4)** Industry-specific software for the special functions needed by different types of business. Examples are software for banking, retail, engineering, architects, theatres and so on.

We will first of all take a closer look at general-purpose applications software beginning with word processing software.

## Word processors

Word processing is the preparation of text for creating, editing and printing of documents. It is the most commonly used type of application software and is probably responsible more than anything else for the initial adoption of computer technology into business. Almost everyone who uses a computer does some word processing.

The basic feature of all word processors is that they provide the facility for the creating, editing, storing and retrieving, and printing of textual material. Many modern word processors also allow users to insert graphics and tables. The overriding advantage of word processing over using a typewriter is the ease with which mistakes can be corrected, leading to substantial gains in productivity. Another big advantage is that documents can be stored in the computer rather than the filing cabinet and therefore ought to be found very quickly when needed.

The document cycle is the name given to using word processing to perform the following tasks:

**(1)** entering
**(2)** editing
**(3)** spell-checking and using a thesaurus
**(4)** saving and retrieving
**(5)** printing a document.

The merging of a number of different files into a single document may also be a part of the cycle.

*Common features of word processing software.* The following list of features is a suggested minimum that you should be able to perform if you are to be judged a competent user of a word processing package.

- ❑ correcting
- ❑ block and move
- ❑ spell check
- ❑ thesaurus
- ❑ mail merge
- ❑ scrolling
- ❑ search and replace
- ❑ placing of headers and footers
- ❑ outlining
- ❑ split screen
- ❑ word wrap
- ❑ font choice
- ❑ justification
- ❑ typeface
- ❑ bold/italic/underline.

## Exercise 10.1

**(a)** Using your chosen word processing package, enter the letter on the opposite page and save it as LETTER1. (The words in italics indicate where you should use your own personal information.)
**(b)** Insert the following paragraph between the first and second paragraphs.

```
  We visited almost every one of the departments. They were all very
attractively laid out and everything on offer was of the highest
quality at a very fair price. You will be very pleased to know I am
sure that we were very tempted to spend much more than we could afford!
However I was the MOST impressed by your staff. All of them that we
came into contact with were very courteous and patient. They did not
did not seem to mind at all how many times my mother changed her mind!
```

Save this as LETTER2.

*your address line 1*
*your address line 2*
*your address line 3*

```
The General Manager
Chungs Superstore
6th Floor
Divine Buildings
47, Pacific Highway
Old Cantonment
ANYTOWN 47HA 7#
```

*Today's Date*

```
Dear Sir
```

```
I am writing to congratulate you! Last week I visited your new
store with my mother so that she could choose a birthday
present. She is usually very hard to please - but on this
occasion we had no problems.
```

```
We also visited your foodcentre in the basement. Again we were
delighted at the good things on offer at very reasonable prices.
We will certainly be visiting again when you have your special
promotions for the forthcoming festive season.
```

```
Yours sincerely,
```

*Your Name*

**(c)** Add a footer to LETTER2 that includes your name and print the letter.

**(d)** Write a short report on the benefits of using word processing software. Your report should be no more than two pages long. It must have paragraphs, be left-justified, have a margins at the top and bottom, and contain no spelling errors. Headings must be in bold and any technical terms used should be in italics. Save your report as REPORT1 and print it out. Change the typeface of your report and print out another version.

**(e)** Using your experience of the above, write a short report on which features of your chosen package are: **(i)** particularly easy to use; **(ii)** particularly difficult to use. You should also comment on how easy or difficult it is to learn how to perform these functions that you have chosen.

**(f)** Would you recommend your package to: **(i)** the school secretary; **(ii)** a school student; **(iii)** your parents for casual use at home? Give reasons in each case.

## Spreadsheets

Spreadsheet software is based on the traditional accounting worksheet and allows users to develop personalized reports. Its biggest advantage is that it has automatic calculation, and does therefore save much tedious (and error-prone) arithmetic. It is an extremely flexible tool, only limited by the imagination of the user.

*Common terms used in spreadsheet work.* The following is a list of terms used when working with spreadsheets. If you are to be judged a competant user, you should know what they mean.

- ❏ column labels
- ❏ row labels
- ❏ cell
- ❏ value
- ❏ cell address
- ❏ cell pointer
- ❏ window
- ❏ formulae
- ❏ recalculation
- ❏ scrolling.

*Spreadsheet analysis.* The display screen and computer memory is divided into a set of cells, in rows and columns. Each cell can store one data item. Data can consist of numbers or a set of words, but is really intended for storing numerical data arranged and manipulated in columns.

The cursor may be moved up or down one cell at a time to choose a particular row and column and enter, delete or edit data. It is possible to set relations between columns or rows and to define processing operations for an entire column.

Many spreadsheets contain a report generator function, including graph commands, which allow users to view the spreadsheet (or just a part of it) graphically. The print options allow users to obtain hard-copy of the spreadsheet, the summaries and the graphs.

## Exercise 10.2

**(a)** Using your own choice of software, create a spreadsheet to help plan a budget for a retail shop for the next three months. Enter anticipated

income and expenses. Income should be from the sales of at least 10 different items. Expenses will include wages, rent, power, telephone, as well as the wholesale cost of goods to be stocked.
**(b)** Develop your spreadsheet by changing profit margins and/or numbers of goods sold.

## Graphics/drawing systems

Many different graphics and drawing packages are available. The minimum capability is one which allows users to produce basic graphical forms such as bar charts, line graphs and pie charts. This type of package is usually referred to as analytical graphics. There are also presentational graphic packages which allow the user to be an artist and compose free-form pictures, or adapt pictures from an existing library of designs. These can be used to produce output on screens, paper or transparencies for a number of different purposes.

*Graphical representations for business use.* The main reason for using graphical representations in business is to improve communication by being able to produce more meaningful reports. Their use is now very common in business, particularly because colour printers are also much more generally available at reasonable cost.

Some spreadsheet packages have analytical graphics capability (or are integrated with the graphics package) to allow the representation of data for easier communication.

## Exercise 10.3

Using your own choice of package, illustrate the budget and expected profit/losses from your spreadsheet exercise by producing bar charts, pie charts and other graphs to illustrate the figures produced.

## Communications software

Such software allows access to remote computers and is needed for access to the Internet, for electronic mail (e-mail) uses and for sharing resources across local area networks. The convergence of computers and telecommunications technologies is becoming increasingly important.

## Exercise 10.4

Investigate commonly available communications packages and write a short report to help your school decide what would be useful to use for Email and access to the World Wide Web.

## Database management systems

Database management software (DBMS) systems allow the user to store large amounts of data that can be easily retrieved and manipulated to a high degree of flexibility in order to produce many different types of report.

*DBMS features.* The following is a list of the basic functions that you should be able to perform if you are to be judged a competent user of any DBMS.

- ❏ creating a database
- ❏ adding data to a database
- ❏ searching a database
  - – relational operations
  - – logical operations
  - – string operations
- ❏ sorting a database
- ❏ modifying database structures
- ❏ creating and printing reports.

DBMS include a data query language which can be used for programming special data retrieval functions. This is discussed more fully later in this chapter.

## Exercise 10.5

**(a)** Create a structure for an employee database with the following information:
Surname
Forename
Address
Date of joining company
Annual salary
Department.
**(b)** Add records for 10 people.
**(c)** Save the database.
**(d)** Try the following operations and produce reports which: **(i)** lists all names and departments; **(ii)** sorts into lastname order and prints them out; and **(iii)** selects and prints all employees in a particular department.

## Integrated software

Integrated software is when the different types of applications package are combined into a single piece of software, often with a common set of commands and a standard user interface. The objective is to allow the user to switch easily between tasks. Such packages are increasingly common. For example, a spreadsheet may be part of an integrated package which also includes a database, a graphics facility, a communications program, a word processor and a time management facility. Thus, it is possible to use one part of the workspace as a database, another as a timesheet and yet another to perform calculations and produce something as complete as a computerized planner.

## Exercise 10.6

Investigate at least two integrated packages. Choose one and write a short evaluation of its features – particularly consider how well it performs the basic functions that we discussed earlier. (Try to actually use it if possible!)

### Evaluating requirements

It is very important when evaluating applications software to ensure that it will meet the requirements of the user. This is no different to the care that must be taken with the specification for a custom-built program.

There are two possible scenarios; the first when the hardware and operating system are already in place, the second when it is not. In the latter case it is the applications software that should be selected first to meet the identified needs. If this is done there is a better chance of the software meeting all the processing needs.

When the hardware is already in place, the choice may be restricted because the ideal solution will not operate on the existing computer configuration.

### Choosing applications software

So much software is available today that it can be difficult to decide what will meet users' requirements, although it is true to say that **industry standards** have emerged and a small number of packages by just a few suppliers do in fact account for the majority of users. The fact that these packages have so many users means that the suppliers are forced to take notice of the views of the users of their software and are able to provide a reasonable level of support and training. In addition the many magazines, journals and books available provide information for both users and prospective users of the more popular packages.

Given these market conditions, there are questions (apart from investigating the features offered and their suitability for the proposed task) that need to be asked when purchasing software. These include:

(1) How much?
(2) What specific tasks does it perform (and do they meet my requirements?).

 (3)   What are the key features?
 (4)   What hardware and operating system are required?
 (5)   How much storage is required?
 (6)   How good is the documentation?
 (7)   Training available? Of what type? Cost?
 (8)   Support available? Where from? When? Costs?
 (9)   Warranty?
(10)   Other users? Where? How many?

## Exercise 10.7

Choose two of the packages you identified for Exercise 10.6. Compile a table to compare them for use by a small business of your choice. Use the 10 items listed above as a guide.

## 10.3  Application program generators

At the end of this section you will be able to:

❑ explain the features of an application program generator and the benefits of the use of one.

### *Definition*

An applications program generator is a software system that produces a computer program in response to a user's needs. The system is a set of pre-coded modules that perform different functions. Users select the functions that they require; the applications generator determines how to perform the tasks and produces the instructions for the program. An applications program generator can be classified as a fourth generation language (4GL).

It is not straightforward to define a 4GL because there are a number of different types and the different producers of such systems define them in a different way to each other. It is better to first examine their characteristics before attempting to define them. Essentially though they are easier to use than third generation languages, both for programmers and users.

4GLs are non-procedural languages – allowing users to specify **what** a program must do, rather than **how** to do it. The consequence of this is that they need only about 10 per cent of the number of statements that a third generation language would require to do the same task. This is clearly a major advantage.

### *4GLs*

4GLs can be classified into categories with facilities ranging from simple data query of random access files to complete application generation languages.

Some of the most comprehensive are described later, but first we will consider how they have evolved.

As program development tools evolved, packages became available which would allow a user to define a file interactively and would then handle the standard requirements of file creation, file manipulation, file interrogation and file amendment. These were combined with packages which accepted a report format from the user. The file that was created was then used to produce a printed report. One example of this is a relational database as described earlier. For a very large number of applications such a package could handle up to 90 per cent of the work.

To allow the user to define more complex tasks using the files created, very high-level commands were incorporated into these packages. The package then became capable of handling most applications, without the need to understand complex programming techniques.

The characteristics of fourth generation languages are summarized in Table 10.1. 4GLs are intended for interactive, on-line operation. Commands and messages are in simple English-like sentences and many of them offer a facility for menu-driven operation. They can therefore be considered user-friendly.

**Table 10.1**   Features of 4GLs

| On-line operation |
| --- |
| User friendly |
| Very high level instructions |
| Non-procedural code |
| Database manager |
| Query language |
| Report generator |
| Intelligent default assumptions |

The translation is handled by an interpreter rather than a compiler. Commands are non-procedural, i.e. they need not spell out every step in the process, but can define a task to be performed. It follows from this that instructions are at a very high level.

Data are generally organized into databases with the use of partially or fully inverted files with a database manager being incorporated as an integral part of the language.

Queries on the data may be defined in a query language developed for the purpose and a report generator is also included as a part of the language. There are intelligent default assumptions and commands rarely need to be given (see Table 10.2 overleaf).

**Table 10.2**  Types of 4GL

> Query languages
> Report generators
> Applications generators
> Decision support systems and
> financial planning languages
> Some microcomputer software

## Query languages

Query languages are designed to allow users to retrieve information from databases and to ask questions about data stored in them. Such requests are very like natural language but they do have a specific grammar, syntax and vocabulary that must be used (in the same way that other computer languages do). This language needs to be learned by both programmers and users, but is not difficult. For example: 'how many items in inventory have a quantity-on-hand that is less than the re-order point?'. The query language will do the following to retrieve the information:

(1)  Copy the data for items with quantity-on-hand less than the re-order point into a temporary location in main memory.
(2)  Sort the data into order by inventory number.
(3)  Present the information on the screen and/or the printer.

The manager now has the information necessary to proceed with re-ordering certain low stock items. The important thing to note is that the manager didn't have to specify how to get the job done, only what needed to be done, In other words, in our example, the user needed only to specify the question, and the system automatically performed each of the three steps listed above.

Some query languages also allow the user to modify databases and add or delete entries in the same way that database management software does.

Some common query languages are:

❑ ORACLE
❑ INTELLECT
❑ SQL.

## Report generators

These are similar to query languages in functionality but do not allow the user to modify the database. They are used (as would be expected from their name) to present reports. Users can specify what should be in the report and how it should look. Report generators contain assumptions about what users require and this is often much simpler than making decisions from nothing.

A report generator is a software utility which, at its simplest, reads a file, extracts specified records and prints all, or part, of them.

Commercial information technology contains a great deal of this kind of activity, so several different types of report generator exist. Some are like the simple **extract and print** – others are much more powerful, and therefore more flexible.

The more powerful report generators are effectively very high-level languages, which are easy to learn and easy to use correctly, because they are formalized and restricted in the way that the commands can be used. Table 10.3 below shows the main features which a powerful report generator will have.

It is possible to produce complete data processing systems with these features and some installations do just that! Installations which use report generators find that they can produce work much more quickly than they did before they introduced them. Users, as well as programmers, can often make effective use of this type of generator, which releases programming effort for the more complex programming jobs. The only commands which a generator needs are parameters to define the relevant aspects of the processing, for example which file to use, which records and which fields.

There are however some disadvantages when using report generators.

(1) No report generator can be as powerful or as comprehensive as a well developed programming language such as C++ or COBOL, but for the routine extraction of data, and the formatting of data files or reports from it, a report generator is often quite acceptable.
(2) Runtime. It is fairly obvious that a highly 'tuned' program in a standard language will probably run more quickly on the computer than a program produced by building blocks. Nevertheless, they are efficient – and it would be misleading to say that all **proper** programs are more efficient at runtime than all **generator** programs.

If a generator is available, it is worthwhile using it because it will save time and enable straightforward processing jobs to be completed quickly, leaving

**Table 10.3** Main features of
powerful report generator

File update
Multifile input and output
Calculations on fields
Control – printing
    – sub-totalling
    – layout
Library routines

more time for the complicated ones which must be done by programming in a language. In addition, it should be noted that report generator programs are very easy to modify. They are clear, logical, readable and therefore comparatively straightforward to maintain.

## Applications generators

These are different to both report generators and query languages which only allow users to specify output- and input-related tasks. Applications generators allow users to specify a complete software application – a program in fact, with the usual format of input, validation of data, process (both logic and computation) and output (usually in the form of reports). Their advantage is that they allow users to reduce the time it takes to produce a working system.

Applications generators accept the specification for a program in a **computer-unable form.** This specification file is read into the generator itself which determines how to perform the tasks and produces the instructions for the computer to carry out the task. As with query languages and report generators, the user of an applications generator does not need to specify exactly how processing tasks are to be performed.

*How they work in practice.* A user could use an applications generator to design payroll runs – to calculate each employee's pay for a certain period and to output printed cheques. Again, as with query languages and report generators, the user doesn't have to specify **how** to get the processing tasks performed.

Table 10.4 below lists the main characteristics of applications generators.

During the input definition, the formats and linking of screens for data input and the data validation procedures may be specified by displaying the requirements on the screen. The types, range and other details of the data may be defined by filling out a form presented by the package. Procedures may be defined through the use of very high-level commands or by completing a questionnaire. Commands may be used to set a view of data for report

**Table 10.4**   Main characteristics of applications generators

| |
|---|
| Program development by inexperienced or non-programmers |
| Input definition by screen painting |
| Data definition by form-filling |
| Procedure definition by questionnaire |
| Report/enquiry definition by answering commands |
| Automatic code generation |
| Automatic generation of complete application |

generation and report formats may be specified by filling out forms. Sample formats can be produced as templates for defining requirements, and outputs can be easily obtained when an applications generator is used. Hence, a prototype can be presented to the user quite quickly for verification before serious work begins on the system. User involvement is possible at every stage, so for a routine application it may not be necessary to acquire any programming expertise at all.

## Exercise 10.8

Make a list of the types of information that would need to be specified and the type of output required to generate a stock control program for a small retail shop.

*Decision support systems and financial planning languages* combine special interactive computer programs and some special hardware to allow senior managers to bring data and information together from different sources and manipulate it in new ways – to make projections, do **what if** analyses and make long-term planning decisions.

These tools belong to a class of applications packages known as management information systems (MIS). These are systems that support management decision making in a rapidly changing business environment. They must supply managers with information quickly, accurately and completely.

## Decision support system

The decision support system (DSS), a set of special computer programs and particular hardware, establishes a sophisticated system to produce information for unstructured decision making. DSS are generally used by top management (although they support all levels of management), combine sophisticated analysis programs with traditional data access and retrieval functions, can be used by people who are not computer specialists and emphasize flexibility in decision making. They are used to analyse unexpected problems and to integrate information flow and decision-making activities. A DSS may use database management systems, query languages, financial modelling or spreadsheet programs, statistical analysis programs, report generators and graphics programs to provide information.

To reach the DSS level of sophistication in information technology, an organization must have established a transaction processing system and an MIS. These two types of systems are not designed to handle unpredictable information and decisions well. DSS are designed to handle the unstructured types of decisions of the what if types of decision that traditional management information systems were not designed to support.

Although most DSS are designed for large computer systems, electronic spreadsheet packages and database management packages are used in business as tools for building a DSS for microcomputers. As microcomputers have become more powerful, more microcomputer-based MIS include a DSS using a DBMS. The popularity of spreadsheet software among managers is due to the fact that it allows managers to examine a variety of business situations – that is, to **see what would happen** if business conditions changed – and to make projections, or guesses, about future developments based on sophisticated computer-based data analysis. DSS designed for large computer systems collect large amounts of data and analyse them in more ways and with greater efficiency than a microcomputer spreadsheet does.

DSS generally fall into two distinct categories: **general** and **institutional**. A general DSS produces information that can be used in making a wide variety of management decisions. The electronic spreadsheet is an ideal tool for the development of general DSS for microcomputers. Large database management systems and natural languages or query languages are used to develop decision support systems for large computer systems. An institutional DSS is much more industry- and function-specific. Examples include a DSS for the medical profession (including hospitals), which supports decision making in the areas of administration, patient diagnosis, determination and monitoring of drug dosages, medical records, etc.; a DSS for the advertising profession, which supports strategy in presenting products; and a DSS for the transportation industry, which supports traffic pattern analysis.

## Exercise 10.9

Choose two distinct industries or types of business. Make a list of the types of activities that are involved.

Some microcomputer software can also be used to create specialized applications – in other words, to create new software. Microcomputer software packages that fall into this category include many spreadsheet programs, database managers and integrated packages.

For example, in a business without computers, to **age** accounts receivable (to penalize people with overdue account balances), someone has to manually calculate how many days have passed between invoice date and the current date and then calculate the appropriate penalty based on the balance due. This can take hours of work. However, with an electronic spreadsheet package, in less than half an hour the user can create an application that will calculate accounts receivable automatically, and the application can be used many times.

Another example of microcomputer software that is used to create new programs is HyperCard originally created by Bill Atkinson of Apple for the

Macintosh, but now available on other machines. This package is a database management program that allows users to store, organize and manipulate text and graphics; but it is also a 'programmable program' that uses a programming language called HyperTalk to allow ordinary users to create customized software by following the **authoring** instructions that are provided with the package.

## 10.4  Use of DMBS and the database query language

At the end of this section you should be able to:

❏ appreciate that the power in a computer-based information system comes from the data
❏ explain what a database is
❏ describe the difference between file management systems and DBMSs
❏ describe how DBMSs software relates to hardware and the user
❏ identify the advantages and disadvantages of the three database models and of DBMSs in general
❏ explain the importance of database administration within an organization.

### *Databases*

In any organization different views of the same data are required by different departments. If each department creates files for its own use, multiple copies of the data will be produced. This creates a lack of data integration.

When one department, for example, the sales department, updates its data files, the remaining data becomes out of date until the other departments receive their notifications and update their own files. The integrity of the information contained in any output reports would, therefore, depend on the file used during processing.

If a department wishes to modify its software system to enhance or update the facilities, the data files often need to be modified too. The converse is also true: any alteration in the organization of data, introduced, perhaps, to improve access time, means that all the programs must also be changed.

Data become unified and independent of programs with the introduction of a central (shared) data facility. Data required in an installation are stored in a set of **database** files which may be accessed by all users, according to their security classifications. The database is maintained and accessed with the help of a software system known as a **database management system** (DBMS). Users may define their own view of the data and may write programs to communicate with the DBMS for data handling.

The set of files developed by the DBMS is based on concepts like **file inversion** and **network structures**. This involves the maintenance of a complete set of file linkages and indices, in such a way that each field can be independently and rapidly accessed and conditions can be set on the view of the database needed for any particular application.

Using the database structure, multiple files may be easily cross-referenced and data accessed as if it were on a single file. Quick data summaries may be produced. A report generator package forms an integral part of the DBMS: a report format may be defined, a restricted view of data may be selected, and a report produced without having to define the procedure to obtain it step-by-step.

The physical organization of data need not concern the user. If this is altered, the corresponding software in the DBMS would change without the user programs having to be altered.

With today's networked computers, the availability of a central database facility makes it possible to access data files from widely different physical locations as a part of a single database. We will look at this in more detail later on when we have a look at the client/server solution.

## The user perspective

Managers need information to make effective decisions. The more accurate, relevant and timely the information, the better informed management will be when making decisions.

## Organization of data

In many companies data used to be (and often still is) collected on a grand scale, often the same element of data was entered more than once and appeared in more than one file – computerized or not. However, the data needed for a report were often unavailable (or at least not available in a form appropriate to the situation) and extracting it from data from uncoordinated files was difficult and time consuming.

By the early 1970s it was apparent that traditional file-handling concepts were no longer adequate to handle the large amounts of data. To improve the quality of management information – and information for users in general – and the ease with which it could be produced, the DBMS was developed.

Database management concepts are the same for large computer systems and for microcomputers. General business users are most likely to be using a microcomputer or a terminal to access data stored in a **database**, i.e. a large group of stored, integrated cross-referenced data elements that can be retrieved and manipulated (usually from a minicomputer or a mainframe) with great flexibility to produce information. It is therefore important to understand not only what a database is, but also what a DMBS is, so that they can be used effectively.

## What is a DBMS?

A DBMS is a comprehensive software tool that allows users to create, maintain and manipulate an integrated base of business data to produce relevant management information. (Integrated means the records are logically related to one another so that all data on a topic can be retrieved by simple requests.) The DBMS software represents the interface between the user and the computer's operating system and database.

In a typical office there is a desk, chair, telephone and a row of filing cabinets. A wide variety of business data is stored in these cabinets. If the files have been carefully organized and maintained, then any piece of data that needs to be retrieved can be located and easily removed. However, if the data have not been properly filed, time and effort will be needed to find it. Further, regardless of how carefully the files have been organized and maintained, it is often also necessary then to retrieve related pieces of data. For example, to review the customer files for invoices for payments due in excess of $2500, each one needs to be located. They then have to be refiled (risking misfiling them). When all the customer folders have been examined, and the appropriate invoices copied, they need to be reviewed and put together in a report. This is very time-consuming. If there are a lot of customers, it would need many hours, if not days!

Now look at the situation in a different way. The environment is the same, except that, instead of filing cabinets, there is a microcomputer or a terminal and DBMS software that has access to a customer database file. In this file a row of customer data is referred to as a record, and an individual piece of data within a record, such as name, is referred to as a field. To get the required invoice data, the following needs to be done:

- ❑ turn on the computer and the printer
- ❑ start up the DBMS software
- ❑ give the command to 'open up' the customer database file (similar in concept to manually opening up the customer drawer in a filing cabinet)
- ❑ give the command to search all the records in the database file and display copies of the records that meet the criterion (that is, in this example, the names of the people with unpaid invoices greater than $2500). In dBASE IV, a popular microcomputer DBMS, the command would look something like:

```
LIST FOR INV_AMOUNT > 2500
```

If you were using SQL (structured query language), the command would look like this:

```
SELECT NAME FROM CUSTOMER
    WHERE INV_AMOUNT > 2500
    ORDER BY NAME
```

In response to this command, all records in the file that have an invoice amount greater than $2500 will be listed on the screen. (The SQL command would also sort the listing into order by name.) This whole procedure would take perhaps five minutes or less.

The DBMS is a software tool designed to manage a large number of integrated, shared electronic **filing cabinets**. The type of data to be stored is described, and the DBMS is responsible for creating the database file(s) and providing an easy-to-use mechanism for storing, retrieving and manipulating the data.

## File management systems versus databases

In small businesses, databases may be both created and operated by the user. In larger businesses, the corporate database is usually created by technical information specialists such as the database administrator, but the DBMS is acquired by the information systems department. Users generate and extract data stored by the DBMS. To design a database the organization must describe its informational needs to designers and specify the type of data needed. Users participate heavily in this process of defining what information needs to be stored in the database.

Since the early 1980s, tremendous advances have been made in developing DBMSs for microcomputers. They are now easy enough for users to learn to operate without assistance and powerful enough to produce valuable management information. Regardless of the size of a business, the capabilities that a DBMS can provide are invaluable. It is one of the most powerful tools available for use as an information resource.

## Data management concepts

You will recall that there are three methods for storing and retrieving data: sequential, direct and indexed sequential. Each method stores records differently within a file, and each method is suited to particular applications and processing requirements.

The DBMS approach for storing and retrieving data in computer-usuable form has evolved to allow users to easily retrieve and update data that is in more than one file. Before describing why the DBMS approach is significant, the traditional system it evolved from – the file management system – is briefly described.

## File management systems

Computers were first used commercially use in 1954, when the General Electric Company purchased a UNIVAC (Universal Automatic Computer) for its research division. At first, the processing performed was straightforward. Applications software programs were usually organized sequentially, stored in a single file on magnetic tape which contained all the elements of data required for processing. The term **file management system** was coined to describe this traditional approach to managing business data and information. However, file management systems did not provide users with an easy way to group records within a file, or to establish relationships among the records in different files. As disk storage became cheaper and its capacity grew, new software applications were developed to access disk-based files. The need to access data stored in more than one file was quickly recognized and created more complex programming requirements.

## Data redundancy

The same data elements appear in many different files and often in different formats. This makes updating files difficult, time consuming and error prone. An example of how this might occur is where, say, a payroll file and a personnel file both contain an employee's ID number, name, address and telephone number, and how having many copies of the same data elements takes up unnecessary storage space.

In addition to wasted space, data redundancy creates a problem when it comes to **file updating.** When an element of data needs to be changed – for example, employee address – it must be updated in **all** the files, a tedious procedure. If some files are missed, data will be inconsistent – that is, **data integrity** is not maintained – and reports will be produced with incorrect information.

Another limitation of file management systems is related to the lack of **program** and **data independence.** This lack of independence means different files established in different arrangements, such as some with the date first and expense items second and others vice versa, cannot be used by the same program. Programs must be written by programmers to use a specific file format. This process takes a programmer a large amount of time and can prove expensive.

To deal with these problems and the ever-growing demands for a flexible, easy-to-use mechanism for managing data, the concept of a database was developed.

## Database management systems

The term *database* describes a collection of related records that forms an integral base of data, which can be assessed by a wide variety of applications programs and user requests. In a DBMS, data need to be entered only once. When the user instructs the program to sort data or compile a list, the program searches quickly through the data (in memory or in storage), copying the required data into a new file for the purpose at hand. However, the user's instructions do not change the original set of data in any way. (Database administrators may change the data later when they update the database.) This is done through software, i.e. the DBMS. However, the software must be considered together with the hardware and the database because the type and capacity of certain hardware components and the size of the database will affect both the sophistication and efficiency of the DBMS software.

## Hardware and storage considerations

Storage capacity is crucial to the operation of a DBMS. The many gigabytes of data that move through large organizations cannot be handled by microcomputers. To manage these databases, large-scale DBMSs need to use very high capacity and high-speed disks for storage. Such database files in a large organization will use a number of disk-storage devices, as well as additional backup ones.

Managers and other users in large organizations usually interact directly with the DBMS via a terminal connected to a large computer. The terminal allows users to communicate their requests for information to the system and view the results immediately. In the past, most information was displayed in the form of text. However, many terminals now have colour graphics capability and users can view information graphically, which is often easier to understand.

Database files are an important business resource and must be protected from damage, loss and unauthorized use. The most common way to protect them is to periodically make backup copies. These copies are usually made on one or more reels of standard half inch magnetic tape. The backup process for large corporate databases requires the involvement of computer operation specialists. The most popular form of backup for a microcomputer hard disks is the **tape streamer,** or **streaming tape unit.** These devices are small, fast and so easy to use that users themselves can perform backup operations.

## DBMS software

A DBMS is an integral set of software programs that provides all the necessary capabilities for building and maintaining database files, extracting the information required for making decisions, and formatting the information into structured reports.

(1) Data independence, e.g. you have created a student database with many student records. After some time, you decide to change the structure of

the student database to include telephone numbers. With a DBMS you can do this and still use the applications program you were using before you changed the database structure, because the data's organization is independent of the program being used.

(2) Establish relationships among records in different files, e.g. the user can obtain all data related to important data elements.

(3) Eliminate data redundancy, e.g. because data is independent of the applications program being used, it can be stored a single time in a file that can be accessed, for example, by the student billing applications program or the grade averaging program.

(4) Define the characteristics of the data, e.g. the user can create a database that has stored in it based on particular informational needs.

(5) Manage file access. For example, the DBMS can 'examine' user requests and clear them for access to retrieve data, thus maintaining data safe from unauthorized access.

(6) **Maintain data** integrity, e.g. because data are not stored redundantly, they only need to be updated in one place.

Using DBMS software, personnel can request that a program be run to produce information in a predefined format or extract information in a specific way. For example, if you are the manager of a school's registration department, you may want to review a report of the classes that currently have space available; however, the manager of the school's finance division may want to use the same data to generate a report on courses that had low enrolment over the past two years to determine whether to continue offering these courses.

The DBMS software usually includes a query language, report writers (for microcomputers only), utilities and an applications program language interface (which is usually called the **Data Manipulation Language,** DML).

## Query language

Most users find a query language for data retrieval to be the most valuable aspect of DBMS software. Traditionally, many managers relied on the information provided by periodic reports. However, this creates a problem when a decision must be made at once and the information required to make it will not be produced until the end of the week. Query languages allow managers to use everyday language to produce information on demand. This information is also in everyday language. To be effective, a query language must allow the user to phrase requests for information in a very flexible fashion.

Some examples of the types of question that a user could ask using a query language when a single file is involved are in, say, a request for inventory information. They might be as follows:

❑ list all items in the inventory database for which the quantity on hand equals zero (immediate orders would have to be placed to restock these items)
❑ list all items in the database for which the quantity on hand is less than or equal to the re-order point (this information would be used to process regular orders for restocking inventory)
❑ list all items in the database for which the unit cost times the quantity on hand exceeds $10,000 (this would show the highest dollar volume items in the inventory).

## Data manipulation language

The user needs the data manipulation language (DML) software in the DBMS to effect input to, and output from, the database files; in other words, all programs, including the query language, must go through the DML. The DML is made up of the technical instructions for the input and output routines in the DBMS. Each applications program that is written needs certain data elements to process in order to produce particular types of information. A list of the required elements of data is contained within each applications program. The DML uses these lists, identifies the elements of data required, and provides the necessary link to the database to supply the data to the program.

## Data dictionaries and transaction logs

When a DBMS has been implemented, the data dictionary and transaction log are constantly in use alongside the database files.

A **data dictionary** is a file that contains the details of the data; it contains the rules for the use of the database files. The information in a data dictionary differs in different DBMSs, but it generally contains the type of information shown in Table 10.5.

**Table 10.5**  Types of information to be found in a data dictionary

**What** data are available
**Where** data are located
**Descriptions** (attributes) of the data
**Ownership** of the data (i.e. who is responsible)
**How** the data are used
**Access** to data (i.e. who may retrieve and who may change data)
**Relationships** between data items
**Lmitations** ( i.e. security and privacy considerations)

The data dictionary is in contant use as a reference tool. When data are requested, the DBMS refers to the data dictionary to find the details of where data can be retrieved from, whether the user has authority and so on. The **transaction log** contains the record of activity that affects the data in a database during a transaction. It is used to backup databases and for rebuilding files if they become damaged or destroyed. It is straightforward to use for backups as all transactions are recorded and the previous day's copy of the database is considered to be the current one, which is then updated using the transaction log. It is important to note that the transaction log is automatic in large systems but not usually provided for microcomputer systems and you need to take account of this in the program design.

## Database models

There are three models for organizing data in a database. These are

❑ hierarchical
❑ network
❑ relational.

These three models have developed since the late 1960s, but the relational model is now used the most extensively.

*Hierarchical database.* In this model, data are organized into related groups similar to a family tree. There are **parent records** and **child records.** Parents records are higher up the tree than child records; each child can have only one parent, i.e. any one record can have only one record above it, but may have many below. The record at the top or highest level, is known as the root record – this is the key to the model and connects the different branches.

The parent–child relationship is known as a **many-to-one relationship.** To store or retrieve records, the DBMS begins at the root and moves downward until the required record is located. Note that there is no connection between separate branches.

The main advantage of this type of database is that data are easily stored and retrieved.

The main disadvantages are:

(1) Records in separate groups cannot easily be linked together, so it is difficult to answer questions such as: 'how much were the expenses for a particular employee in a given month?'.
(2) If a parent is deleted, all the children are automatically deleted.
(3) Updating is complex and requires the programmer to know all the links.
(4) There is often data redundancy, since some data must necessarily be stored in more than one tree.

*Network databases.* These are similar to the hierarchical model, but each record can have more than one parent, thus overcoming the main limitation of hierarchical databases because it allows for relationships between records in different groups.

The main advantage is that network databases can provide sophisticated logical links between data. The main disadvantage is that the user is limited to retrieving data that can be accessed using the links that have been established (as in a hierarchical database).

*Relational databases.* A relational database is made up of many tables (known as **relations**) in which related data items are stored. Each relation can be considered conceptually as a file and is known as an **entity.** It has a number of rows (similar to records in a file) and columns (similar in concept to fields). Rows are called **tuples** and columns **attributes.**

In a relational database, complex logical relationships between records can be expressed reasonably easily. They can cross-reference data and hence retrieve it automatically. Users do not need to understand the structure to the same degree as is necessary in the other models since it is addressed by content rather than by address.

The disadvantage is that it can take a long time to access data (and therefore is the most likely method with smaller databases such as those used on personal computers).

## Database design

Database design is a complex and specialized task which involves matching a design to the overall information needs of an organization. A modular approach, department by department, is usually the preferred method.

Database design has two distinct phases: logical and physical design.

## Exercise 10.10

Make a list of the different departments in a company. For each one make a list of its informational needs. Now consider all the different needs to produce a general plan of information needs across the departments of the company.

## Logical database design

Logical database design is a representation of what the data actually are, rather than how they operate, i.e. it is a description from a business perspective, rather than a technical one.

Logical design involves defining user needs, analysing data elements and logical groups, and creating the data dictionary. Each element of data and the relationship between them must be identified. Two differing viewpoints must be included; the **schema** (the overall database and the relationships within it) and the **subschema** (the way in which particular records are linked to serve specific purposes and/or users).

The first stage defines users' information needs and logically groups them – this is called **information requirements analysis.** Table 10.6 gives an example of data that two different departments in a company require to be collected for each employee.

**Table 10.6**   User information needs

| Personnel department | Payroll department |
| --- | --- |
| Name | Name |
| Home address | Home address |
| Telephone number | Pay rate |
| Starting date | Deductions |
| Department | YTD pay |
| Job title | |
| Salary grade | |
| Date of last review | |
| Date of next review | |
| Performance rating | |
| Office | |
| Telephone extension | |

## Exercise 10.11

Use Table 10.6 to identify:

**(a)**  the redundant data elements
**(b)**  the natural groups into which they can be organized
**(c)**  the groups that might be needed for specific applications programs.

The next stage in the design is to identify the reports and related data that will be required from the database for each report.

## Exercise 10.12

Using Table 10.6, what data elements will be required for reports on the dates that performance evaluations are due?

The final stage in the logical design is to combine and refine the logical subsets of data, i.e. the subschema, into the overall schema. The schema contains a description of all the data elements to be stored, the logical records into which they will be grouped and the number of individual database files or relations to be maintained within the framework of the DBMS. It also describes the relationships amongst the data elements and the structure (i.e. hierarchical, relational or network model).

## Physical database design

This involves the specification of how data is arranged and stored. The objective is to store it so that retrieval and updating can be performed as efficiently as possible. A major consideration is the frequency that certain items will be required by users for particular purposes. If there are specific known patterns, speed and efficiency can be maximized for those items.

## Database administration

The database administrator coordinates the use of the database. This person has six main responsibilities as outlined below.

(1) Database design – plays a key role in both logical and physical design phases, guides the definition of the database content and data dictionary, sets coding, backup/restart procedures.
(2) Database implementation and operation – guides the use on a day-to-day basis, i.e. adding, deleting, controlling access, detecting and repairing losses, instituting recovery, restart and backup procedures.
(3) User coordination – receives and reviews user requests for support, establishes feasibility, resolves redundant or conflicting requests, establishes priorities. Enforces standards for data access, storage formats, data element names, etc.
(4) Backup and recovery – prepares the plan for the regular backing up of the database and establishes the procedures for recovering from failures due to either hardware or software.
(5) Performance monitoring – responsible for making sure that the DBMS meets needs. Regular monitoring ensures that if problems occur, they can be readily identified and steps taken to remedy them.
(6) System security – this usually involves the issuing of passwords and other security measures to control the access to the database.

## Summary

This section has concentrated upon database concepts. The main advantages and disadvantages of a database approach are given in Table 10.7.

**Table 10.7**  Advantages and disadvantages of a database approach

| Advantages | Disadvantages |
| --- | --- |
| No data redundancy | Complexity (need for technical expertise) |
| Easy file updating | Higher costs |
| Data independence | |
| Easy program maintenance | |
| Increased user productivity | |
| Increased security | Vulnerability |
| Standardization | |

## 10.5  Client/server computing

Client/server computing is rapidly becoming the universally accepted model for enterprise-wide systems. It is often spoken of in the same breath as **downsizing** and **distributed** computing, but it is different because it is a fundamental change from the traditional notion of centralized data processing.

### Definition

There are a number of different definitions of client/server to be found in the literature; they tend to be based upon the different types of application. Client/server computing is a concept in which an application is divided into multiple tasks that are executed on different hardware platforms, of which one is an intelligent workstation or PC (client), to achieve a net advantage.

This definition makes the following three key assumptions:

❑ that it is feasible to divide a single application into self-contained tasks
❑ that these tasks can be performed by different machines
❑ that one of the machines involved will be a PC or 'intelligent workstation'.

The client/server model assumes that computing is a dialogue (or many dialogues) between different hardware elements which together make up the whole task. Historically, the elements have been general-purpose desktop computers (the clients) and special purpose processors (the servers) dedicated to performing only one type of function.

The idea of client/server architecture arose because the critical departure from conventional mainframe systems (as represented by networks of PCs or workstations where intelligence is at the user end of the system) is a fundamental requirement – i.e. processing is distributed. In understanding the client/server model it must be realized that processing can occur in different physical or logical areas in the system. Once this is accepted it becomes easy to understand a separation between client and server at almost any level.

The main advantage of client/server systems is that each component, with its own set of tasks, can be optimized for a different set of operations, thus taking the best advantage of the computer on which it is installed. The server component responsible for data storage and management is optimized for data integrity, security and transaction performance. The client component assumes the responsibility for presenting the information to the user and is therefore optimized for presentation, usability and ease-of-use. This division of responsibilities makes a lot of sense in today's computing environment where many, if not all, of the employees in an organization are equipped with computers for word processing, spreadsheet analysis, electronic communications, and so on. These PCs are often under-utilized by such tasks, and can be better used by diverting some of their processing potential towards a distributed, corporate client/server approach.

To illustrate, clients and servers can be separate machines with servers providing particular functions like printing or database management, or they can be separate processors running on multicomputer systems or even on a single machine. Server processes may display different levels of granularity – for instance, print-spooling is a 'coarse-grained' process while functions, procedures or subroutines may be considered 'fine-grained' server processes. The distinction between client and server, then, is that the client initiates a request and the server fulfils it. Clients and servers may be parts of processes, whole processes, entire programs, small computers, complete networks or even – in an increasingly popular view – large mainframes.

## Distributed computing

The granularity of the client/server process is reflected in the different levels or forms distributed computing in current use.

Distributed presentation is, in effect, the new technology equivalent of time-sharing. Presentation logic – which includes graphical-user interfaces (GUIs) themselves and the presentation managers which sit above them – reside on client platforms and applications and database management reside on servers. The GUI is the client.

Remote data management puts presentation logic and applications on client platforms and database management on servers. This is currently the most widely used form of client/server computing, focusing on the use of database servers, and represents some 80 per cent of current spending on client/server systems. A typical definition of client/server computing from a financial software specialist (MCS Ltd) slightly extends this category: *'Client/server architecture is the term used to describe distributed information processing across a network. Software is split so that low-cost PCs (clients) provide the user interface (or screen display) and local data processing while a single more powerful computer (the server) stores files, provides central processing power, access to other networks, and network management and administrative functions.'*

In distributed data or database management, presentation logic and applications are found on client platforms, and database management is shared between multiple server platforms. In such a configuration, individual procedures or functions within the database management system may properly be described as the servers.

Distributed process (or distributed logic) puts presentation logic on each client and database management on the server. Applications are split between clients and server, so that procedure calls may be made by one client process to another on a remote platform. Typical examples are transactional monitors in distributed OLTP applications. This is the most flexible form of client/server computing and the one predicted to grow most in the next few years. An interesting prospect is offered by effecting a 'merger' between client/server and centralized mainframe architectures. An idea currently being floated by a number of mainframe vendors is that the mainframe itself could become the database server in a client/server system.

The client/server approach allows considerably more productive and versatile use to be made of raw data: 'what-if' spreadsheet models, real-time simulators, GUIs, graphics, hypermedia, presentations and visualization techniques all help make data more meaningful because they enable computer systems to provide management information and decision support functions, not merely statistical summaries, tables of figures or form views. They do this by allowing end-users to call on sophisticated processing abilities at the desktop. However, they still need raw data and they need to be able to extract that data from the increasingly large amount that organizations add to day-by-day. The problem has been to combine mainframe levels of data handling experience and PC-type information management. The logical answer is to introduce mainframes into the PC environment using client/server architecture.

The benefits are undeniable: user-friendly information, virtually unlimited storage capacity, high levels of security, reliability and performance, without the need to completely rethink information technology strategy or development plans. It is widely believed that mainframes will one day be redundant. While this is almost certainly correct, it is unrelated to the concept of client/server. The mainframe is likely to survive within the concept of client/server for many years to come, as a machine optimized for throughput, availability and raw data handling. A recent survey has found that in large installations of more than 1000 users, mainframe-based client/server configurations may well be the most economical on a cost-per-user basis after taking into account local area network administration, support, training, and local printing and disk-storage costs.

In summary, client/server systems offer a great deal of flexibility while allowing full access to important data. Since the major functional components of the system are separated from one another, it becomes a simple task to add to new front-end pieces that accomplish different tasks. For example, a spreadsheet program can be used as a SQL server front-end to analyse important corporate data. At the same time, an order entry system, perhaps created with a high-productivity development tool such as the Microsoft Visual Basic programming system, can be used to enter new data or to query and update existing data. Graphical report-writing tools can be used concurrently with these other applications to provide detailed insight into corporate activities. Since the SQL server interfaces are published and well known, any number of tools can be used safely. Commonly used front-end components can be used to build desired systems and, regardless of which tool or application is chosen, security and integrity of data are consistently and safely applied using the same rules for access.

## *Exercise 10.13*

Explain the main advantages of using the client/server solution.

## *Summary exercise*

**(1) (a)** List four benefits of purchasing off-the-shelf packages such as spreadsheets and database management systems.

    **(b)** Describe one example of an application which demonstrates how each of the following packages is used: **(i)** spreadsheets; **(ii)** database management systems.

    **(c)** Describe what is involved in the **feasibilty study** phase of the system development life cycle and list the people who participate in it. (IDCS 3/94.)

**(2) (a)** Describe fully the layout of a typical spreadsheet display screen.

    **(b)** Explain the following spreadsheet features: cell formula; numerical cell format; macro. (IDCS 2/94.)

**(3)** A personnel record system contains employee records of: employee number, employee name, dept. code, salary.

    **(a)** Describe how, using a database management sytem package, these records can be created making clear any validation which would be used.

    **(b)** Describe how the names of all the employees in a department would be retrieved.

    **(c)** State one method of improving the speed of data retrieval.

**(d)** If there is also a file containing department records of: dept. code, dept. name, manager code (an employee number), explain how the name of the manager in a given department may be found. (IDCS 4/93.)

# 11
# Operating systems

## Objectives

At the end of this chapter you should understand:

❑ what operating software is, and why it is important to the programmer
❑ the main tasks carried out by operating systems
❑ the role of systems software.

## 11.1 Introduction

Operating systems are developed for specific hardware. There may be a choice of operating systems and the same operating system could be 'reconfigurable' to other hardware configurations. The actual system used affects the way in which programs may be implemented and often even the program design. The facilities offered by systems can be quite different and they also vary in how easy they are to use. Programmers must therefore, have a knowledge of the operating system that is being used.

## 11.2 Definition

An operating system is a suite of programs that controls the resources of, the processes in, and the detailed actions of the processor in a computer. It provides the link between the programmer and the hardware, ensuring that a program can actually be executed by providing the resources (e.g. memory, input, output) that it needs. In other words, the operating system is the manager of the computer, making sure that everything is controlled correctly.

## 11.3 The main tasks

As we have said, the facilities of operating systems can vary widely. Obviously for a stand-alone microcomputer, with only one user at any one time, some features, such as balancing the concurrent needs of several users, are not necessary. We will, however, discuss the general features of all operating systems.

### 11.3.1 System start-up (booting)

The part of the operating system that resides in main memory (internal instructions) is the most important since without these instructions the computer cannot operate. These instructions are loaded from storage when the computer is first turned on (called booting) and ensure that the hardware actually functions. Internal instructions must reside in main memory at all times while the computer is on.

### 11.3.2 Control

The operating system controls everything that happens in a computer system from access (e.g. in larger systems where users cannot begin an interaction without logging in with a valid user name and password), allocation of resources such as memory, input, storage and output devices, and the provision of systems tools to users' applications programs.

To illustrate this, let us consider first what the operating system is doing when you begin to type your program into a computer.

❑ If you are using a shared system, you will first enter your name and password so that the computer can check whether you are an authorized user.

❑ You might choose to type in your program using a word processing facility and perhaps choose that particular applications program from a menu. The operating system will ensure that that particular facility is available to you at your request, including allocating some storage for you to save your file when you choose to do so.

❑ If you request a printout, a message is sent by the operating system to the printer so that it is ready to receive your data for printing.

❑ When you decide to leave your session on the computer, it is the operating system that makes sure your work is saved in secondary storage with the correct labelling so that you can find it again.

### 11.3.3 Assignment of resources

When a computer is first booted up, the supervisor program is activated. This program resides in main memory and calls up other systems software when it is required. Once the other program is no longer needed, the supervisor takes control again. As well as the supervisor, other programs in the operating system are important to the functioning of the computer.

One is the command language translator, which reads instructions to the supervisor to allow users to do such things as retrieving, saving, copying, deleting or moving files. These instructions are written in 'job-control language' (JCL). In fact, many users increasingly are using modern graphical interfaces and interacting via a mouse where the actions are chosen from a menu – but the mouse choice actually then calls up the JCL and it is this that is communicated to the supervisor. Although this might seem to be easier, it actually only is if what you want to do is on the menu!

### 11.3.4  Scheduling of resources

This function of the operating system is almost transparent to most users, but in large systems with many users the system needs to track what is being used and by whom all the time. Even with a single user PC-based system, you might have noticed that you may have to wait, for example, for printing to finish before, for example, you can retrieve or save a file – in this case it is the operating system that has decided that the printing needs to use the memory before it can be used for other tasks. The operating system does in fact schedule the different jobs to make the most efficient use of the system. This procedure is one of a number of techniques which are known as interleaved processing (see section 11.4 below).

### 11.3.5  Monitoring

Another function of the operating system is to monitor (i.e. keep track of) all activities while processing is being done. It might terminate programs that have errors, or use up too much memory; at the same time sending out a message to indicate what the problem is. It will also monitor the peripherals and, again, send out a message if there is a problem (e.g. printer out of paper). In cases of peripheral failure on large systems, error recovery routines are triggered which help in the diagnosis of faults.

Security is another monitoring function of the operating system, e.g. the checking of users' passwords and related access with appropriate messages being sent when necessary. Additionally, statistics such as length of time logged on, last log-on, etc. are recorded, which can be used for accounting purposes.

## 11.4  Interleaved processing

This is the general term given to those facilities of an operating system that enable more than one job and/or user to perform tasks. There are a number of variations, which are discussed below.

## 11.4.1 Multiprogramming

Multiprogramming is when a number of different applications programs can be stored in the main memory at any one time. The CPU however only works on one of them at any one time, but when a program requires some other part of the computer to do something (e.g. a printer or backing storage device) the CPU moves on to another program, returning to the initial program when it needs it.

Multiprogramming is possible because the CPU works very much faster than any other operation such as retrieving data from a disk, and can perform many thousands of operations while input/output operations are being executed.

## 11.4.2 Multitasking

Multitasking is a particular instance of multiprogramming where two or more programs from a single user run at the same time on the computer. It means that you can for example, edit one program while another one is running. It is important to realize that the computer can only do one job at a time, but because it can work so quickly, it appears to the user that it is actually doing more than one concurrently.

Multitasking is particularly useful when any particular program requires a long processing time (such as a search of a large database) and you want to do another job at the same time – without this facility, you would simply have to wait – or do something else off the computer.

This interleaving of a single user's tasks is very similar to the Windows environment, with which many of you will be familiar.

## 11.4.3 Time-sharing

In a time-sharing system, many user stations or terminals are supported simultaneously; in other words, the users share time on the computer based on assigned time slices. As an example, there might be 100 programs in the system and each one is allocated a time slice of a tenth of a second (slices are probably much smaller than this – and all are not necessarily equal). The CPU will work on the first one for the assigned time slice allocated, then move on to the next one and so on. The advantage of this is that no one program dominates the CPU and short programs are not held up by long ones.

Time-sharing is similar to multiprogramming and multitasking, except that with the latter job tasks are based on program priorities, whereas with time-sharing jobs are allocated a specific length of time and programs are processed one after the other. It is common today to find computers that combine both these methods of interleaved processing for maximum processing capability.

The processing requirements of an operating system with time-sharing capabilities are very high – it is not unusual for such systems to require another smaller computer (called a front-end processor) to schedule and control all the user requests. The front-end processor allows the main computer to concentrate solely on processing applications as quickly as possible.

### 11.4.4 *Virtual storage (virtual memory)*

Virtual storage, sometimes known as virtual memory, is when the disk is used to extend main memory. It is particularly useful when a program is very long, since it enables a program to be broken into modules, or small sections, that can be loaded into main memory when needed. Modules not currently in use are stored on a very high-speed disk (secondary storage) and retrieved one at a time when the operating system determines that the current module has completed executing.

In the past, all computer operating systems were designed so that an entire program had to be loaded into main memory before it could begin to execution. As a result, the size and sophistication of a program was limited by the amount of main memory available.

Virtual storage can work in one of two ways; either by paging or segmentation. In both of these methods the operating system first puts the programs to be processed onto the virtual storage area on the disk. They are here divided either into fixed-length pages or variable-length segments (depending upon the type of operating system). As an example, if a program was 100 kilobytes long and the paging system uses 10 kilobyte pages, then the program would be divided into 10 kilobyte lengths. As the CPU processes the program, it stores only a few pages at a time – as the other pages are required for execution, they are selected from the virtual storage area and brought into the CPU to overwrite the pages that are no longer needed. If it is needed again, it is brought in again – all the original pages on the virtual memory area remain unchanged. The process is illustrated in Figure 11.1.

Segmentation is similar to paging, but the segments are of a variable length, depending upon the logic of the program. As in paging, those parts of the program in main memory that are not required are overwritten by other segments. This technique, while allowing for the processing of large programs, does require additional time because of the swapping of pages/segments into memory. Not all large systems use virtual memory because of this; some PC-based applications (most word processing software) do use it because of the relatively small area of main memory that are available for use. Computers with virtual memory usually also feature multitasking, since this feature enables the computer to process as if it contained an almost unlimited supply of main memory.

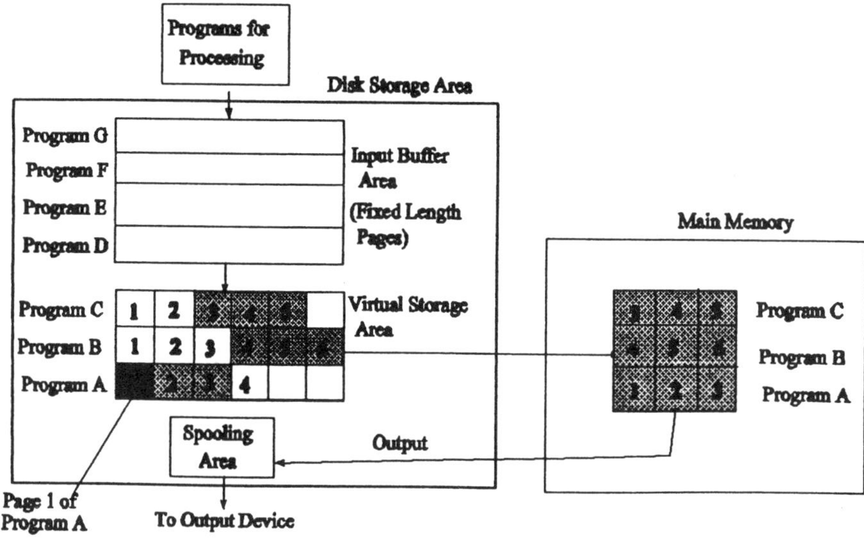


**Figure 11.1** Virtual storage based on a paging system.

## 11.4.5 Multiprocessing

Multiprocessing (or parallel processing) is when there are two or more CPUs linked together. Work is performed in parallel at the same time, i.e. several jobs can be executed on several machines (contrast this with multiprogramming where several jobs are executed concurrently on a single machine).

It is common to find a number of lower-cost PCs working together, rather than one large machine, because in this way jobs can be processed more quickly for a lower cost. Parallel processing techniques are also used to build fault-tolerant computers, where an immediate automatic back-up is available should a component fail in the first machine.

You may come across the term **coprocessing**. With this method, although it is similar to multiprocessing, there is an important difference. In co-processing, the CPU works in parallel with a specialized processor which performs a special function only (e.g. graphics or particular mathematical functions). It is not true parallel processing, because that requires the CPUs to all be capable of all functions.

## 11.5  Systems software

Systems software is the general name given to the programs that coordinate the various parts of the computer system so that it works efficiently. It can be divided into several classifications which are described below.

Systems software is written to work with a particular type of microprocessor and is incompatible with machines that do not use that type of processor. The level of sophistication of systems software depends on the size of the computer it operates and the task it is intended to perform.

### 11.5.1 *Internal command instructions*

As we have already mentioned, the most important piece of systems software is the operating system itself, and particularly that part of it that resides in main memory. These are known as the internal command instructions, and the computer cannot operate without them. They are loaded from storage when the computer is first turned on. This is called booting for microcomputers and initial program load for mainframes. Internal instructions must reside in main memory at all times while the computer is on.

### 11.5.2 *External command instructions (often referred to as utilities)*

External command instructions perform housekeeping tasks, which are concerned with desktop management and file and storage management. Utilities reside in secondary storage and are called in by the supervisor when required. They are written by users in a command language, e.g. in DOS, the PC disk operating system, we use commands such as 'ERASE C:\REPORT\FIRST.DOC' to tell the computer to delete a file called FIRST.DOC, which is on drive C in the directory REPORT. The command language for each operating system is unique to that system.

Utilities are provided so that programmers do not have to write routines for the commonly used functions that are required very frequently. Examples of utility programs are:

❑ sort utilities, which can sort records in files according to user-specified keys. We see examples of these in database packages such as Dbase III
❑ spooling software, which assists with input and output to disks, tapes and printers, by holding data in special areas to avoid holding up the CPU and slowing down processing
❑ windowing software, which allows users to create and display different parts of the same application, or parts of different applications at the same time
❑ editors, which are provided for changing for text and graphics
❑ desktop functions such as calendars, calculators, clocks, cardfiles, notepads, etc.

### 11.5.3 *Language processors (language translators)*

Language processors, or translators, convert the high-level language of the user's software into the only language the computer can understand – machine language. Some low-level languages, called assembly languages, were created using abbreviations to help programmers avoid the tedious and time-consuming task of writing programs in machine language (zeros and ones). High-level languages were developed to make the job even easier. However, both high-level and assembly languages must be translated into machine language for the CPU to use them. The translation can be done by interpreters, which convert software instructions from source code to object code a line at a time and thus allow for on-the-spot error correction, or compilers, which convert the whole source program at once and create a program in object code that the computer can understand (called an object program) and save.

Figure 11.2 shows how source code in a computer language is prepared for, and processed by, a CPU.

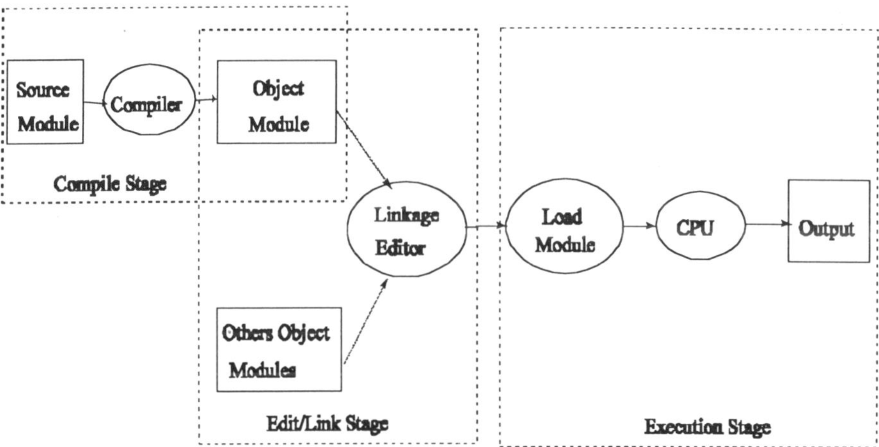


**Figure 11.2**   Showing the stages a source module goes through to output.

## Summary

An operating system is a suite of programs that controls the resources of, the processes in, and the detailed actions of the processor in a computer. It provides the link between the programmer and the hardware, ensuring that a program can actually be executed by providing the resources (e.g. memory, input, output) that it needs.

The facilities of operating systems can vary widely but most provide the following facilities:

❏ multiprogramming
❏ multitasking
❏ time-sharing
❏ virtual storage (virtual memory)
❏ multiprocessing.

Systems software is the general name given to the programs that coordinate the various parts of the computer system so that it works efficiently. There are three main classifications:

❏ internal command instructions
❏ external command instructions or utilities
❏ language processors (language translators)

## Exercise 11.1

**(1) (a)** Describe briefly the use to the programmer of file libraries and operating system logging.
**(b)** Explain the process of linking to produce an executable program. (IDCS 4/93.)
**(2)** What are the major functions of an operating system?
**(3)** Give three examples of a utility program and explain what each one does.
**(4)** Match each term with its description:
**(a)** windowing software
**(b)** compiler
**(c)** linkage editor
**(d)** spooling software
**(e)** interpreter
**(f)** operating system

1    A language translator which reads, translates and executes source programs a line at a time.
2    Enables a user to edit a document while printing out another.
3    Creates several independent boxes of information on the display screen.
4    Binds object modules together.
5    A piece of systems software which is critical to the operation of a computer.
6    A language translator which creates an object module.

# 12
# Case study

## 12.1  A computer system for a shop

This case study scenario is suggested as the basis of a programming project. It is possible to restrict the size of the project by adapting the scenario by varying the requirements.

## 12.2  The shop system

The shop could be of any type, but the following criteria are important to provide a sufficiently detailed task

(a)  a range of goods is on offer
(b)  the shop has a number of different suppliers
(c)  some goods go out of date (e.g. perish or go out of fashion).

## 12.3  Background

A local shop has requested that you develop a computer system to support its sales activities. There is a manager and a maximum of 10 sales staff all of whom are paid by performance.
  The following facilities are to be provided.

(1)  Stock control – each item bought and sold is logged onto the computer.
              – items are to be categorized.
(2)  Finance control – weekly, monthly and annual figures for income and expenditure.

(3) Wages control – this is based upon a fixed wage plus a percentage for all staff except the manager, who receives a fixed wage plus a percentage of all sales.

(4) A number of statistics (e.g. daily takings, cost of wastage, analysis of money taken per hour, current value of stock, length of time it takes for stock to be sold, stock that is almost out-of-date).

(5) Statistics of weekly, monthly and annual sales figures of all goods.

(6) Additional functions such as: writing off stock, employing staff, sacking staff, are also required.

The task is to design and implement a computer system to support the local shop.

## 12.4 Suggested approach (as discussed in Chapter 3)

(1) Decide upon the exact requirements. For example, you might decide to do stock control only and this could be further restricted by having only a few different types of goods.

(2) Design the data required by the shop for its stock, finances and staff. Describe the data by means of data structure diagrams of the data to be input for processing, and the data to be output.

(3) Produce program structures (make sure that you have correspondence between the program and data structures).

(4) Analyse your program structure in a top-down manner by refining each layer of the design until all the necessary actions and conditions have been identified at their appropriate levels.

(5) Design your tests.

(6) Code and test your programs.

(7) Ensure that you document all your work.

# Appendix
# Pseudo-code definition

❑ Keywords are defined in upper case, e.g. READ, IF, FUNCTION, CASE
❑ values are defined in lower case, e.g. next-number, a, operator response
❑ types are defined with an upper-case first letter, e.g. Integer, Address, StudentRecords
❑ the pseudo-code has five basic types: Integer, Real, Character, Boolean, String.

(a) The assignment symbol ' : = ' means 'takes the value of':

c : = a + b

means c takes the value of a plus b.

(b) Sequencing is indicated by indentation.

(c) Keywords allow data input to and output from the program:
   READ to input data from a backing store,
       e.g. READ next-number;
   WRITE to output data to backing store,
       e.g. WRITE stock-record;
   ACCEPT to input data from a keyboard.
       e.g. ACCEPT operator-response;
   DISPLAY to output data to a screen,
       e.g. DISPLAY error-report;
   PRINT to output data to a printer,
       e.g. PRINT name, code

**(d)** There are three looping constructs:

    **(i)** REPEAT

        command-sequence;

      UNTIL condition;

    **(ii)** WHILE condition

        command sequence;

      ENDWHILE;

    **(iii)** FOR ( $i = a$, $i < b$, $i + 1$ )

        command sequence;

      ENDFOR

**(e)** Conditional branching may use the IF–THEN–ELSE construct :

  IF condition

    THEN

    command sequence 1;

    ELSE

    command sequence 2;

    ENDIF;

  Multiple branching (or selection) with nested IFs:

  IF condition 1

    THEN

      command sequence 1;

    ELSE IF condition 2

      THEN

        command sequence 2;

    ELSE IF condition 3

      THEN...

      ............

    ELSE

      default command sequence;

  ENDIF;

**(f)** Alternative selection ladder – the CASE structure:

  DO CASE OF index

    CASE index condition 1

      command sequence 1;

    CASE index condition 2

      command sequence 2;

    CASE index condition ...

      :

    CASE index condition N

      command sequence N;

    OTHERWISE

```
    default command sequence;
      ENDCASE;
```

(g) Procedures and functions are called by their names. They are defined in the code as:

```
PROCEDURE xyz (list-of-parameters)
  body-of-procedure
ENDPROCEDURE

FUNCTION xyz (list-of-parameters): result-type
  body-of-function
ENDFUNCTION
```

Parameters to be passed to the function or procedure are written in brackets, followed by their type. For example,

```
PROCEDURE writechar (i:Integer, c:Character)
```

The type of function, i.e. the result value is written after the brackets. For example,

```
FUNCTION ok (i:Integer): Boolean
```

(h) An array is defined using

```
ARRAY [lower-bound, upper-bound] OF array-type
```

For example

```
ARRAY [1,10] OF Character
```

defines an array of 10 characters.

(i) A data records is defined using

```
record-type = RECORD
list-of-fields
ENDRECORD
```

For example,

```
Address = RECORD
           number     : Integer
           street     : String
           town       : String
           country    : String
         ENDRECORD
```

(j)  A pointer type is defined using

pointer-type = $\wedge$ record-type

For example,

AddressPtr = $\wedge$ Address

The keyword NIL is used to defined a pointer to nothing.

# Answers to exercises

Note that programming solutions in pseudo-code are examples only. There are many different correct ways of doing things such as screen displays, etc.

You will enjoy the practice more if you use a computer language and test out your own solutions on your computer.

## Chapter 1

### Exercise 1.1

Real, integer, real, char (or integer).

### Exercise 1.2

**(a)** 33,  **(b)** 17, **(c)** −68, **(d)** 9, **(e)** −29

### Summary exercise 1A

Suggested answers in pseudo-code
**(1)**  *use variables area, radius of type real*
  *constant pi = 3.142*
  *DISPLAY 'enter radius of circle'*
  *ACCEPT radius*
  *area:= pi * radius * radius*
  *DISPLAY 'area of circle is', area*
**(2)**  *Use variables area, length, width of type real*
  *DISPLAY 'enter length and width of carpet in metres'*
  *ACCEPT length, width*

```
        area := length * width
        DISPLAY 'Area of carpet needed is', area
```
**(3)** *use variables number, square, cube of type real*
```
        DISPLAY 'enter number to be used'
        ACCEPT number
        square := number * number
        cube := number * square
        DISPLAY 'the square of your number is', square
        DISPLAY 'the cube of your number is', cube
```
**(4)** A reserved word is a word used as part of a programming language and it cannot therefore be used for a variable name.

## Exercise 1.3

**(a)** $a > b$ is false, $b = c$ is true, $2 * a = b$ is true, $c > a$ is true.
**(b)** *xyz* is displayed.

## Exercise 1.4

**(a)** action
    no action
    action
    action
**(b)** action
    no action
    no action
    action

## Exercise 1.5

**(a)** print yes
    print no
**(b)** print b,c
    print a
    print b, c

## Exercise 1.6

```
use variables sales,wage of type real years of type integer
DISPLAY "enter sales for this month"
ACCEPT sales
DISPLAY enter number of years employed
ACCEPT years
IF years > 3
```

```
    wage := sales * 0.15 * 1.1
ELSE wage := sales * 1.1
DISPLAY wage
```

## Exercise 1.7

```
use variables index, expenditure of type integer
ACCEPT index
DO CASE OF index
   CASE index = 1
     expenditure:= 4 * 3 * 100
       DISPLAY expenditure
  CASE index = 2
   expenditure:= 2 * 4 * 100
   DISPLAY expenditure
  CASE index = 3
   expenditure:= 1 * 5 * 100
   DISPLAY expenditure
  CASE index = 4
   expenditure:= 2 * 7 * 100
   DISPLAY expenditure
OTHERWISE DISPLAY "entry is invalid"
```

## Summary exercise 1B

```
(a) use variables number of type integer
    DISPLAY 'enter a number between 1 and 100'
    ACCEPT number
    IF number <2 OR > 99
    DISPLAY 'number out of range'
(b) use variables a,b,c
    DISPLAY 'enter lengths of sides of triangles
    ACCEPT a, b, c
    IF (a + b) >= c OR (a + c) >= b OR (b + c)>= a
       DISPLAY 'triangle cannot be drawn'
    ELSE DISPLAY 'triangle can be drawn'
(c)   use variable choice of type char
      DISPLAY 'choose the house category required'
      DISPLAY 'type A or B or C'
      DISPLAY 'category A: $200 per week'
      DISPLAY 'category B: $400 per week'
      DISPLAY 'category C: $800 per week'
      ACCEPT choice
    Do CASE of choice
```

```
        CASE choice = A
            print 'house is 1 bedroom with car parking area'
        CASE choice = B
            print 'house is 2 bedrooms with garage'
        CASE choice = C
        print 'house is 3 bedrooms, detached with double garage'
            OTHERWISE  print 'entry is invalid'
    ENDCASE
```

## Exercise 1.8

**(a)**
```
REPEAT
DISPLAY 'Enter your number or 999 to finish'
ACCEPT number
IF number <> 999
   SQUARE := NUMBER * NUMBER
   DISPLAY 'The square of your number is', square
ELSE
   DISPLAY 'Goodbye';
UNTIL number = 999
```
**(b)**
```
N:= 0
REPEAT
DISPLAY 'Enter a name or stop to finish'
ACCEPT name
N:= N + 1
UNTIL N = 20 OR name = 'stop'
```

## Exercise 1.9

**(a)**
```
COUNT:= 0
LETTER:= ' '
WHILE LETTER <> '.'
ACCEPT LETTER
COUNT := COUNT + 1
ENDWHILE
DISPLAY 'THE NUMBER OF LETTERS WAS', COUNT
```
**(b)**
```
DISPLAY 'Enter a number'
ACCEPT NUMBER
WHILE NUMBER < = 0 OR NUMBER > = 10
   DISPLAY 'NUMBER NOT IN RANGE'
   DISPLAY 'ENTER NUMBER AGAIN'
   ACCEPT NUMBER
ENDWHILE
```

## Summary exercise

(1) **(a)** A reserved word is one which is used by the computing language.

**(b)** A variable may change its value during the running of a program, but a constant keeps the value that it was given at the beginning of a program.

**(c)** The repeat until loop must always run at least once because the test is at the end of a program loop segment. The while conditional test takes place at the start of the loop, hence the loop may not need be entered for termination to happen.

(2) 'Overdrawn' is a Boolean variable.

(3) USE Variables A, B, SUM of type REAL
```
      ANS of type CHARACTER
REPEAT
DISPLAY 'ENTER 2 NUMBERS'
ACCEPT A, B
SUM:= A + B
DISPLAY 'THE SUM IS'; SUM
DISPLAY 'ENTER S IF YOU WISH TO STOP'
ACCEPT ANS
UNTIL ANS = S
```

(4) USE VARIABLES A,B,C,N, SCOREA, SCOREB, SCOREC OF TYPE REAL
```
SCOREA := 0, SCOREB:= 0, SCOREC:= 0
FOR (N = 1, N < 20, N + 1)
DISPLAY 'ENTER SCORES A, B OR C'
ACCEPT A, B, C
SCOREA:= SCOREA + A
SCOREB:= SCOREB + B
SCOREC:= SCOREC + C
ENDFOR
DISPLAY 'SCORE A IS' SCOREA
DISPLAY 'SCORE B IS' SCOREB
DISPLAY 'SCORE C IS' SCOREC
```

(5) USE VARIABLES  CHOICE OF TYPE CHARACTER
```
      AREA, CIRC, VOL, RADIUS OF TYPE REAL
REPEAT
DISPLAY 'CHOOSE YOUR CALCULATION OR STOP'
DISPLAY 'TYPE THE LETTER NEXT TO YOUR CHOICE'
DISPLAY 'A: AREA OF CIRCLE'
DISPLAY 'C: CIRCUMFERENCE OF CIRCLE'
DISPLAY 'V: VOLUME OF SPHERE'
DISPLAY 'S: TYPE S TO STOP'
ACCEPT CHOICE
DO CASE OF CHOICE
```

```
CASE CHOICE  = A
DISPLAY 'ENTER RADIUS OF CIRCLE'
ACCEPT RADIUS
AREA = 3.142 * RADIUS * RADIUS
DISPLAY 'AREA IS' AREA
CASE CHOICE  = B
DISPLAY 'ENTER RADIUS OF CIRCLE'
ACCEPT RADIUS
CIRC = 2 * 3.142 * RADIUS
DISPLAY 'CIRCUMFERENCE IS' CIRC
CASE CHOICE  = V
DISPLAY 'ENTER RADIUS OF CIRCLE'
ACCEPT RADIUS
VOL = 3.142 * RADIUS * RADIUS * RADIUS
DISPLAY 'VOLUME OF YOUR SPHERE' VOLUME
CASE CHOICE = S
DISPLAY 'THE PROGRAM WILL NOW STOP'
OTHERWISE
DISPLAY 'ENTRY ERROR, PLEASE TRY AGAIN'
UNTIL CHOICE = S
```

## Chapter 2

### *Exercise 2.1*

**(a)**    DSD – Pack of cards in four suits

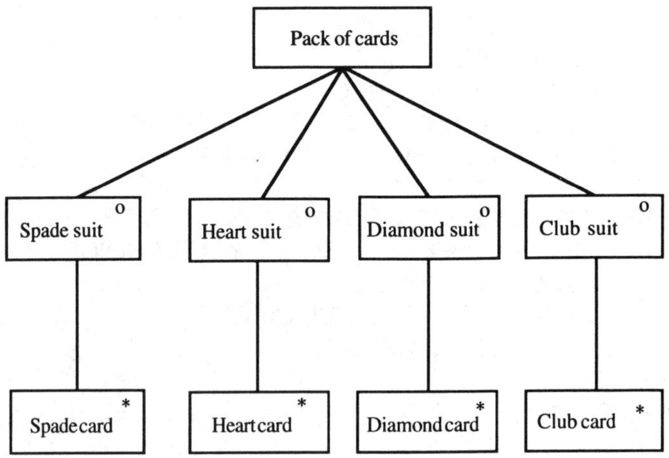

**(b)**

**(c)**

**(d)**

**(e)**

School
Class *
Student *
Book
Preface
Chapter *
Epilogue
Library
'A' Books
'B' Books
'C' Books
'D' Books
'E' Books
Book with 'A' author *
Book with 'B' author *
Book with 'C' author *
Book with 'D' author *
Book with 'E' author *
Play
Act 1
Act 2
Act 3
Scene *
Scene *
Scene *

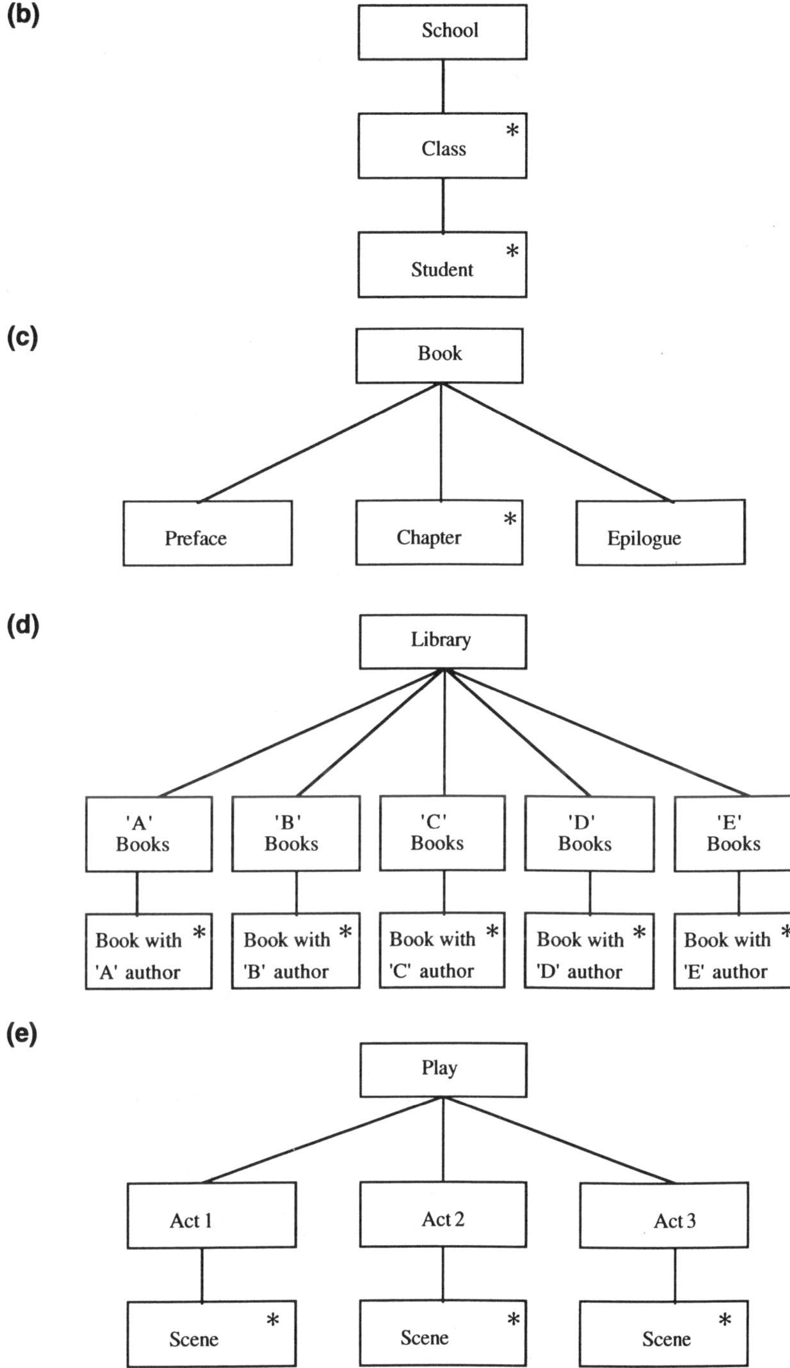

## Exercise 2.2

**(a)** The file should consist of records containing:

| | |
|---|---|
| name | string of 30 chars |
| cat | string of 15 chars |
| subscription | real number |
| paid | one char |
| address | could be, e.g. 3 lines, 20 chars |
| tel. No. | integer |

Any sensible interpretation of this would be acceptable in an examination. If asked for more details more may be required, e.g. record name or field lengths.

**(b)** As above no one answer is correct. Answer should show the knowledge of field storage requirements of different variable types.

e.g. patient_name
patient_address
age
sex

as a header record followed by records detailing illness

problem_name
problem_description
treatment_details
etc.

e.g.

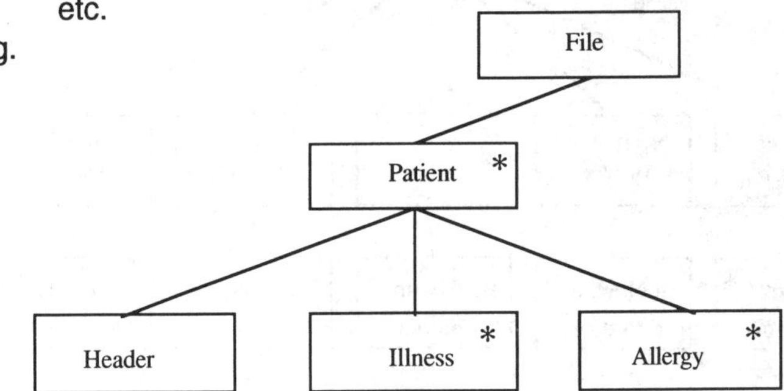


For instance, file is organized by patient with each patient having a set of records which could consist of a header record followed by records of each illness and treatment.

**(c)**
```
Item:  record
    product_number  :   array[1..6] of character;
    product_name    :   array[1..18] of character;
    quantity_in_store:  integer;
    price_per_item  :   real;
    supplier_name   :   array[1..24] of character;
end record;
```

**(d)** For example

| | |
|---|---|
| employee_name | string 30 chars |
| monthly_sal | real |
| tax_d | real |
| employee_no | string 8 chars |

## Exercise 2.3

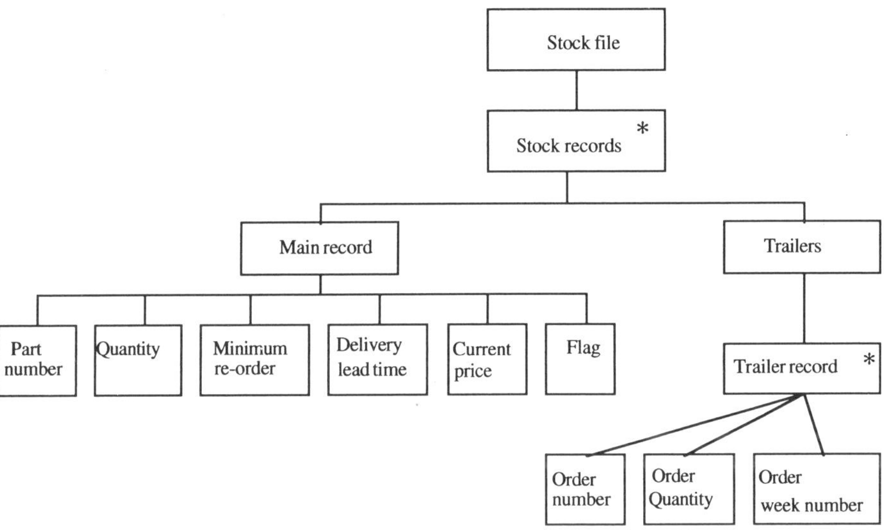


## Exercise 2.4

**(a)**

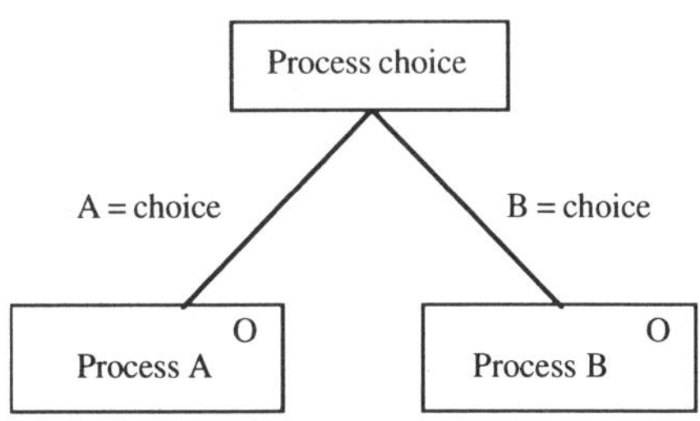

**(b)**

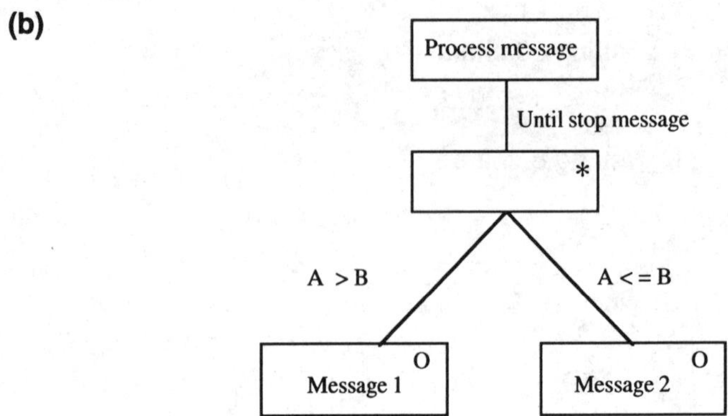


## Exercise 2.5

**(a)**

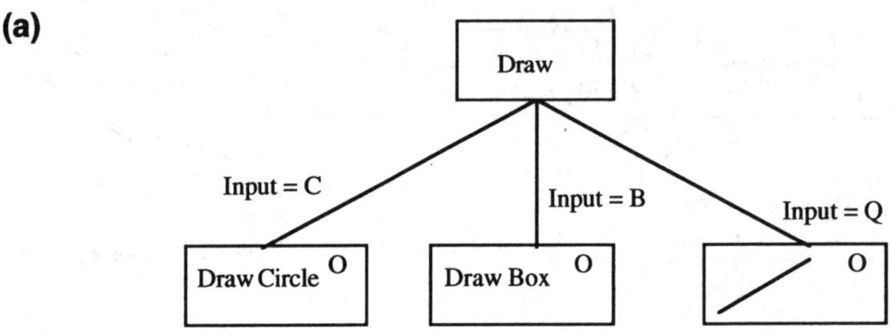


**(b)**

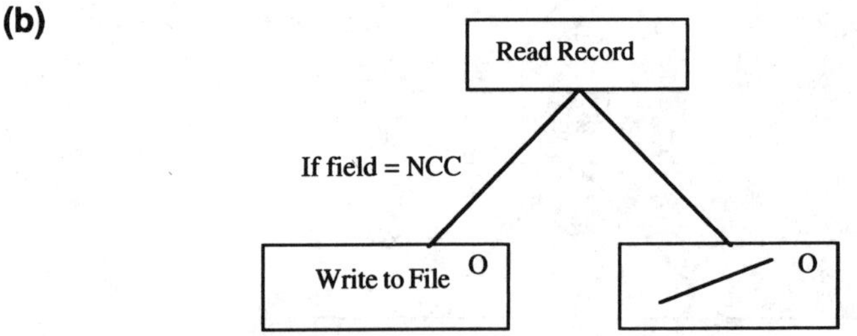

## *Summary exercise*

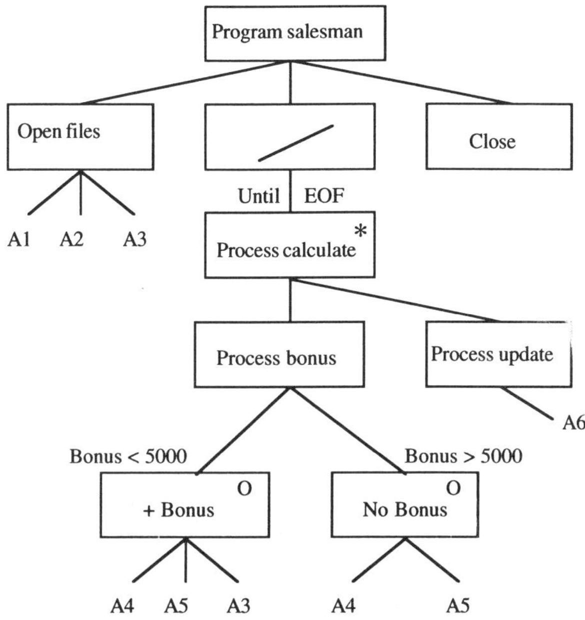


A1: Open salesman file for reading
A2: Open wages file for writing
A3: Read salesman record
A4: Calculate percentage commission
A5: Add bonus
A6: Write to file

# Chapter 3

## *Exercise 3.1*

**(a)**

**(b)**

**(c)**

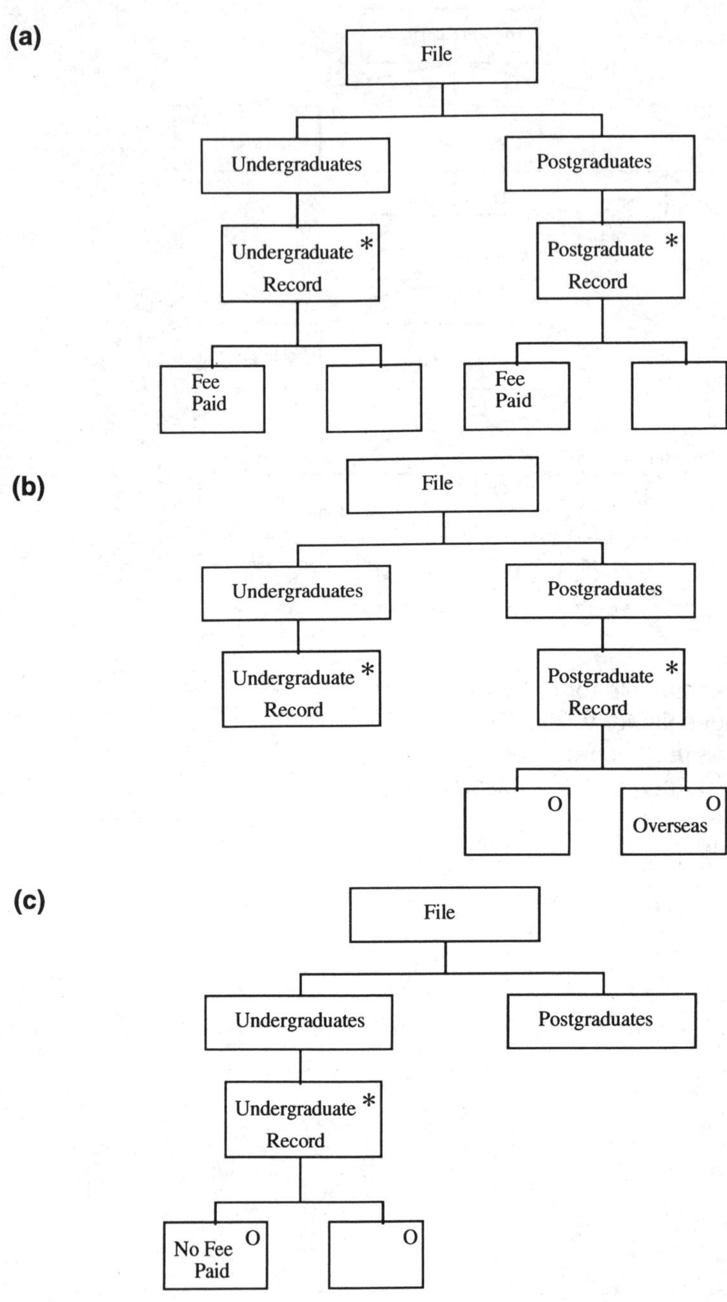

## *Summary exercise*

**(1)** Possible answers:

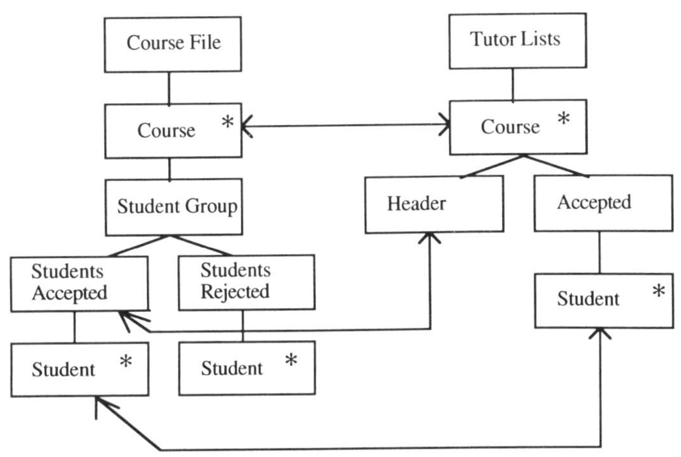

**(2)** Possible answers:

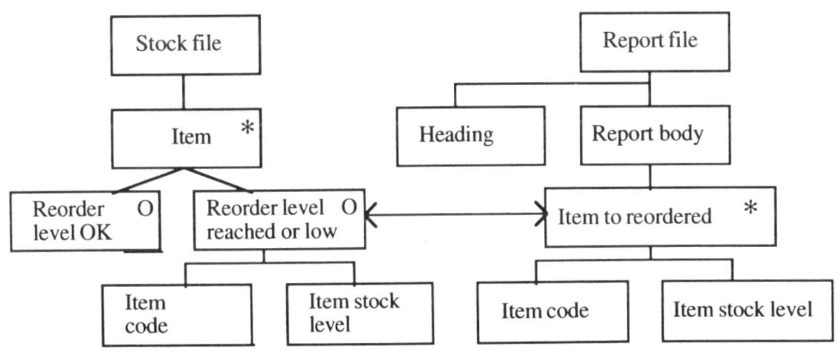

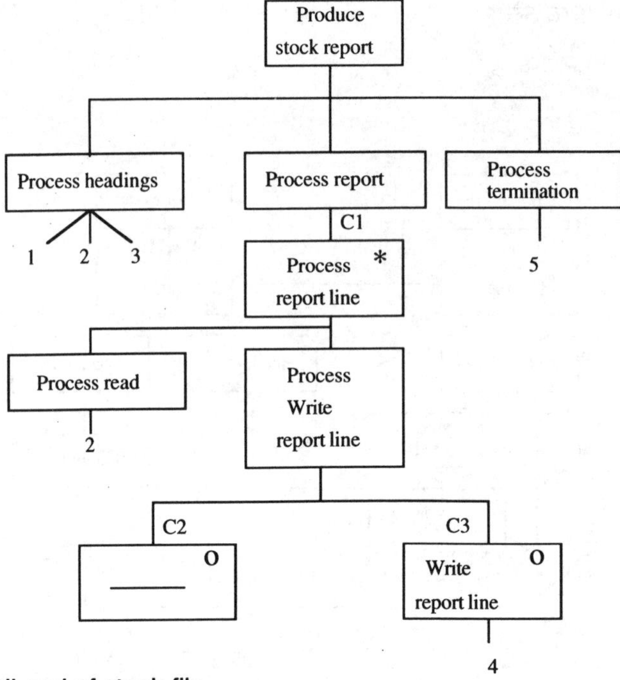

C1    Until end of stock file
C2    If re-order level OK
C3    If re-order level too low or reached
1     Open stock file
2     Read stock record
3     Write headings to report
4     Write report line
5     Close stock file

## Chapter 4

### Exercise 4.1

Assists in building a structured program
Easier to test small modules of code
Easier to debug
Can reuse code that is reliable.

### Exercise 4.2

**(a)** Three of hearts, Queen of spades, ace of diamonds.
**(b)** cards[12], cards[37], cards[40].

## Exercise 4.3

Note any alternative variable names will do!
**(a)** item-type = RECORD

|  |  |
|---|---|
| first_name | : String(20); |
| initials | : String(5); |
| last_name | : String(20); |
| room_number | : String(6); |
| site | : String(7); |
| tel_no | : Integer; |

ENDRECORD

one_item : item_type;

**(b)** The table could be declared as tel_list array[1..100] of item_type.

**(c)** Initialize table index to 1;
WHILE( more records in the file and room in the array)
   READ record into table;
   increment table index by 1;
ENDWHILE
Any similar algorithm is an acceptable answer.

**(d)** n holds the number of elements in the table
read input_site
for I in range 1 to n
do
  if (site = input_site)
    then print first name and last name
  endif;
enddo;


## Exercise 4.4

**(a)** There are many sort algorithms that you might have written. An examiner would look for the following: a named sort; correctness (you can test that on your computer); and the clarity of the algorithm – pseudo-code is better than an explanation in words.

**(b)** You might have answered this using a language or a DBMS package. An examiner would look for the following: an explation of how the file is created; a definition of the record structure; field names and types in the record structure; and correct field types.

**(c)** Here an examiner would look for the following: a mechanism for looking through all the records in the file (a loop or an appropriate DBMS retrieval statement); a condition to check the employee name against the required number; and an explanation of how the required value would be input to the program.

## Chapter 5
*Summary exercise*

**(a)** The condition stub
The condition entry
The action stub
The action entry.

**(b)** If a procedure has a large number of related decisions, the flow chart becomes complex. In such cases, decision table is preferred.

**(c)**

| Invoice settled? | 7 days | 14 days | 5 days | ELSE |
|---|---|---|---|---|
| Discount? | 10 % | 7 % | 5 % | Refer to manager |

**(d)** Coding from the table by hand using a preprocessor which converts the table into a source program for input to the compiler. Using a program which interprets the table.

## Chapter 6
*Exercise 6.1*

Largest and smallest should not be initialized to zero. Instead, largest should be set to numbers(count) and Smallest should be set to numbers(count)
Count should be initialized to 2.
Loop should be controlled by WHILE Count = < 20.

*Exercise 6.2*

| Statement | | x | ch | word | ch "." | ch  to " " |
|---|---|---|---|---|---|---|
| A | 1 | 10 | | | | |
| A | 2 | 10 | O | | | |
| A | 3 | 10 | O | | TRUE | |
| A | 4 | 10 | O | | TRUE | TRUE |
| A | 5 | 10 | O | O | TRUE | TRUE |
| A | 6 | 9 | | O | TRUE | TRUE |
| A | 7 | 9 | N | O | TRUE | TRUE |
| A | 3 | 9 | N | O | TRUE | TRUE |
| A | 4 | 9 | N | O | TRUE | TRUE |
| A | 5 | 9 | N | NO | TRUE | TRUE |
| A | 6 | 8 | N | NO | TRUE | TRUE |
| A | 7 | 8 | E | NO | TRUE | TRUE |

Repeat steps 3–7 giving

| A | 7 | 7 |   | ENO | TRUE | TRUE |
|---|---|---|---|---|---|---|
|   |   |   |   |   |   |   |
| B | 3 | 7 |   | ENO | TRUE | TRUE |
| B | 4 | 7 |   | ENO | TRUE | FALSE |
| B | 7 | 7 | T | ENO | TRUE | FALSE |
|   |   |   |   |   |   |   |
| C | 3 | 7 | T | ENO | TRUE | FALSE |
| C | 4 | 7 | T | ENO | TRUE | TRUE |
| C | 5 | 7 | T | TENO | TRUE | TRUE |
| C | 6 | 6 | T | TENO | TRUE | TRUE |
| C | 7 | 6 | E | TENO | TRUE | TRUE |

Repeat steps 3–7 for letters E, S, T giving

| C | 5 | 4 | T | TSETENO | TRUE | TRUE |
|---|---|---|---|---|---|---|
| C | 6 | 3 | T | TSETENO | TRUE | TRUE |
| C | 7 | 3 | . | TSETENO | TRUE | TRUE |
|   |   |   |   |   |   |   |
| D | 3 | 3 | . | TSETENO | FALSE | TRUE |
| D | 8 | 4 | . | TSETENO | FALSE | TRUE |
|   |   |   |   |   |   |   |
| E | 9 | 4 | . | TSETENO | FALSE | TRUE T printed |
| E | 10 | 5 | . | TSETENO | FALSE | TRUE |
| E | 9 | 5 | . | TSETENO | FALSE | TRUE S printed |
| E | 10 | 6 | . | TSETENO | FALSE | TRUE |
| Repeat steps 9–10 until x = 10 printing TSETENO | | | | | | |
| E | 9 | 10 | . | TSETENO | FALSE | TRUE |
|   |   |   |   |   |   |   |

## Chapter 7

### Exercise 7.1

Possibilities are:

| For use | For maintenance |
|---|---|
| input specification | program specification |
| output specification | program design – pseudo-code |
| operating instructions | – structure chart |
| error messages/recovery | program listing/code |
| user reference manual | program testing – plan/data/run |
| tutorial | data dictionary/glossary of variable |
| sample runs | amendment history |

### Exercise 7.2

Meaningful data names
Line indentation
Use of comments
Goods structure/modular
Avoidance of code tricks.

### Exercise 7.3

Input specification
Program design
Testing strategy
Data dictionary
Program listing
User manual, etc.

### Exercise 7.4

Understanding and using the system maintenance
Learning to use the system from scratch and without any other sources of help
Knowledge of how the system behaves under different condition.
Communicating between personnel
Assessing the progress of the project, etc.

# Chapter 8

## *Exercise 8.1*

**(a)** The following is one possible instruction set. Note, instructions may be allocated in a different order. Three bits are needed for the eight instructions and in an eight-bit computer there would be five bits left.

000 – load
001 – add
010 – subtract
011 – store
100 – load constant
101 – branch
110 – branch if greater than zero
111 – stop.

**(b)** The following are outlines of what will happen for each instruction.
*Load*; place contents of store onto highway A, pass through the CPU, onto highway C, into the Accumulator and onto highway B.
*Add*; place contents onto highway A, use CPU to add contents of highway B, place result on highway C, pass into the Accumulator and onto highway B.
*Subtract*; place contents onto highway A, use CPU to subtract contents of highway B, place result on highway C, pass into the Accumulator and onto highway B.
*Store*; place contents of Accumulator onto highway B, pass through the CPU, onto highway C and into the STORE.
*Load Constant*; place constant on highway A, pass through CPU, onto highway C,into the Accumulator and onto highway B.

**(c)** To extend the instruction set to 16, you need four-bits. Additional instructions could be; multiply, divide, decrement, more branch instructions, load a constant and clear accumulator.


## *Exercise 8.2*

**(a)** The mnemonics should all be three letters and be sensible representations of the instructions.

LDA – load
ADD – add
SUB – subtract
STO – store
LDC – load constant
BRA – branch
BGT – branch if greater than zero
STP – stop.

**(b)** RESULT := MULT1 $*$ MULT2

```
    LDC #0                      !(loads constant 0)
    STO RESULT
    LDC #12                     !(loads constant 12)
    STO MULT1
    LDC #10                     !(loads constant 10)
    STO MULT2
    L1: LDA MULT1
        ADD RESULT
        STO RESULT
        LDA MULT2
        SUB #1                  !(subtract 1)
        STO MULT2
        BGT L1
        LDA RESULT
        STP
```

## Exercise 8.3

**(a)** Using the detailed examples of fac(3) and fac(2) the following solution can be devised.

```
fac(4)
    fac(4) = 1, if 4 == 0 : FALSE
    fac(4) = 4 * fac(3)
        fac(3) = 1, if 3 == 0 : FALSE
        fac(3) = 3 * fac(2)
            fac(2) = 1, if 2 == 0 : FALSE
            fac(2) = 2 * fac(1)
                fac(1) = 1, if 1 == 0 : FALSE
                fac(1) = 1 * fac(0)
                    fac(0) = 1, if 0 == 0 : TRUE
                ...fac(1) = 1 * 1
            fac(2) = 2 * 1 * 1
        ..fac(3) = 3 * 2 * 1 * 1
    fac(4) = 4 * 3 * 2 * 1 * 1
fac(4) = 24.
```

**(b)** fac(−1) will result in an infinite recursion as there is no test for negative values. The following improvement to the function will solve the problem; answer

```
fac :: integer → integer          || declaration
fac(x) = x, if x < 0              || for  negative  values  just  return
                                       value
fac(x) = 1,  if x == 0           || fac(0) = 1, terminating condition
```

fac(x) = x * fac (x–1), otherwise   || fac(x)  =  x  *  fac  (x–1),  general condition

The number of recursions can be reduced by making fac(1) and fac(2) special cases along with fac(0).

fac : : integer → integer          || declaration
fac(x) = x, if x < 0               || for  negative  values  just  return value
fac(x) = 1,  if x < 2              || fac(0) = 1 or fac(1) = 1, terminating condition
fac(x) = 2, if x == 2             || fac(2) = 2, special condition
fac(x) = x * fac (x–1), otherwise  || fac(x)  =  x  *  fac  (x–1),  general condition

This stops the two cases where the end of the recursion simply multiplies the result by 1.

**(c) (i)**  FUNCTION fac(i : Integer) : Integer
```
       IF i=0
          THEN
             RETURN 1
          ELSE
             RETURN i * fac(i–1)
          ENDIF
       ENDFUNCTION
```
**(ii)**  FUNCTION fac(i : Integer) : Integer
```
       fact : Integer
       fact := 1;
       WHILE i<>0
          fact := fact * i;
          i := i – 1
       ENDWHILE
       RETURN fact
       ENDFUNCTION
```

## Exercise 8.4

**(1)** Students should be able to use the example to produce the following solutions:

**(a)** you_can_get_from(a,c):-
track(a, b),                     YES : selects first track from a.
you_can_get_from(b, c).
you_can_get_from(b, c):-

```
track(b, c),                          YES : selects first track from b.
you_can_get_from(c, c).               YES : using you_can_get_from(HERE,
                                            HERE).
```

Success!

```
(b)  you_can_get_from(d, a):-
     track(d, e),                     YES : selects first track from d.
     you_can_get_from(e, a).
     you_can_get_from(e, a):-
     track(e, X),                     NO : no tracks from e.
     you_can_get_from(X, a).
     you_can_get_from(d, a):-
     track(d, X),                     NO : no more tracks from d.
     you_can_get_from(X, a).
```

Failure!

```
(c)  you_can_get_from(b, e):-
     track(b, c),                     YES : selects first track from b.
     you_can_get_from(c, e).
     you_can_get_from(c, e):-
     track(c, X),                     NO : no tracks from c.
     you_can_get_from(X, e).
     you_can_get_from(b, e):-
     track(b, e),                     YES : selects second track from b.
     you_can_get_from(e, e).          YES : using you_can_get_from(HERE,
                                            HERE).
```

Success!

```
(d)  you_can_get_from(b, d):-
     track(b, c),                     YES : selects first track from b.
     you_can_get_from(c, d).
     you_can_get_from(c, d):-
     track(c, X),                     NO : no tracks from c.
     you_can_get_from(X, d).
     you_can_get_from(b, d):-
     track(b, e),                     YES : selects second track from b.
     you_can_get_from(e, d).
     you_can_get_from(e, d):-
     track(e,X),                      NO : no tracks from e.
     you_can_get_from(X, d).
     you_can_get_from(b, d):-
     track(b, X),                     NO : no more tracks from d.
     you_can_get_from(X, d).
```

Failure!

**(2)** The following facts would be required:
    station(a).
    station(b).
    station(c).
    station(d).
    station(e).

**(3)** Students will obviously choose different names but the following provides some guidance on the structure of the answer expected.
    –facts
    male (fred).                        – fred is male
    female (mary).                      – mary is female
    male (denis).
    female (helen).
    male (martyn).
    male (ian).
    parent-of (fred,denis).             – fred is parent-of denis
    parent-of (mary,denis).             – mary is a parent of denis
    parent-of (denis,martyn).
    parent-of (helen,martyn).
    parent-of (denis,ian).
    parent-of (helen,ian).
    rules
    father-of (X,Y) :- male(X), parent-of (X,Y).
    mother-of (X,Y) :- female(X), parent-of (X,Y).
    brother-of (X,Y) :- male(X), parent-of (A,X), parent-of (A,Y).
    sister-of (X,Y) :- female(X), parent-of (A,X), parent-of (A,Y).
    grandfather-of (X,Y) :- male(X), parent-of (X,A), parent-of (A,Y).
    grandmother-of (X,Y) :- female(X), parent-of (X,A), parent-of (A,Y).

There are many more that the students could include such as parent-of, grandparent-of, son-of, daughter-of, child-of, grandson-of and grand-daughter-of.


## Exercise 8.5

**(1)** A class defines the properties (data and mechanisms) associated with something, such as a Person, a Chair, a Desk and a Window.

An instance is a specific instantiation of a class, with particular characteristics, for example all the desks in the class room are instances of the class Desk and all the students in the classroom are instances of the class Person but they are all individuals.

Note that there can be many instances of an object that have exactly the same characteristics, e.g. many chairs are the same but are different instances. It is unusual to find two classes with exactly the same or even similar properties.

(2)   **(a)**

Chair:   data →   no. of legs     → Integer
                         size of seat    → Area
                         back               → Boolean
                         swivel             → Boolean
                         wheels            → Boolean

         mechanisms                 → pick-it-up
                                                make-it
                                                break-it
                                                return-number of legs
                                                return-size

**(b)**

Window: data       open       → Boolean
                          locked     → Boolean
                          height     → Real
                          width      → Real
                          shape      → Shape

         mechanisms              → open-it
                                            close-it
                                            lock-it
                                            unlock-it


## Exercise 8.6

**(a)** Students should come up with a range of answers but it is important that they develop some intermediate abstract classes. The following is just a small example:

Shape
    RoundShape
        Circle
        Oval
        Ellipse
    MultiSidedShape
        ThreeSidedShape
            Triangle
                Isoceles
                Equilateral

            FourSideShape
                Rectangle
                Square

**(b)** Students should come up with a range of answers but it is important that they develop some intermediate abstract classes. The following is just a small example:

Furniture
    SleepingFurniture
        Bed
            SingleBed
            DoubleBed
            BunkBed
            CampBed
        Hammock
    SittingFurniture
        Chair
            ArmChair
            UprightChair
        Settee
            TwoSeater
            ThreeSeater
            FourSeater
    StoringFurniture
        Wardrobe
        Cupboard
    WritingFurniture
        Desk
        Table

## *Exercise 8.7*

**(a)** For the shape hierarchy the following polymorphic mechanisms could be considered: area of shape – where calculation of area would be dependent on the shape; size of shape – where calculation of size would be dependent on the shape; draw shape.

**(b)** For the furniture hierarchy the following polymorphic mechanisms could be considered: height – this would have a different meaning for each type of furniture; length – this would have a different meaning for each type of furniture; width – this would have a different meaning for each type of furniture; capacity – this would have a different meaning for each type of furniture.

## Exercise 8.8

**(1) (a)** PileOfPlates     data     →     top-of-pile
number-of-plates
stack-of-plates

mechanisms → add-plate
remove-plate

**(b)** LineOfPeople     data → length-of-queue
front-of-queue
queue-of-people

mechanisms → add-person
remove-person

**(c)** RailwayNetwork     data → stations
number-of-stations
number-of-tracks
network

mechanisms → add-station
add-track
remove-station
remove-track

**(2)**    **(a)** PileOfPlates is a subclass of Stack
   **(b)** LineOfPeople is a subclass of Queue
   **(c)** RailwayNetwork is a subclass of Graph

**(3)**

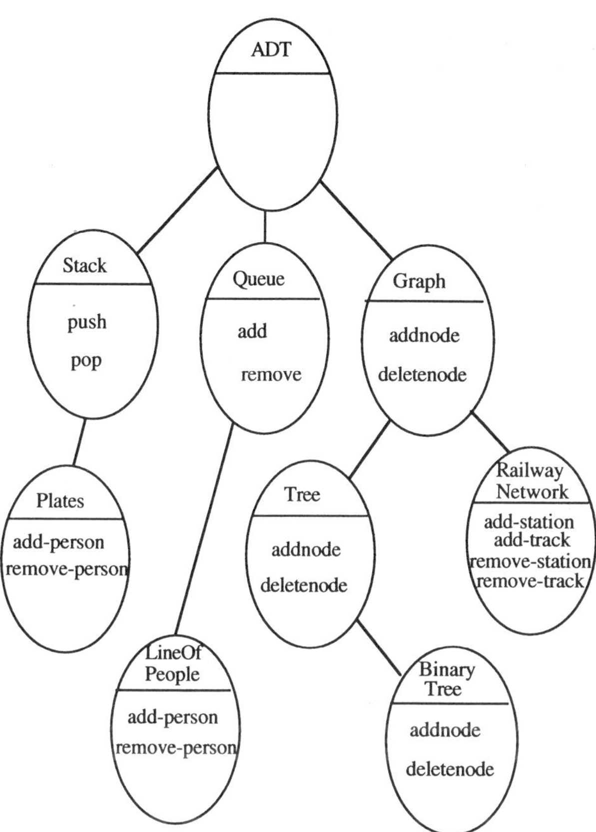



## *Exercise 8.9*

**(a)**    ch= getc(filein);
putc(ch, fileout);
scanf(filein, "Hello World, I am %s \n", &str);
str = "Charlie";
printf(fileout, "Hello World, I am %s \n", str);

**(b)**    str = fgets(&str, &n, filein)          gets a line of $n - 1$ characters from a file
str = gets(&str)                       gets a line from standard input
i = fputs("hello world!", fileout)    puts a string to a file
i = gets("hello world")               puts a string to standard input

## *Exercise 8.10*

**(a)** myFile := WriteFileStream openEmpty: 'myname.txt'.
   myFile  nextPut: #M;
           nextPut: #a;
           nextPut: #r;
           nextPut: #t;
           nextPut: #y;
           nextPut: #n;
           nextPut: cr.
           myFile close.

**(b)** myFile := ReadFileStream open: 'myname.txt'.
   myFile reset.
   ch := myFile next.
   myFile close.


## Chapter 9

### *Exercise 9.1*

**(a)** A chess board:
   BoardRow = ARRAY [1,8] OF ChessPiece
   ChessBoard = ARRAY [1,8] OF BoardRow
   There would be a similar solution to the draughtsboard.
   Rubic's cube
   Row = ARRAY[1,3] OF Colour
   Square = ARRAY[1,3] OF Row
   Cube = ARRAY[1,6] of Square

**(b)** Marks = ARRAY[0,100] of Integer
   Each element in the array holds the number of students who scored that many marks in the examination. So if 10 students score 37 marks, location 37 would have the value 10.

| | |
|---|---|
| popular-mark | : Integer |
| average-mark | : Integer |
| total-mark | : Integer |
| num-marks | : Integer |
| marks | : Marks |
| popular-mark | := 0 |
| total-mark | := 0 |
| num-marks | := 0 |

   FOR (i = 0; i< = 100; i + 1)
     IF marks[i] > marks[popular-mark]
     THEN
       popular-mark := i

```
  ENDIF
  num-marks := num-marks + marks[i]
  total-marks := total-marks + marks[i]*i
ENDFOR
average-mark := total-marks / num-marks
DISPLAY popular-mark
DISPLAY average-mark
```

## *Exercise 9.2*

**(a)**
```
Element =  RECORD
              int : Integer
              ptr : Element
ENDRECORD
  ElementPtr = ^Element
  front : ElementPtr
  current    : ElementPtr
  int   : Integer
  elem: Element
  initialise(front);
  WHILE no-more-input
    ACCEPT int
    createelement(elem, int)
    IF front=NIL
    THEN
      firstelement (front, elem)
    ELSE
      current := front
      WHILE current<> NIL AND current^.int < elem^.int
          current := current^.ptr
      ENDWHILE
      IF current=NIL
      THEN
          addelementafter(current, elem)
      ELSE
          addelementbefore(current, elem)
      ENDIF
    ENDIF
  ENDWHILE
```
**(b)** The only change that needs to be made is in the WHILE loop testing the value of the new element with the elements already in the list. This will have to be changed to:

```
WHILE current<> NIL AND current^.int > elem^.int
    current := current^.ptr
ENDWHILE
```

## Exercise 9.3

**(a)**
```
Queue = ARRAY [1, 500] of Element
front : Integer
back : Integer
queue : Queue
FUNCTION addelement (elem : Element) : Boolean
  back := back + 1
  IF back=501
  THEN
    back := 1
  ENDIF
  IF back = front
  THEN
    back := back − 1
    RETURN FALSE
  ELSE
    queue[back] := elem
    RETURN TRUE
  ENDIF
ENDFUNCTION
FUNCTION removeelement () : Element
  front := front + 1
  IF front = 501
  THEN
    front := 1
  ENDIF
  RETURN queue[front]
ENDFUNCTION
PROCEDURE initialise
  front := 0
  back := 0
ENDPROCEDURE
```

**(b)**
```
QueueElement = RECORD
      data : DataType
      next : Queue
ENDRECORD
Queue = ^QueueElement
front : Queue
```

```
  back : Queue
  PROCEDURE addelement (element : QueueElement)
    IF front = nil
    THEN
      front := ^element
      back := ^element
    ELSE
      back^.next := ^element
      back := ^element
    ENDIF
  ENDPROCEDURE
  FUNCTION removeelement () : QueueElement
    temp : Queue
    temp := front
    front := front^.next
    IF front = NIL
    THEN
      back := NIL
    ENDIF
    RETURN temp
  ENDFUNCTION
  PROCEDURE initialise
    front := NIL
    back := NIL
  ENDPROCEDURE
```

## Exercise 9.4

**(a)**
```
  Stack = ARRAY [1, 500] of Element
  top : Integer
  stack : Stack
  FUNCTION push (element : Element) : Boolean
    IF top = 500
    THEN
      RETURN FALSE
    ELSE
      top := top + 1
      stack[top] := element
      RETURN TRUE
    ENDIF
  ENDFUNCTION
  FUNCTION pop (element : Element) : Boolean
    IF top > 0
```

```
     THEN
        top := top - 1
        element := stack[top + 1]
        RETURN TRUE
     ELSE
          RETURN FALSE
        ENDIF
     ENDFUNCTION
     PROCEDURE initialise
        top := 0
     ENDPROCEDURE
(b) StackElement=    RECORD
                  data : DataType
                  next  : Stack
     ENDRECORD
     Stack = ^StackElement
     top: Stack
     PROCEDURE push (element : StackElement)
        IF top <> NIL
        THEN
           element^.next := top
        ENDIF
        top := ^element
     ENDPROCEDURE
     FUNCTION pop (element : StackElement) : Boolean
        IF top=NIL
        THEN
           RETURN FALSE
        ELSE
           element := top^
           RETURN TRUE
        ENDIF
     ENDFUNCTION
     PROCEDURE initialise
        top:= NIL
     ENDPROCEDURE
```

## *Exercise 9.5*

**(1)** Station =   RECORD
                name : Character
                next : Stationptr
                tracks : Trackptr
                ENDRECORD
      Track =   RECORD
                station : StationPtr
                next  : TrackPtr
                ENDRECORD
      StationPtr = ^Station
      TrackPtr = ^Track
      front : StationPtr
      back : Station Ptr

**(a)** PROCEDURE addstation (station : Station)
        IF front=nil
        THEN
            front := ^station
            back := front
        ELSE
            back^.next := ^station
            back := ^station
        ENDIF
      ENDPROCEDURE

**(b)** PROCEDURE addtrack (stationptr : StationPtr, track : Track)
        IF stationptr^.tracks = NIL
        THEN
            stationptr^.tracks := ^track
        ELSE
            track.next := stationptr^.tracks
            stationptr^.tracks := ^track
        ENDIF
      ENDPROCEDURE

**(2)**

|   | a | b | c | d | e | f |
|---|---|---|---|---|---|---|
| a | o | x |   |   | x |   |
| b |   | o | x |   | x |   |
| c | x | x | o | x |   |   |
| d |   |   |   | o | x |   |
| e |   |   |   |   | o | x |
| f |   | x |   |   |   | o |

## *Exercise 9.6*

**(a)** Tree =RECORD
        int : Integer
        left : TreePtr
        right : TreePtr
        ENDRECORD
     Treeptr = ^Tree
**(b)** top : TreePtr
     curr : TreePtr
     elem : Tree
     int : Integer
     PROCEDURE createelement (elem : Tree, int : Integer)
       elem.int := int
       elem.left := NIL
       elem.right := NIL
     ENDPROCEDURE
     PROCEDURE addelement (element : Tree, treeptr : TreePtr)
       IF treeptr = NIL
       THEN
         treeptr := ^element
       ELSE
         IF treeptr^.int > element.int
         THEN
           addelement(element, treeptr^.left)
         ELSE
           addelement(element, treeptr^.right)
         ENDIF
       ENDIF
     ENDPROCEDURE
     WHILE no-more-input
       ACCEPT int
       createelement(elem, int)
       addelement(elem, top)
     ENDWHILE
**(c)** PROCEDURE display-tree (tree : TreePtr)
       IF tree<>nil
       THEN
         display-tree(tree^.left)
         DISPLAY tree^.value
         display-tree(tree^.right)
       ENDIF
     ENDPROCEDURE

**(d)** The way to change the program is to alter the condition on the IF statement in the addelement procedure, the > should become a <, as shown below:

```
PROCEDURE addelement (element : Tree, treeptr : TreePtr)
   IF treeptr = NIL
   THEN
      treeptr := ^element
   ELSE
      IF treeptr^.int < element.int
      THEN
            addelement(element, treeptr^.left)
      ELSE
            addelement(element, treeptr^.right)
      ENDIF
   ENDIF
```

# Chapter 10

**It is not possible to provide many answers in this chapter as solutions will depend upon your choice of software.**

## *Exercise 10.11*

| Personnel department | Payroll department |
|---|---|
| Name | Name |
| Home address | Home address |
| Telephone number | Pay rate |
| Starting date | Deductions |
| Department | YTD pay |
| Job title | |
| Salary grade | |
| Date of last review | |
| Date of next review | |
| Performance rating | |
| Office | |
| Telephone extension | |

Tinted areas indicate redundant data items. There are four natural groupings: employee data, position data, performance data, Salary Data.

| Employee data |
| --- |
| Employee number |
| Name |
| Home address |
| Home telephone number |

| Position data |
| --- |
| Employee number |
| Department |
| Job type |
| Office |
| Telephone extension |

| Performance data |
| --- |
| Employee number |
| Starting date |
| Date of last review |
| Performance rating |
| Date of next review |

| Salary data |
| --- |
| Employee number |
| Pay rate |
| YTD pay |
| Deductions |

## Exercise 10.12

Employee number
Name
Starting date
Date of last review
Performance rating
Date of next review
Staff grade
Pay rate

## Summary exercise

**(1) (a)** Examiners will award one mark for each point such as:
compatibilty and portability
cheaper than developing in-house
due to widespead use, more robust and reliable

**(b)** Examiners will award two marks for demonstration of spreadsheet knowledge;
one mark for an application and one for a relevant example, and similarly for a DBMS.

**(c)** Examiners will award two marks for each of the following:
description, user involvement, participation of systems analysts and senior programmers, activity of investigation and documentation.

**(2) (a)** Diagram – one mark. Data area and areas at top and bottom – two marks.
Explanation of data areas include column labels – two marks.
Menu line/input edit line/ message help lines  up to three marks.

**(b)** Contents of cell is an expression – one mark.
Examples given – up to two marks.
Additional explanation – one mark.
The way a cell displays a number – one mark.
At least two example illustrations up to three marks.
Stored action that can be called again – one mark.
Usually keystrokes and special functions – one mark.
Illustrative examples – up to two marks.

## Chapter 11

*Exercise 11.1*

**(1) (a)** File libraries contain subprograms, functions and procedures. These can be shared. Save development time, duplication of work. Operating system logging: keeps a record of system events, identifies time, date, identity of action, used to implement security trace, file access, etc.

**(b)** Linking uses: Object code produced by compiler, other object code from subroutines called, code from libraries, produces an executable code file that can run alone.

**(2)** Failure and recovery. Security and control of logins. File management. Accounting and statistics. Reporting of faults

**(3)** Possible answers are:

sort utilities, for sorting records within files according to user-specified keys

spooling software, to handle input and output to disks, tapes and printers, by holding data in special areas

windowing software, for creating and and displaying different parts of the same application, or parts of different applications at the same time

editors, for changing for text and graphics.

**(4)** 1e, 2d, 3a, 4c, 5f, 6b.

# Bibliography

These books provide further reading for those students who wish to explore topics in more detail. They cover topics to a deeper level than that required for the International Diploma, but students may wish to study particular aspects to a higher level.


## Programming theory

Martin and McClure, *Software Maintenance: The Problem and its Solutions.* Prentice-Hall (1983).

Myers, *The Art of Software Testing.* John Wiley (1979).

Myers, Clack and Poon, *Programming with Standard HL* (1993).

## Programming languages

Bal and Grune, *Programming Language Essentials.* Addison-Wesley (1994).

Charlton, Leng and Little, *A Course on C.* McGraw-Hill (1992).

Gazdar and Mellish, *Natural Language Processing in PROLOG.* Addison-Wesley (1989).

Lewis and Papadimitriou, *Elements of the Theory of Computation.* Prentice-Hall (1981).

Martin, *Introduction to Languages and the Theory of Computation.* McGraw-Hill (1991).

Watt, *Programming Language Concepts and Paradigms.* Prentice-Hall (1990).

## Professional issues

Bott, *Professional Issues in Software Engineering.* Pitman (1991).

## Systems design and development

Avison and Fitzgerald, *Information Systems Development: Methodologies, Techniques and Tools.* Blackwell (1988).
Budgen, *Software Design.* Addison-Wesley (1993).
Gray and London, *Documentation Standards.* Business Books (1970).
Hanly, *Problem Solving and Programming in C.* Addison-Wesley (1993).
Jones, *Systematic Software Development*, 2nd edition. Prentice-Hall (1990).
King, *Current Practices in Software Development: A Guide to Successful Systems.* Prentice-Hall (1979).
Morgan, *Programming From Specifications*, 2nd edition. Prentice-Hall (1994).
National Computing Centre, *Data Processing Documentation Standards.* NCC (1977).
National Computing Centre, *Decision Tables in Data Processing.* NCC (1977).
Sommerville, *Software Engineering*, 3rd edition. Addison-Wesley (1989).
Van Vliet, *Software Engineering – Principles and Practice.* John Wiley (1990).
Von Mayrhauser, *Software Engineering: Methods and Management.* Academic Press (1990).
Zeigler, *Programming System Methodologies.* Prentice-Hall (1983).

## Algorithms and data structures

Brassard and Bratley, *Algorithms, Theory and Practice.* Prentice-Hall (1988).
Harel, *Algorithmics: the Spirit of Computing*, 2nd edition. Addison-Wesley (1992).

## Databases

Elmasri and Navathe, *Fundamentals of Database Systems*, 2nd edition. Addison-Wesley (1994).

## Natural language processing and knowledge representation

Gazdar and Mellish, *Natural Language Processing in PROLOG.* Addison-Wesley (1989).
Smith, *Computers and Human Language.* Oxford University Press (1991).

## Communications

Halsall, *Data Communications, Computer Networks and OSI*, 3rd edition. Addison-Wesley (1991).
Hutchinson and Sawyer, *Computers, The User Perspective.* Richard D. Irwin (1990).
Stallings, *Data and Computer Communications*, 4th edition. Macmillan (1994).

## Operating systems

Bacon, *Concurrent Systems.* Addison-Wesley (1993).
Silberschatz and Galvin, *Operating System Concepts*, 4th edition. Addison-Wesley (1994).

The following are particularly useful for programming examples.

## Programming languages
Borland, *Using Turbo C*, 2nd edition. Osborne/McGraw-Hill (1989).
Holmes, *Pascal Programming*, 2nd edition. DP Publications (1990).

## Algorithms and data structures
Burgess, *Structured Program Design using JSP.* Hutchinson (1987).
King and Pardoe, *Program Design using JSP.* Macmillan (1985).
Judith Knapp, *Data Structures for Business Programming.* Mitchell (1989).

# Index